DEEDS OF
HEROES

For Natalia

DEEDS OF HEROES

The Story of the
Distinguished Conduct Medal
1854–1993

MATTHEW RICHARDSON

Pen & Sword
MILITARY

First published in Great Britain in 2012 by
PEN & SWORD MILITARY
an imprint of
Pen & Sword Books Ltd
47 Church Street
Barnsley
South Yorkshire
S70 2AS

ISBN 978 1 84884 374 5

A CIP catalogue record for this book is
available from the British Library

Typeset in Ehrhardt
by Chic Media Ltd

Printed and bound in England
by CPI Group (UK) Ltd, Croydon, CR0 4YY

Pen & Sword Books Ltd incorporates the imprints of
Pen & Sword Aviation, Pen & Sword Family History, Pen & Sword Maritime,
Pen & Sword Military, Pen & Sword Discovery, Wharncliffe Local History,
Wharncliffe True Crime, Wharncliffe Transport, Pen & Sword Select,
Pen & Sword Military Classics, Leo Cooper, Remember When,
The Praetorian Press, Seaforth Publishing and Frontline Publishing

For a complete list of Pen & Sword titles please contact
PEN & SWORD BOOKS LIMITED
47 Church Street, Barnsley, South Yorkshire, S70 2AS England
E-mail: enquiries@pen-and-sword.co.uk
Website: www.pen-and-sword.co.uk

Contents

List of Illustrations

Foreword

With its 139-year history and with thousands of awards made in that time, it would be difficult to describe every act of gallantry associated with the Distinguished Conduct Medal, but we must remember that each medal awarded has its own unique story. Matthew Richardson, with his intimate knowledge of the medal and of military history (as shown in his previous writings on the Leicestershire Regiment) has in this book *Deeds of Heroes* given a detailed, informative account of the medal, from its inauguration by Queen Victoria to the last award. This gives us a definitive history of one of our most important, but least known, military awards.

Not only does this dedicated work name many of the award holders but also gives an insight into the lives of soldiers and conditions in which they fought, the effect it had on their careers, and their life after service. From the citations, personal accounts of individual acts of bravery, and eyewitness statements, you will be able to follow the history not only of the DCM but also of worldwide military conflicts from 1854 to 1993. Battlegrounds such as the Crimea, the mud-filled trenches of the Great War, my own Falklands War and the final award earned during the Ulster 'troubles' are well documented and have a well-deserved place in this book, but the author also includes awards made for lesser known actions by British and Commonwealth soldiers in the Ashanti campaign in Ghana, the Boxer Uprising in China, and the jungles of Vietnam, to name but a few.

Of course, one thing has not changed over time and that is the bravery and unselfish actions of recipients of the DCM. Matthew has gone a long way to immortalise their memory in this book, and to give them their rightful place in military history.

Julian Burdett DCM

Introduction and Acknowledgements

The Distinguished Conduct Medal, which before 1993 ranked second highest in the British awards system, was actually instituted before the Victoria Cross. In its 139-year history it has been awarded for some incredible feats of gallantry, as will quickly become apparent as the pages of this book unfold. Indeed, many recipients of the DCM only narrowly missed out on the award of the VC. Yet their awards and their heroism have to a great extent been overshadowed by those of VC recipients in the media and mainstream press.

Indeed, one of my chief reasons for writing this book was the fact that acres of paper and gallons of ink have been expended on the Victoria Cross, and yet scarcely anything beyond bare lists of names has been written about what was for over a hundred years Britain's second tier gallantry award for land forces.

I felt that the recipients of the Distinguished Conduct Medal, the so-called 'live man's VC', deserved at least one book chronicling their achievements in some detail. Frankly, I was surprised that a similar book had not been written already, and the further I got into it the more gripping I found the breathtaking accounts of heroism, whether from the age of sword and lance or from that of laser-guided bombs.

My ambition in writing this book has not been to chronicle every single action that resulted in the award, which would in any case be impossible in the space available. Nor is its purpose to provide reference lists of DCM awards, which are readily available elsewhere. Rather, the remit of this book is to analyse the social context of the medal, why it was created, and why it was abolished, and what it meant to the men who won it. I have used examples to illustrate how those who won the award influenced the outcome of the actions in which they participated, and to contrast the differing circumstances, often a hundred or more years apart, which resulted in the award of a DCM. Above all, wherever it has been possible I have allowed the DCM recipients to describe the action in their own words. This I believe brings an immediacy to the events and is also humbling as we, the readers of the early twenty-first century, contemplate how we might have reacted in similar circumstances.

I would like to thank Augie Herchenratter DCM for permission to use his story in this book, and Bob Vrbanac at the *Waterloo Chronicle* for allowing me to quote from the article about Augie published in that newspaper. Thanks are due also in this regard to Owen Lackenbauer, author of the article. Tamara Bell at the Melbourne *Herald & Weekly Times* was most helpful in providing clearance for material I wished to use, as was Michael Sadan at *The Times* online archive.

I feel very fortunate and greatly privileged to have met the recipient of one of the first DCMs of the Second World War, John Sheppard of the 1st/5th Leicesters, whose story forms a key part of this book, and I thank him warmly for his help over the years. Karen Rattigan provided me with photographs of her late father and much additional information for which I am grateful. Celia Green at the Regimental Museum of The Royal Welsh at Brecon was a great help. My old friend Patrick Gariepy allowed me unlimited access to his marvellous collection of photographs.

Bernard Lewis in South Wales provided me with valuable information, as did Bev Lewis. A tremendous number of members of the British Medal Forum (an invaluable internet resource for collectors) provided me with advice. It seems iniquitous to single some out individually for praise and not others, but without the help of Leslie Guy, Gerry O'Neill, Peter Sharpe, Steven Todd, Jeff Ritsick, Irv Mortenson, Dan FitzGerald, Dick Flory, Captain Michael W Clare CD (Retd), Alastair Jack, John Meyers, Steve Rosbotham, Howard Williamson, Steve Danaher, Paul Williams, Derek Bird, Mark Simner, Stuart Brown and Alex Jolley this book would have been so much the poorer. Mike Downey also significantly contributed to the content of the book with important material, and I am also immensely grateful to him.

I am, it is no exaggeration to say, thrilled and delighted that Mrs Margaret Holmes has allowed me to quote from her father Frank Richards' book *Old Soldiers Never Die*. Frank Richards DCM MM has been a hero of mine ever since boyhood, when reading of his exploits first sparked my interest in the events of the First World War. To have the presence of this 'Old Sweat' in the book has truly lent it gravitas. I am tremendously grateful to Mrs Holmes for permission to quote from her father's classic war memoir, and to David Langley for putting us in contact in the first place. Dr John Krijnan was also most helpful in this context in supplying photographs. Similarly, Mrs Heather Wilson very kindly allowed me to quote from her grandfather's diary, published as *Blue Bonnets, Boers and*

Biscuits, and I thank her also. Barry Sue allowed me to quote from his father's marvellous book *Blood on Borneo,* which I strongly recommend as an outstanding Second World War memoir. Carla Rathmanner at HarperCollins Australia was most helpful in providing permission to quote from James Allan's book *No Citation.* Georgia Glover at David Higham Associates provided permission to quote from Charles McCormack's *You'll Die in Singapore.*

I am greatly indebted to Major Peter Ratcliffe DCM for permission to quote from his superb book *Eye of the Storm,* also to Toby Buchan at Michael O'Mara Books who facilitated this for me. Audrey Portman and Ian Uys in South Africa were a great help. I am particularly grateful to Ian for permission to use information from his book *Rollcall,* a superb account of the South African Brigade in Delville Wood. Lisa Hooson at Pen and Sword Books and David Feebery allowed me to quote from *Guardsman and Commando,* for which I am most grateful. Martin Middlebrook, always generous with his material, kindly allowed me to quote from *Operation Corporate, The Story of the Falklands War.* General Sir Frank Kitson permitted me to use material from his book, *Gangs and Counter Gangs,* for which again I am tremendously grateful.

My thanks also extend to Emma Lefley at the National Army Museum, and to Jonathan Smith for their help in finding photographs. Mark Quayle kindly allowed me to quote from the Spink archives.

I have tried hard to obtain permission for use of all copyright material quoted within this book. However, if you believe you are the copyright holder of material used and are not acknowledged as such, please contact the publisher. In particular, it was not possible to trace the families of Arthur Chambers, Edward Humpries, James Gerrard and Reginald Evans, all quoted herein, but I thank them nonetheless for making the original material publicly accessible. Likewise, the descendants of Derrick Nabarro could not be traced, but acknowledgement is made to Cassell Plc (a division of the Orion Publishing Group) as publishers of *Wait For The Dawn.* Neither could the heirs of William Moore now be traced, but acknowledgement is made to Leo Cooper/Pen & Sword as publishers of *Panzer Bait* for the extracts used herein.

Nimrod Dix at Dix Noonan Webb is worthy of special mention, for granting permission for me to use material from the DNW archive. Dix Noonan Webb are perhaps Britain's foremost auctioneers of military medals, and their archive of past sales is an enormous resource. Without the tremendous support provided by Dix Noonan Webb, this book would have been so much the poorer. Richard Davies at the University of Leeds was, as ever, tremendously helpful and I thank him, Kasia Drozdziak and all of the Special Collections staff warmly. Rupert Harding at Pen & Sword once again supported my ideas. He and Ralph Daly both read an early draft of the book, and each offered much useful advice and criticism, for which I thank them both.

I am deeply honoured that Julian Burdett DCM has graciously agreed to provide the foreword to this book. I was at school when the actions for which his DCM was awarded took place, but I still remember vividly reading each morning's newspaper coverage from the Falklands conflict. To also have Julian's first-hand account of those events here is a terrific endorsement, and I thank him warmly.

To my family, once again I say thank you for allowing me to indulge my obsessions. To Natalia, for listening to me ramble about people she has never heard of, to Lucie and Katie again for your interest. To Mum and Dad, thank you for helping me locate those obscure books.

Finally, I will close by observing that it is lamentably easy for an author to cause offence by omission. There are unquestionably hundreds - indeed thousands - of men whose bravery in the face of the enemy deserves not to go unrecorded, and who for reasons of space I have been unable to mention by name in this book. Nonetheless, I salute each and every one of them, and from them or their families I ask their forgiveness for the fact that - on this occasion - I was not able to mention them.

Matthew Richardson
Douglas, Isle of Man, 2011

Chapter 1

In the Beginning
1854–1913

The Crimean War of 1853 to 1856 was the catalyst for a number of changes, both within the British Army and also to the relationship between the British people and their soldiers. The war was widely reported in the press, more so than any other war up to that point. It was also the first war to be extensively photographed. The British public had a clearer picture of what the war meant to the ordinary soldier involved in it than in any previous conflict. They followed each and every turn in *The Times* over their breakfast tables, and they were as appalled by the mismanagement of the war, and the incompetence of those planning it, as they were impressed by the stoicism of the ordinary British soldier.

Ill equipped, with the wrong kind of clothing, and with inadequate and unsanitary medical arrangements, the plight of Britain's soldiers fighting abroad struck a chord with middle England. For the first time the idea began to grow in the minds of the middle classes of an 'unwritten contract' between the Army and the nation. If the nation expected soldiers to die on its behalf on a far away battlefield, then the least that soldier could expect in return from the nation that sent him there was to be adequately clothed, fed, and cared for should he be wounded. No one took a keener interest in these ideas than that very middle class monarch, Queen Victoria.

A number of reforms grew out of the Crimean debacle. The most obvious was that of the army medical services, which had been championed by Florence Nightingale and others like her. The British Army's main hospital was a filthy hovel built on top of a cesspit at Scutari. The wounded were treated with indifference and the death rate appalling. The ministrations of Nightingale and others if nothing else shamed the military authorities into implementing at least the basics of good medical practice, as far as it was understood at that time. Other reforms concerned the rewards that soldiers could expect for their sacrifice on the battlefield. Queen Victoria personally oversaw the creation of a medal for bravery, which was instituted in 1856 and which was to bear her name - the Victoria

Cross - which could be awarded to all ranks, officer and private soldier alike.

However, two years earlier in 1854, another medal had been instituted, which again would recognize heroism on the battlefield, though perhaps of a lesser order than that required for the Victoria Cross. This was the Distinguished Conduct Medal (DCM), and it differed significantly from the Victoria Cross by virtue of the fact that it was only open to those of the rank of sergeant or below.

This medal had arisen purely because of a change in official attitudes towards soldiers of the rank and file. In previous generations the British private soldier was regarded with unconcealed contempt by the military establishment. The Duke of Wellington is reputed to have described the rank and file as:

> ...the scum of the earth, recruited for drink ... and it is really remarkable what fine fellows we have made of them.

In some cases in the past, in the absence of any official reward for NCOs and below, individual officers had taken it upon themselves to purchase at their own expense medals for the reward of good or gallant behaviour. These regimental medals for good shooting or bravery were the precursors of the modern system of military honours and awards, but were uncommon even at the time, and these officers were in a minority.

It was widely believed that soldiers in the Georgian army were held to their task only by the threat of flogging or other savage punishments. After Waterloo, Wellington remained commander-in-chief of the Army until his death, and it is no exaggeration to say that in the years that followed the ending of the Napoleonic Wars the British Army fossilised. Wellington was resistant to any form of change (both in the Army and in society at large). In his view, his army had been adequate for the defeat of Napoleon, the greatest enemy Britain had ever faced, so why change anything.

Wellington maintained his iron grip on the Army until the bitter end, and it was no coincidence that much needed military reforms, in equipment, tactics and supply, only began to follow in the wake of the Duke's death in 1852. Around the same time, a new sense of enlightenment was creeping across Victorian Britain. Queen Victoria's German husband Prince Albert encouraged a new era of progressive thinking, the questioning of old ideas and new approaches to problems. Albert's ideas were encapsulated in his pet project, the Great Exhibition of 1851, in which inventions and mechanical marvels from across the globe were showcased at Kensington Gardens. Now, there was more of an understanding abroad that in some cases men were better led than driven, and that military merit when exhibited should be encouraged and rewarded.

Flogging was not finally abolished in the British Army until 1881, but the maximum number of lashes was reduced from 250 in 1854. In 1860, the Duke of Cambridge introduced a new punishment code by which soldiers were divided into two classes. Soldiers of the first class could not be punished by flogging, and this was the class to which all new recruits entered. Only repeated defiance of authority would reduce a soldier to the second class, in which he could receive corporal punishment.

The catalyst for the creation of the DCM was the war in the east. Growing expansionism on the part of the Czar had led to war between Russia and Turkey in the Crimea. The imminent collapse of the ramshackle Turkish Empire had alarmed Britain and France sufficiently for them to send an expeditionary force to try to prop up the Turks. By the winter of 1854, Britain had been at war with Russia in the Crimea for just over six months. The Battle of the Alma had been fought in September, Balaclava in October and Inkerman in November. Time and again the ordinary British soldier had demonstrated his heroism in the face of sometimes overwhelming odds, and the stoicism of the British redcoat was already becoming the stuff of legend. In terms of scale, even taking into account skirmishes and battles in the conquest of India, the conflict was the largest military undertaking Britain had been involved in for almost forty years. The mood of the country was strongly of the view that more should be done officially to recognise this sacrifice and fortitude.

The Times newspaper carried a letter dated 19 December 1854, which read:

> The attention of the public being now much directed to the proper mode of rewarding those who distinguish themselves in the present war, it has occurred to me that a very suitable mode would be by attaching to each of our orders of knighthood a new dignity by creating Officers of the Orders of the Garter, Bath, Thistle & St Patrick. A soldier who had eminently distinguished himself (as Captain Butler and Major Naysmith at Silistria) might be created an Officer of the Order of the Garter, and those nearly as deserving might have given to them the decoration of any of the other orders.
>
> The plan would, it appears to me, satisfy those who ask for the creation of an English 'Legion of Honour', and such a decoration would be more highly prized than a medal given indiscriminately to all who 'are present' in a campaign, and would also afford a means of

rewarding the devotion of our medical officers and of the commissariat.

In the case of private soldiers being so decorated, there might be also conferred on them a pension for a limited number of years, with liberty to study, free of charge, at Sandhurst.[1]

The letter was signed 'A Civilian' and if the civilian's idea that studying at Sandhurst might be more of an incentive to a soldier in the ranks than a gratuity with which to feed and clothe his family seems a shade naïve, it at least illustrates the point that the matter of finding a method for rewarding private soldiers was high in the public consciousness. The very same day that the letter was penned, in the House of Commons Captain George Scobell MP rose to move:

That an humble Address be presented to Her Majesty praying that she would be graciously pleased to institute an 'Order of Merit,' to be bestowed upon persons serving in the Army or Navy for distinguished and prominent personal gallantry during the present war, and to which every grade and individual, from the highest to the lowest, in the United Services, may be admissible. The hon. and gallant Member said, that if he received any intimation from the Government that they would take this subject into favourable consideration he should be content to leave it in their hands. He was convinced that if some such an Order as that referred to in his Motion were immediately instituted it would be tantamount to reinforcing our army of the Crimea, so great would be its effect on the spirits and temper of the troops. The real question before the House was whether the medals and orders at present distributable were sufficient for the purposes of the great war such as that in which the country was now involved. Now the Order of the Bath was entirely confined to the upper ranks of the Army and Navy, for no one under the rank of major in the Army, or captain in the Navy, could partake of the distinctions of that Order. That showed it must be vastly too exclusive, and that its regulations demanded immediate alteration. Then, again, a custom prevailed of giving medals to the Army and Navy for certain battles, which applied as well to those actually in action as those out of it; but that custom had no reference to individual bravery, and many ships taking no part in an action would get the medal equally with those obliged to bear the brunt of the fight. He thought, therefore, since the grant of medals under existing rules did not sufficiently distinguish personal merit, some change was imperatively required.

At the present moment the country was engaged in a war which demanded the putting forth all its strength; but it was a question whether there were those incentives and inducements to the display of courage and endurance on the part of our soldiers and sailors which there ought to be. The soldiers of the Crimea were fighting side by side with the army of France, which possessed an Order which extended down to the meanest drummer-boy in the ranks. He thought, therefore, that the present was a most appropriate juncture for the institution in this country of an Order similar in its character. If, however, he should receive the assurance of the Government that the matter would be taken up by them, and that the objects of his Motion met their cordial assent, he was quite willing not to press the matter further – but under no other circumstances would he consent to committing the subject to their hands.[2]

For the Government, future Prime Minister Lord John Russell stated that he:

... thought that a proposition of this kind ought properly to come from the Crown. He could, however, assure the hon. and gallant Gentleman that the whole question was under consideration; while he was at the same time quite willing to admit that the Order of the Bath did not appear to him to comprehend all the persons who ought to receive it. [3]

The matter was indeed in hand for as the debate was in progress the *London Gazette* was going to press carrying details of a new Royal Warrant. This stated, under date 12 December 1854, that:

It is ... Our will and pleasure to extend the provisions of Our Royal Warrant of the 13th April 1854, and with the special view of marking Our sense of the distinguished service and gallant conduct in the field of Our army now serving in the East, in the Crimea, or elsewhere, under the command of Field Marshal Lord Raglan, to order and direct that the commanding officer of each regiment of cavalry shall be allowed to recommend one sergeant, two corporals, and four privates, and the commanding officer of each regiment of infantry, and of each battalion of Foot Guards, and of the Rifle Brigade, shall be allowed to recommend one sergeant, four corporals, and ten privates, to receive a medal and gratuity of

For a sergeant £15
For a corporal.............£10
For a private £5

The gratuity to be placed in the Regimental Savings' Bank, there to remain in deposit at interest until his discharge from Our service, and to be deemed to be his personal property...[4]

It will be noted that the title 'Distinguished Conduct Medal' was not used initially to describe the medal, and does not appear to have come into common usage as shorthand for the more cumbersome 'Medal and gratuity for distinguished conduct in the field' for some little time after the award was instituted. Nonetheless, Distinguished Conduct Medal is the term used hereon in. Likewise, no citations were published for early awards. This can make it somewhat difficult to establish exactly why a decoration was granted. There is in any case some speculation that the medal was not in every instance awarded for a specific act of gallantry. Some awards may well have been for consistent good service over a period of time, and there is strong evidence that the lieutenant-colonels commanding some battalions in the Crimea had either misunderstood the purpose of the new medal or were choosing to interpret the warrant in their own terms, for in certain battalions every award made went to old soldiers with track records of good service. Some of these officers clearly perceived the new award as a simply an extension of the Meritorious Service Medal or Army Long Service and Good Conduct Medal, and as a way to get a few extra pounds for some of their veteran soldiers before the Army turned them out onto a cold and hard civvy street.

Not all of the new awards fell into this category however. One of the first was made to Private John Forrest, who was recommended for the award on 26 March 1855. He was born near Biggar, Lanarkshire, in February 1820, and enlisted in the Scots Fusilier Guards at Glasgow in February 1841, aged twenty-one years. A tall man for the Victorian era, standing at nearly 6 feet, he would have appeared a good deal taller with the bearskin worn by the Scots Fusilier Guards. For reasons not recorded he deserted his regiment in July 1845 and was at large until August 1847, when he was tried by court martial. He was sentenced to three months' hard labour and the forfeiture of his earlier service. Further disciplinary action was to follow in April 1850, when he was apprehended by the civil authorities for assault. This time he received twenty days' imprisonment.

Yet his apparent bad character was not to prevent Forrest from distinguishing himself with the 1st Battalion in the Crimea, in which theatre of war he served from February 1854 until March 1855, including the battles of Alma, Balaclava and Inkerman, and the operations before Sebastopol. The Guards regiments won distinction for their great gallantry at the Battle of the Alma, the first major set-piece Battle of the Crimean

War, which occurred on 26 September 1854. After initially allowing the British and French armies to land in the Crimea unopposed, it was on the banks of the River Alma that the Russians decided to make a stand. Their two redoubts stood either side of the road to Sebastopol, and effectively blocked any further Anglo-French advance. Having first crossed the river, the Guards brigade fought its way up the slopes of the opposite bank towards the Russian positions. They met a withering Russian fire but carried on; here the Scots Fusilier Guards gained the regiment's first VCs, namely those awarded to the Colour Party under Captain R J Lindsay, who carried and protected the Queen's and Regimental Colours (the regiment's most prized possessions) in the battle.

It is possible that Forrest's subsequent award of the DCM was in some way connected with the gallant actions of the Colour Party here, but he was also involved in a bayonet charge and a good deal of bloody hand-to-hand fighting at the Battle of Inkerman a little over a month later. Indeed, he was seriously wounded here by a Russian musket ball. He was not alone, for the regimental history states that of the nineteen officers and 372 other ranks of the Scots Fusilier Guards engaged at Inkerman, one officer, five sergeants and fifty-nine rank and file were killed or died of wounds, and eight officers, five sergeants, two drummers and ninety-nine rank and file were wounded. Forrest was finally discharged in London in December 1855, his service record states:

> ... in consequence of being unfit for further service from a severe gunshot wound in the right hand at Inkerman (two middle fingers amputated).[5]

By then in possession of two Good Conduct Badges, his pre-desertion service had also been reinstated on his record. Forrest received an increase in his pension in April 1870, was admitted to the Royal Hospital, Chelsea, as an in-pensioner in December 1874 and died in January 1883, aged sixty-three years.

A confirmed Inkerman DCM was awarded to Colour Sergeant Charles Walker of the 55th Regiment (latterly the Border Regiment). Charles Walker was born at St Mary's Gate, Derby, and enlisted at Trowbridge on 20 June 1840, aged twenty years, a skinner by trade. He served for over twenty-one years, including service in July 1841 at the walled town of Ching-Kiang, during the First China War. In 1844, he was promoted to corporal but six months later was reduced to the ranks for leaving the barracks without permission. In 1846, the regiment was stationed in Ireland during the time of the potato famine and, in 1849, was posted to

Gibraltar, where Walker was again promoted to corporal. He was promoted to colour-sergeant in November 1855. In the Crimea the regiment was part of the 2nd Division, serving under General De Lacy Evans, where it fought at the Alma River, at Inkerman and before Sebastopol, including the attack on the Quarries in June 1855, and the final attack on the Redan. It was at Inkerman, when thirty men of the 55th, led by Major Daubenay, attacked a whole Russian battalion, that Sergeant Walker distinguished himself and ultimately received the Distinguished Conduct Medal. The Museum of the Border Regiment in Carlisle Castle holds a number of recommendations for the Victoria Cross for officers and men of the 55th in the Crimea. These reveal that Walker was in fact originally recommended for the VC, the statement reading:

> [For] distinguished gallantry at the Battle of Inkerman 5th November 1854, in recapturing one of our Field Guns which was being dragged away by some of the enemy – and which but for the gallant and determined conduct of Sergeant Walker would have been carried off by the Russians.[6]

The incident was vouched for by an eyewitness, Private Thomas Leyland, 55th, and submitted for consideration by Lieutenant-Colonel H C B Daubenay, Commanding Officer of the 55th. Walker's extraordinary gallantry at Inkerman is further described by Kinglake in his book *The Invasion of the Crimea*, volume VI, which records:

> In the earlier moments of the audacious attack the Colour Serjeant – Charles Walker, a man of great size and strength – had wielded the butt-end of his rifle with prodigious effect, and now, when English and Russian soldiers became so jammed together that none could make use of his weapons, the huge Colour Serjeant was still fiercely driving a rank through part of the closely compressed crowd; doing this more or less by the power of his mighty shoulders and arms, but also by the dint of the blows he rained on right and left with his fists, and those which he maintained with his feet against the enemy's ankles and shins.[6]

His DCM was announced in Army Orders of 20 August 1856, together with a £10 annuity, for gallantry at the Battle of Inkerman. He continued in the rank of Colour Sergeant until his discharge on 15 August 1861. He was appointed a Yeoman of the Guard in 1864, and in 1881, aged fifty-nine, was employed at the Royal Army Clothing Depot. He was at this time living with his wife and family at St George's, Hanover Square, London.

Walker died at Clapham on 15 May 1886. One is tempted to wonder if his path in later life ever crossed with that of a fellow soldier of the 55th Regiment also decorated with the DCM in the Crimea, one Private George Dolan. Dolan received the medal as well as the French Legion of Honour for saving the life of his colonel, and lost his arm in the storming of the Redan at Sebastopol. Like many old soldiers, especially those who had been injured, he fell upon hard times. In May 1861 he was brought up before Middlesex Magistrates for stealing a pair of boots from the landlord of the Hoop and Grapes public house, Broadway, Westminster. Dolan claimed to have been intoxicated at the time and believed he had been given the boots. The bench, who must have been aware of Dolan's previous service and his decoration, and possibly as a result were sympathetic, acquitted him.

Between the battles of the Alma and Inkerman occurred the most notorious incident of the Crimean War: the famous (or perhaps better described as infamous) Charge of the Light Brigade. The charge took place during the Battle of Balaclava on 25 October 1854, and the incident was a microcosm of the Crimean War as a whole, with indecisive British leadership and poor staff work, juxtaposed against the almost immeasurable heroism of the ordinary rank and file soldier. The fiasco occurred when Lieutenant General the Earl of Lucan, in command of the cavalry, received an order from the army commander Lord Raglan, which stated that:

> Lord Raglan wishes the cavalry to advance rapidly to the front, follow the enemy, and try to prevent the enemy carrying away the guns. Horse artillery may accompany. French cavalry is on your left. Immediate.

Raglan in fact wished the cavalry to prevent the Russians taking away the naval guns from the redoubts that they had captured on the reverse side of the Causeway Heights, the hill forming the left side of the valley (from the point of view of the cavalry). Raglan could see what was happening from his high vantage point on the west of the valley, but Lucan and the cavalry were unaware of what was going on owing to the lie of the land where they were drawn up. The order was carried by Captain Louis Edward Nolan, who when Lucan questioned it, is reputed to have declared, whilst pointing at a well dug-in Russian battery at the head of the valley:

> There is your enemy, there are your guns sir!

Lucan duly ordered his brother-in-law, the Earl of Cardigan, commander of the Light Brigade (consisting of the 4th and 13th Light Dragoons, 17th

Lancers, and the 8th and 11th Hussars) to charge the Russian guns, which were defended by an estimated 5,000 Russian infantry and cavalry. The resulting debacle has become part of folklore, largely due to Alfred Lord Tennyson's poem eulogising the 'Gallant 600'. With undoubted heroism, the officers and men of the Light Brigade rode into an inferno of Russian fire, and although they reached the guns, the brigade was almost annihilated, suffering approximately fifty per cent casualties. A number of Distinguished Conduct Medals were awarded for this incident, and rightly so.

Among those who charged was Frederick Short. Born at Windsor, he originally enlisted in the 3rd Light Dragoons in December 1843, aged eighteen years. In the following summer he transferred to the 4th Light Dragoons. Eleven years later in July 1854, Short reached the rank of sergeant. The same year he travelled with his regiment to the Crimea. He was to serve with distinction in that campaign, and in particular in the famous charge, in which his horse was so badly wounded that it died shortly afterwards. During the action, Short personally accounted for several enemy artillery drivers using his sword. This fact is confirmed by a fellow soldier of the 4th Light Dragoons, R S Farquharson, in his memoir *Reminiscences of Crimean Campaigning and Russian Imprisonment*:

> Lieutenant Jolliffe and Sergeant F. Short of ours did some good hard work at the guns. The former cleared off a number of gunners with his pistol, and the latter disposed of several drivers, and their horses as well, thus materially preventing the enemy from removing the guns. On account of this, Short gained for himself the Medal for distinguished conduct in the field.[8]

Advanced to Troop Sergeant-Major in February 1855, Short was awarded his DCM in the following month. In April 1860 he was attached to the Yorkshire Hussars Yeomanry Cavalry as an Instructor on the Permanent Staff, and served with them until rejoining the 4th Hussars - as his regiment was now titled - in January 1868, the month of his final discharge. He had been awarded his Long Service and Good Conduct medal in February 1863. To have one eyewitness account of an early Distinguished Conduct Medal action is fortunate, but to have a second description of the same incident is remarkable, particularly so when it comes from the recipient himself. Short gave his own account of the charge in an affidavit submitted for the famous Calthorpe vs. Cardigan court case in June 1863. Colonel Calthorpe had published a book entitled *Letters from a Staff Officer in the Crimea,* in which he had suggested that in the Charge of the Light

Brigade, its commander Lord Cardigan was guilty of cowardice, not having been present on the field at the most critical point. Calthorpe had stated that an able a horseman as Cardigan could not possibly have been carried to the rear as he stated, simply because his horse took fright. The matter came to court, and Short was called as a witness. He stated:

I have been a Troop Sergeant-Major for eight years. The regiment now called the 4th Hussars was formerly called the 4th Light Dragoons.

I remember the charge of the Light Cavalry Brigade at Balaclava. I was on the extreme left of the right hand squadron in the front rank during the charge. At the commencement of the charge the 8th Hussars were in line with the 4th Light Dragoons and the 11th Hussars were somewhat in advance of our lines.

I am certain that the entire of the 4th Light Dragoons who were not disabled charged right up to the Russian battery. On arriving at the guns the Russians were retreating with them from their original positions. The 4th endeavoured to take possession of these guns. Lieutenant Jolliffe (now Captain, retired) was next to me. I was slightly in advance and attacked the drivers of the guns while Lieutenant Jolliffe shot with his revolver the gunners sitting on the guns. I distinctly saw him do that. I state positively that I cut down at least six drivers.

Whilst we were so engaged, several scattered parties of Cossacks got to our rear, as did also a regiment of Russian lancers which formed to our left rear on our return. We were then ordered to form on the 17th Lancers, but, as we found out, the troops which we had taken for the 17th were Russian lancers. However, we got back in front of them without being molested by them. On returning to the place we originally started from, I saw, for the first time since we had departed, the Earl of Cardigan, who must have arrived before us, and he came up and said, 'Men, it was a hare-brained trick, but it was no fault of mine.' I heard some of the men, who were naturally still rather excited, say, 'Never mind, my Lord, we are ready to go again.' Lord Cardigan replied, 'No, no, men, you have done enough.' I heard no command given that day by Lord Cardigan, whilst we were so engaged, that is to say from the time we started to our return.[9]

Whilst serving with the Yorkshire Hussars, Short kept an inn in the Chapel Allerton district of Leeds. Sadly he was not able to make a success of the business and was declared bankrupt in 1870. By a sad irony, as a result of his bankruptcy he also lost his military pension, which must have further increased his financial difficulties. He attended the first Balaclava Banquet in 1875, became a member of the Balaclava Commemoration Society in 1879, and died at Kilmersdon, Somerset, in May 1886, aged sixty-one years.

Another equally awe-inspiring Charge of the Light Brigade DCM was awarded to Corporal John Allen, 13th Light Dragoons. Allen was born on 14 February 1826 at Englefield, near Reading. He joined the 13th Light Dragoons in 1842 and was present with the regiment throughout the Crimean War, taking part in the affair at Bulganek on 19 September 1854, and the Battle of the Alma on the following day. He was promoted to the rank of Corporal on 1 October 1854. At Balaclava on 25 October, the 13th Light Dragoons were in the Light Brigade on the right of the line. Allen rode in the famous charge in the third line and though he had his horse killed under him, he survived unscathed. He afterwards took part in the Battle of Inkerman and in the siege of Sebastopol. He was promoted to Sergeant on 7 August 1855, received his Long Service and Good Conduct medal after eighteen years' service in 1862, and retired in the rank of Squadron Sergeant-Major. Allen was present at the Balaclava Banquets held in 1875 and 1892, and was one of the survivors of the charge who signed the Loyal Address on the occasion of Queen Victoria's Golden Jubilee in 1887. In that same year he took over as landlord of the Swan Hotel in Leek, Staffordshire, and died there at the age of sixty-eight on 30 July 1894.

The same day as the Light Brigade was destroyed, 25 October 1854, a far more successful charge was made by the cavalry of the Heavy Brigade, though this has largely been overshadowed in the public consciousness by the events surrounding the Light Brigade earlier in the day. Among the men who charged with the Heavy Brigade was Private Michael Macnamara of the 5th Dragoon Guards, who was later to be awarded the Distinguished Conduct Medal for his part in the fighting. Again, we have an eyewitness account of these events, in the form of a letter from Corporal Joseph Gough, 5th Dragoon Guards:

> We had no infantry up at the time, except the highlanders, who formed squares, and popped them off nicely, so they retired from them. In the meantime, another lot of cavalry came to attack us. I suppose they thought we should run. At first we thought they were our Light Brigade till they got about twenty yards from us; then we saw the difference. We wheeled into line. They stood still, and we did not know what to do. The charge sounded and away we went into the

midst of them. Such cutting and slashing for about a minute, it was dreadful to see; the rally sounded, but it was no use - none of us would come away until the enemy retreated; then our fellows cheered as loud as ever they could. When we were in the midst of them my horse was shot; he fell, and got up again, and I was entangled in the saddle; my head and one leg were on the ground. He tried to gallop on with the rest, but fell again, and I managed to get loose. While I was in that predicament a Russian lancer was going to run me through, and I could not help myself. Macnamara came up at the time, and nearly severed his head from his body; so, thank God, I did not get a scratch. I got up, and ran to where I saw a lot of loose horses; I got one belonging to one of the Enniskillens, and soon was along with the regiment again.[10]

Macnamara's DCM was recommended in January 1855.

Another member of the Light Cavalry Brigade to be decorated with the DCM in the Crimea was John Breeze. He was born in Stepney in about 1818, and enlisted into the 11th Hussars at Hounslow in March 1841. He sailed for the Crimea in May 1854 and served there until invalided in May 1855. It is not known for certain if he actually took part in the famous charge at Balaclava. However, he attended the first Balaclava Banquet on 25 October 1875, and his portrait was published in the *Illustrated London News* on 30 October of that year, where he was described as one of the 'Survivors of the Light Cavalry Brigade'. This much was true. He is recorded as a survivor in the 1877 Balaclava Commemoration List, but not in the 1879 edition. His gravestone states 'formerly of the 11th Hussars and one of the Balaclava Six Hundred', but of course this epitaph was written by those who came after him.

What is more certain is the fact that he lost his right arm at the Battle of Inkerman on 5 November 1854, the circumstances being described by the Regimental Sergeant-Major, George Loy Smith, in his book *A Victorian R.S.M.*:

The Chasseurs d'Afrique now went past us at a gallop and passed over the brow of the hill. We halted about 200 yards from the top. The enemy must have known we were there, for they dropped their cannonballs just over the brow of the hill so that they passed through us about breast high. One struck a horse's head knocking it to pieces, then took off Sergeant Breese's [sic] arm, taking the three bars and leaving the crown. It then struck Private Wright, who was riding a Russian horse, full in the chest, passing through him. He fell out of the saddle close to my horse's feet. His horse then galloped away and we never saw it again.[11]

Breeze was to suffer further hardship when during the great storm of 14 November, he and many other injured were left lying unattended outside Balaclava Harbour. He was then taken to Scutari hospital, where Sergeant-Major Smith visited him on 22 November:

> On asking the sergeant whose arm was struck off at Inkerman, how he was, he said his arm had been amputated a second time, and that he suffered greatly and feared he should not live he had had such a dreadful diarrhoea. Having heard that Dutch cheese was an excellent thing for diarrhoea, I went out to the bazaar and bought one. He ate a large piece at once, the next day he was much better, after that he improved daily and was quite well as far as his health was concerned. Before I left Scutari, he often thanked me, saying the cheese saved his life.[12]

Sergeant Breeze was successfully recommended for the Distinguished Conduct Medal on 10 January 1855, with a gratuity of £10. His was one of eight DCMs awarded to men of the 11th Hussars for services in the Crimea. Invalided home, he was presented with his Crimea medal by Her Majesty Queen Victoria, at Horse Guards Parade, on 18 May 1855. He left the Army that same month and was appointed to the Queen's Body Guard as a Yeoman in the same year. Breeze rose to become Sergeant-Major of the Fourth Division of the Guard, and was reported to have been a favourite of Queen Victoria, attending the 1887 Jubilee, for which he received the bronze medal. He died at Battersea on 11 October 1889, and was buried two days later in Battersea Cemetery.

~ 0 ~

It must have seemed to the Victorians that no sooner had one catastrophic military campaign in the east drawn to a close than another one, potentially even more serious, blew up. This time it was not merely the question of the balance of power in a far corner of Europe that was at stake. Rather it was the entire future of Britain's hold over her greatest overseas possession, India, which in 1857 came into question. The embers of the Indian Mutiny (or the First Indian War of Independence) had been smouldering for some time before catching light. The shabby treatment of the Indian nobility by the Honourable East India Company (HEAC), which governed India on behalf of the British Crown, was the cause of much humiliation and simmering resentment. Although there were regular British Army regiments stationed in India, 'John Company' as the HEAC was known controlled India largely through its own army, some regiments of which were European, and others of which were native. Here again there was seething discontent. In native regiments, the white British officers treated their soldiers with disdain. Mixing of castes in Hindu regiments caused humiliation, and there was a general distrust of the British and their methods. Many sepoys were fearful that the British secretly wanted to convert them to Christianity, and planned to do this by making them outcasts within their own communities. Matters came to a head with the introduction of a new musket and cartridge, which soldiers were required to bite. The rumour, spread largely by the Indian princely rulers, was that the cartridges were greased with a mix of pork and beef tallow. The former was abhorrent to the Muslim sepoys, the later holy to those of the Hindu faith. The first hint of trouble came at Barrackpore, where a sepoy named Mangal Pandey refused to handle the cartridges. Pandey's stand was one of the first sparks. Soon after, in May 1857, European men, women and children were murdered in Meerut by disgruntled sepoys, and before long central India was in outright revolt.

For both sides the city of Delhi was of symbolic importance; the mutineers marched there at the start of the revolt and after slaughtering as many British as they could find, installed the ageing mogul emperor as their leader. The British, gathering reinforcements from across India, camped before Delhi's enormous walls, and tried to contain the mutineers whilst they brought up siege guns large enough to batter a way through them. The 8th (King's) Regiment was among those units that assembled on the ridge before Delhi. The 5,000-strong British force was ready to make its assault on 14 September 1857. The King's Regiment, reduced now through disease to about 250 all ranks, served in Number 2 Column, under Brigadier Jones of Her Majesty's 61st Regiment, and stormed through a breach in the walls of Delhi at the position known as the Water Bastion.

Among them was James Henry Robinson, by trade a 'Writing Clerk'. He was born in Kilbride, near Arklow, County Wicklow, around 1821. He enlisted into the 40th Regiment of Foot at Athy, Wicklow, on 18 February 1845. The date is particularly significant for in that year Ireland was in the grip of the Great Famine. Thousands were dying of starvation as the potato crop failed. By February, after a hard winter things must have been desperate even for a literate man like Robinson and out of sheer desperation like so many of his compatriots, he opted to join the Army. On 1 June of that year he transferred to the 8th (King's) Regiment, and a year later on 18 March 1846 he managed to purchase his discharge for the not inconsiderable sum of £20, leaving the Army at Portsmouth. Curiously, however, and for reasons about which we can now only speculate, Robinson chose to re-enlist in the 8th just one month later. The regiment had now left for India, and he followed them on 1 August, rejoining regimental headquarters on 20 December 1846. He was already a lance corporal, and thenceforth promotion was rapid: he was made corporal on 14 October the following year, sergeant, on 10 November 1848, and became sergeant-major on 11 February 1857.

After a terrific battering of the walls, the attacking columns attempted to storm Delhi through a number of breaches, Robinson taking part in that by the so-called Water Bastion, by the Jumma River. Once the men got though the gaps in the walls, they were met with a fusillade of fire. Mutineers on the flat roofs of the houses fired down into the columns fighting their way through the narrow streets, whilst cannon fired grapeshot into them, further thinning their ranks. In a grim illustration of the damage that could be inflicted by mid-nineteenth century weaponry, Robinson was wounded by a musket ball, which severely fractured the lower end of the humerus of his right arm, with the result that the arm was permanently crippled, and his forearm bent at a right angle to the arm.

He was sent down country and invalided, receiving his discharge as medically unfit at Chatham on 3 May 1859. He went to live in Dublin on a small pension but quickly found it hard to survive. Assuming that he was right-handed, the wound would almost certainly have prevented him from writing and he probably found it impossible to return to his original trade of clerk. He applied for an increase in pension but was turned down in July 1859. On 6 March 1860, however, a submission was made on his behalf for the award of the DCM. In this period the medal was linked to two types of monetary award, the annuity and the gratuity. The DCM with annuity was to be given to NCOs with the rank of sergeant or above, while the DCM with gratuity, ranging from £5 to £15, was available to all those below commissioned rank. The gratuity was paid out of a special fund set up when the DCM was instituted in 1854, but by 1857 this fund was virtually exhausted. The result was that only the DCM with annuity for sergeants and above was awarded for services in the mutiny, and even then only twenty-two sergeants received it. Robinson was one of them, and was decorated with the DCM with annuity of £10, for 'his meritorious service and gallant conduct in the field more especially in the field before Delhi in September 1857'. He received an increase to his pension on 12 May 1868 bringing it to 1s.10d. per day, and the annuity for the DCM was raised to £15 in 1880. Robinson died from chronic gastritis in a rented room at 34 Usher's Quay, Dublin, on 4 December 1890.

Whilst India had been the focus of British imperial expansion in the first half of the nineteenth century, with the suppression of the mutiny by 1858 the sub-continent was pacified, and British control there would not be seriously challenged again for almost a hundred years. In the second half of the nineteenth century, Britain's imperial ambitions were played out instead for the most part in Africa. The opening up of the Dark Continent to Europeans led to a 'scramble for Africa', as the British, French, Belgians and Portuguese carved out their share. In West Africa, some thirty DCMs were awarded for the 1873-74 Ashantee campaign (actually the third of the four Anglo-Ashanti wars). The Ashanti were a people who occupied the interior of what is now Ghana. Traditionally, they had ruled over the coastal peoples, who in the nineteenth century had begun to look to the British for protection from the Ashanti. In 1871 Britain purchased from Holland the Dutch Gold Coast, including Elmina, which was also claimed by the Ashanti. The Ashanti subsequently invaded the new British protectorate, triggering war. General Garnet Wolseley, with 2,500 British troops and several thousand West Indian and African troops, was sent to suppress the Ashanti. He fought the Battle of Amoaful on 31 January 1874, and later that month the Battle of Ordahsu. Some British accounts pay tribute to the hard fighting of the Ashanti at Amoaful, particularly the tactical insight of their commander, Amanquatia:

> The great Chief Amanquatia was among the killed. Admirable skill was shown in the position selected by Amanquatia, and the determination and generalship he displayed in the defence fully bore out his great reputation as an able tactician and gallant soldier. [13]

The capital, Coomassi, was abandoned by the Ashanti and was briefly occupied by the British and burned. In July 1874, the Asantahene, the defeated ruler, was forced to sign up to harsh British terms in the Treaty of Fomena, which ended the war. One of the DCMs gained in the Ashanti campaign was awarded to Sergeant Charles Page of the Royal Engineers. Page was born in the Parish of St Pancras, London, and was a carpenter prior to enlisting into the Royal Engineers at Chatham, on 16 November 1861. The recommendation submitted by J Browne, Deputy Adjutant General RE, and dated Horse Guards, 17 April 1874, states:

> 7067 Sergeant Page, Charles. Worked unceasingly in charge of large working parties of natives. He was continuously alone and

unsupported. At the action at Amoaful he behaved with great gallantry, encouraged the black labourers to advance and was frequently exposed when in charge of road making parties, especially on the afternoon of the 30 January 1874.[14]

The medal was presented by Her Majesty Queen Victoria at Windsor Castle on 16 May 1874. On that same occasion the Queen presented a further DCM for Amoaful, this one being awarded to Sergeant William Street of the 42nd Royal Highlanders (The Black Watch). The 42nd played a leading role in the Ashanti Campaign, in particular during the successful advance to Coomassie through the dense jungle of the West African interior. William Street was not, however, a Scot, for he was born in the Parish of Aston-Remenham, near Henley-on-Thames, Berkshire. He attested for the 42nd Regiment at Westminster in January 1858, aged eighteen. His DCM was awarded for the Battle of Amoaful, on 31 January 1874, where he was wounded, his recommendation making reference to:

> The cheerful disregard of personal danger of Sergeant-Instructor of Musketry Street, though badly wounded in the thigh.[15]

Whilst the British were struggling to suppress the peoples of West Africa and bring an imperial hegemony to bear over that part of the Dark Continent, a similar conflict was raging in southern Africa. Numerous once proud and independent African peoples had been brought under Britain's sway in the relentless expansion in the Cape. It should not however, be thought that the British had matters all their own way. Native peoples were more than capable of inflicting bloody and decisive defeats on the invaders. The best known example of this is the Anglo–Zulu War of 1879, when after engineering a pretext to cross the Buffalo River and suppress the Zulu Kingdom of Cetshwayo, the British under Lord Chelmsford were severely defeated at Isandlwana. The battle at Rorke's Drift that followed is probably the most famous action in the history of Britain's colonial adventures, if not the most famous moment in Britain's entire military history, thanks to the celebrated movie *Zulu* (1963) starring Michael Caine.

The tiny garrison of Rorke's Drift was surrounded by an enormous Zulu army for more than twenty-four hours, before the attackers were eventually driven off. An unprecedented eleven Victoria Crosses were awarded for this action, the most ever granted for a single battle. Yet only five awards of the DCM were made for Rorke's Drift, which makes this the antithesis of the usual relationship between the two awards.

One of the five went to John Cantwell, who was born in the parish of St

James, Dublin, and enlisted into the 9th Regiment on 6 November 1868, aged twenty-three years six months. He transferred to the Royal Artillery on 1 April 1872 and joined 'N' Battery on 1 July 1877. He arrived at the Cape of Good Hope on 9 January 1878, and subsequently took part in the advance into Zululand. He was promoted to bombardier-wheeler on 29 July 1878, but reverted to gunner on 21 January 1879, in which rank he was present at the defence of Rorke's Drift. He was awarded the Distinguished Conduct Medal for his part in the defence of the hospital within the compound. After they had set fire to the thatched roof, the Zulus were fought off at bayonet point, whilst the patients had to be removed from room to room. Some sources show Cantwell as wounded, though this is unconfirmed. He returned to England on 31 March 1879, and his DCM was presented to him by Her Majesty the Queen at Windsor Castle on 8 March 1880. He was discharged at Woolwich on 19 July 1887 as medically unfit for further service and went to live with his wife and daughter at Pietermaritzburg, South Africa.

The most famous DCM of the Zulu War is undoubtedly that of Colour Sergeant Frank Bourne. The character of Bourne appears in the film *Zulu* which did so much to create interest in the events of the Zulu War in the late twentieth century. However, the actor portraying Bourne on screen was a much older man than he had actually been at the time. He was in fact only twenty-three years old when promoted to the rank of colour sergeant, and was known as 'the kid' as a result. Frank Bourne was the last survivor of Rorke's Drift when he died aged eighty-nine in 1945. He was born at Balcombe, in Sussex, in 1855, the son of a labourer on the railways, and enlisted on 17 December 1872 for the 24th Regiment of Foot. He was clearly an intelligent and reasonably well educated man for his station in life, as evidenced both by his rapid promotion and the fact that in the early years of his service he acted as unpaid secretary to several other men who could barely read or write, penning their letters home and reading the replies. Bourne gave a first-hand account of the events leading to his award of the DCM for services at Rorke's Drift in *The Listener* magazine (published by the BBC) in December 1936:

> ... about 4.30, the enemy from 500 to 600 strong, came in sight round the hill to our south, and driving in my thin red line of skirmishers, made a rush at our south wall. They were met and held by a steady and deliberate fire for a short time, then being reinforced by some hundreds, they made desperate and repeated attempts to break through our temporary defences, but were repulsed time and again. To show their fearlessness and their contempt for the redcoats and

their small numbers, they tried to leap the parapet, and at times tried to seize our bayonets, only to be shot down. Looking back one cannot help but admire their fanatical bravery. About 7 o'clock they succeeded, after many attempts, in setting fire to the hospital. The small numbers we were able to spare defended it room by room, bringing out all the sick who could be moved before they retired. Privates Hook, R.Jones, W.Jones and J.Williams were the last to leave, holding the door with the bayonet when all their ammunition was expended. The Victoria Cross was awarded to these men and they fully deserved it.

The Zulu had collected the rifles from the men who they had killed at Isandhlwana, and had captured the ammunition from the mules which had stampeded and threw their loads; so our own arms were used against us. In fact this was the cause of every one of our casualties, killed and wounded, and we should have suffered many more if the enemy had known how to use a rifle. There was hardly a man even wounded by an assegai, their principal weapon.

Lieutenants Chard and Bromhead and the men received the thanks of parliament, the officers being promoted to the rank of Major. I was awarded the Distinguished Conduct Medal with annuity of £10, the same as awarded to the Victoria Cross, and awarded a commission, but as I was the youngest of eight sons and the family exchequer was empty, I had to refuse it at the time. Now just one word for the men who fought that night; I was moving about amongst them all the time, and not for one moment did they flinch, their courage and bravery cannot be expressed in words. For me they were an example of my soldiering days.[16]

~ 0 ~

The Second Afghan War of 1878-80 came about through the perceived threat to British India, which resulted from Russian overtures towards Afghanistan. The British had always feared Russia's ambitions towards India, the jewel in her imperial crown, and regarded Afghanistan as a vital buffer state, preventing the mighty Russian army pouring through the Khyber Pass and on into India. With the Emir of Afghanistan favourably disposed towards the Russians, India was vulnerable and the British were prepared to fight to depose him. Indeed, the war eventually resulted in de-facto British rule over Afghanistan, through pro-British puppet rulers. In late 1878, three large British columns totalling 40,000 men crossed the border from India into Afghanistan to subdue the country. After battles at Ali Musjid and Peiwar Kotal, which the British won, the war appeared to be over and a treaty was forced upon the Afghans. However, fighting flared anew as the British resident in Kabul was murdered. The war entered a second phase in 1879 as British troops fought to occupy the remaining portion of the country.

Howard Hensman, special correspondent of the *Allahabad Pioneer*, wrote a history of the Second Afghan War. He gives the following details, in a description of the attack on the Asmai Heights on 1 December 1879:

> Colonel Jenkins then worked his way under a heavy fire along the crest, which has a total length of a quarter of a mile; and there only remained the southern sangar, built on the peak of the hill, to be taken. In this sangar, which was unusually strong, were forty or fifty men who, by their fire, checked the advance for some time. Major Stockwell, with a few Highlanders, passed through a gap in the wall which runs down the ridge, and galled the ghazis by a cross fire. Private Gillan, of the 72nd, climbed up the wall, and, creeping along the top, pulled out a standard from among the stones of the sangar.[17]

Patrick Gillan was born in the Parish of Mary Hill, Glasgow, and joined the 72nd Highlanders in August 1877. His papers confirm that he was discharged to the Reserve in August 1889. His character was then described as: 'Bad, owing to drunkenness and absence', but also that he was 'awarded Distinguished Conduct Medal for gallantry at assault of the Asmai Heights, Kabul, 1st December 1879.'[18]

One of the most remarkable fighting DCMs of the Victorian period was also awarded during the Second Afghan War, to a soldier by the name of John Woods, an Irishman born in the Parish of Benow, Cork, in 1852. Woods enlisted into the 5th Fusiliers (later the Royal Northumberland Fusiliers) in Glasgow, on 18 June 1870, aged eighteen years and a carpenter by trade. He was soon posted to India to serve with the 1st Battalion, where he reached the rank of sergeant in May 1877. The 5th Fusiliers were heavily engaged during the Afghan war, taking part in various small actions during 1879. However, it was in 1880 that the action occurred for which Woods, now a colour sergeant, was to be decorated.

On 18 May 1880, Headquarters and 200 men of the 5th Fusiliers, with other details, crossed over the Kabul River into the Besud district, and forming part of the force commanded by Brigadier-General J Doran, were engaged in the defeat of the Safi tribe near the village of Beninga on the following day. Twenty-five of the enemy shut themselves up in a tower, and resisted to the last. Several of them made an attempt to fight their way out but were met hand to hand by Colonel Rowland, Captain Kilgour, Colour Sergeant Woods, and Private Openshaw, and were killed; five who still remained alive were subsequently despatched, after a desperate fight in the fort itself, by Captain Kilgour and Colour Sergeant Woods, who had charged in to bring matters to a close.

The following details of this incident were published in the despatch from Brigadier-General Doran, dated Besud, 27 May 1880:

> ... a desperate hand to hand fight ensued, in which three Afghans were killed ... as soon as the conflict in the courtyard had ended Co. Sergeant Woods with dashing gallantry rushed up the debris and disappeared into the tower, closely followed by Captain Kilgour, and there these two found and slew five desperate men at bay. A finer display of courage cannot well be imagined.[19]

In July 1880, Captain Kilgour and Colour Sergeant Woods were recommended for the Victoria Cross, and other men in the party for the Distinguished Conduct Medal. However, the Commander-in-Chief refused to confirm these awards and Captain Kilgour instead received the brevet of major, whilst a DCM recommendation for Woods was submitted to Her Majesty Queen Victoria on 4 June 1881. Woods finally received his medal at a presentation by the Queen at Osborne House, on 17 August 1881.

Because of the initial Victoria Cross recommendation, Colour Sergeant Woods was required to make a statement regarding his part in the action at Besud, in which he described the incident in his own words. This is a remarkable document and makes for gripping reading (it is worth noting beforehand, however, that when Woods uses 'sword' he appears to mean 'bayonet'. Mid nineteenth-century bayonets could in extremis be used as swords):

> At the taking of the tower, on the 19th May 1880, myself and Pte Openshaw charged into a small place at the foot of the tower - Pte Openshaw shot one and before he had time to recover himself another of the enemy attacked him and gave him a severe wound on the wrist. Col Rowland got wounded at this time.
>
> I also noticed Pte Longworth of the 12th Regiment on my right engaged with the enemy. I saw one of the enemy making a severe cut at him with one of those long knives, and saw he could not parry it. I tried to do so but failed as the knife gave him a severe wound on the shoulder. My sword had got bent a few seconds before this by one of the enemy jumping out of the tower at me. I transfixed him with my sword and

the weight of his body bent it in the manner described. I then helped to despatch any of the enemy I saw at the bottom of the tower.

I then made a charge for the hole in the tower and was met at the entrance by a fellow I took for one of the priests as he flung a book of the Koran in my face and attacked me at the same time with a hatchet; he flung the hatchet at me but I warded the blow with my rifle. I must have put the sword through his heart, as his death appeared to be instantaneous. After withdrawing my sword my foot slipped and I fell, about four of them caught my sword and tried to drag me in but my rifle was loaded so I pulled the trigger and blew their hands and fingers off. I at once got to my feet and engaged with the nearest fellow. I put my sword through his windpipe and the weight of his body falling before I could withdraw it bent it more and made it useless. I got the fellow's sword and shield and used that. They then commenced to hurl their rifles at me and one struck me on the forearm and gave a bruise which is rather painful.

One fellow fired at me inside, he was kneeling down but fortunately missed me. I thought it had hit Capt Kilgour who was just in the rear of me, I forgot to mention his name before. He was second into the tower and it was not his fault that he was not first and did some splendid work when he did get in. When I first got into the tower I thought there were about twenty of the enemy there, but I could not exactly say. I can't remember anyone but Capt Kilgour following me into the tower as I was much too occupied with the work that had to be done.[20]

For reasons now unknown, a few weeks after receiving the DCM, Woods went absent without leave for about three months. It may be tempting to speculate that he was suffering from what we might now describe as post-traumatic stress disorder (PTSD). Whatever the reason, his regiment was less than sympathetic. When he returned, he was immediately demoted to private and transferred out of the regiment into the Durham Light Infantry, and a month later he moved on again to the Grenadier Guards. Woods nevertheless continued with his military career, and went on to regain non-commissioned rank.

At the Battle of Maiwand on 27 July 1880, a British column was ambushed by an Afghan army, and the 66th (Royal Berkshire) Regiment was almost totally destroyed. The regiment was trying to hold its ground when on the flank the Bombay Grenadiers, attempting to form hollow squares, were driven back onto it. A chaotic retreat followed until the Berkshires attempted to make a stand at the village of Khig. Some 216 men were killed and nearly thirty wounded in this disastrous affair, with more men picked off as stragglers as they attempted to reach Kandahar. The Berkshires lost their Colours, and most of the regimental documents. One sergeant and five soldiers received the DCM for their part in this battle. Private William Clayton was one of those awarded the DCM for gallantry at Maiwand in rescuing an officer, Lieutenant Hyacinth Lynch, who was dangerously wounded. The medal was presented to him by Her Majesty the Queen at Osborne House on 17 August 1881. This was not his only reward, however, as he also received a silver-cased pocket watch with a finely engraved inscription on the inner case reading:

> Presented by Lieut. H. Lynch, 66th Regt. to W. Clayton, as a token of gratitude for his gallant conduct in rescuing him while wounded on the Battlefield of Maiwand. 27th July, 1880.[21]

It is interesting to note that Lynch's sword was found six years after the battle in the possession of an Afghan general. It was removed from him and returned to its proper owner. Lynch retired to write his memoirs as a major, and left his blade to the regimental museum, where it is still held.

In the Second Afghan War, almost as soon as one area was suppressed, fighting seemed to spring up anew somewhere else. No sooner had an Afghan army at Kabul been dispersed than another besieged a British force at Kandahar. Having fought at the Battle of Charasia in October 1879, and in the operations around Kabul in the following December, Private William McGillivray accompanied General Roberts on his famous march from Kabul to relieve Kandahar in August 1880. McGillivray was born in 1849 in the Parish of Petty, Inverness, and enlisted into the 92nd Highlanders at Dublin on 26 March 1867, a ploughman by trade. In the Battle of Kandahar on 1 September 1880, he was dangerously wounded by grapeshot in the left arm and hand, three bullets causing considerable damage, according to his discharge papers 'equivalent to the loss of a limb'. The circumstances that led to the award of the DCM were described in Lord Roberts' despatch published in the *London Gazette* of 3 December 1880. McGillivray was one of ten officers and men of the 92nd Highlanders and 2nd Gurkhas who 'showed great gallantry and forwardness in the attack on the Afghan entrenchment near the foot of the Baba Wali Pass.'[22] McGillivray's wounds led to his eventual discharge from the Army, at Aberdeen, on 15 August 1882. He was then aged thirty-three, and stated his intended place of residence to be Dulcross Station, by Inverness.

~ 0 ~

The Sudanese war of 1884 was provoked by the rise in the Sudan of the Madhi, a leader revered by his followers as a holy man, whose coming to purify Islam was foretold in the Koran. The Madhi capitalised on Sudanese resentment of rule by neighbouring Egypt, and urged the Sudanese people to cease paying taxes to the Egyptian Government. Egyptian forces sent to arrest him were repulsed with bloody losses and soon the Sudan was in open revolt. Britain's support for Egypt was founded upon her need to protect the Suez canal, the main sea route to India. The British Government, under Liberal prime minister William Gladstone, was reluctant to become involved in Egypt's problems in the Sudan, and instead urged the Egyptians simply to cut their losses and withdraw their garrisons. General Charles Gordon was dispatched to the Sudan to organise the withdrawal of Egyptian military and civilian personnel, but to the fury of Gladstone, he chose to disregard his orders and instead tried to hold the Sudan against the Madhist forces almost single-handed. He allowed himself to be besieged at Khartoum, necessitating an Anglo-Egyptian relief effort.

The 10th Hussars left India bound for home after completion of their tour of duty in February 1884, but instead found themselves diverted to Suakin, where they arrived on 18 February. They at that time possessed no horses but General Valentine Baker Pasha, their former commanding officer, handed over three hundred of his Egyptian Gendarmerie horses, for which British sailors made nosebags, and head and heel ropes. On 29 February the 10th Hussars fought at the Battle of El-Teb where they made two brilliant charges against the enemy. Among them was Trooper Frank Hayes, an Irishman who was born at Island Bridge, Dublin, in 1856, and who had joined the 10th Hussars as a musician on 29 December 1877. There are various published accounts of Trooper Hayes' gallantry in the battle. Cassell's *History of the War in the Soudan* states:

> Private Frank Hayes of the 10th Hussars showed great courage in the second charge here, in dismounting, attacking, and killing a chief who was endeavouring to escape. Finding that his horse would not face the spear, he undauntedly attacked the Arab on foot, and killed him in single combat.[23]

Other accounts state that Hayes, a noted pugilist, found himself surrounded and, being unable to wield his sword effectively on horseback, dismounted, and dispersed his assailants with his fists. Hayes went on to fight with his regiment at the Battle of Tamaai on 13 March 1884, and two days later a remarkable poem about him was published in *Punch* magazine entitled *A Tale of the Tenth Hussars!*:

When the sand of the lonely desert has covered the plains of strife,
Where the English fought for the rescue, and the Arab stood for his life;
When the crash of the battle is over, and healed are our wounds and
    scars,
There will live in our island story a Tale of the Tenth Hussars!

They had charged in the grand old fashion with furious shout and swoop,
With a 'Follow me, Lads!' from the Colonel, and an answering roar from
    the troop;
From the Staff, as the Troopers past it, in glory of pride and pluck,
They heard, and they never forgot it, one following shout, 'Good luck!'

Wounded and worn he sat there, in silence of pride and pain,
The man who'd led them often, but was never to lead again.
Think of the secret anguish! think of the dull remorse!
To see the Hussars sweep past him, unled by the old White Horse!

An alien, not a stranger; with heart of a comrade still,
He had borne his sorrow bravely, as a soldier must and will;
And when the battle was over, in deepening gloom and shade,
He followed the Staff in silence, and rode to the grand parade;

For the Tenth had another hero, all ripe for the General's praise,
Who was called to the front that evening by the name of Trooper Hayes;
He had slashed his way to fortune, when scattered, unhorsed, alone,
And in saving the life of a comrade had managed to guard his own.

The General spoke out bravely as ever a soldier can –
'The Army's proud of your valour; the Regiment's proud of their man!'
Then across that lonely desert, at the close of the General's praise,
Came a cheer, then a quick short tremble on the lips of Trooper Hayes.

'Speak out,' said the kindly Colonel, 'if you've anything, Lad, to say;
Your Queen and your dear old country shall hear what you've done to-
    day!'
But the Trooper gnawed his chin-strap, then sheepishly hung his head;
'Speak out, old chap!' said his comrades. With an effort, at last, he said –

'I came to the front with my pals here, the boys, and the brave old tars,
I've fought for my Queen and country, and rode with the Tenth Hussars;
I'm proud of the fine old regiment!' - then the Colonel shook his hand -
'So I'll ask one single favour from my Queen and my native land!

'There sits by your side on the Staff, Sir, a man we are proud to own!
He was struck down first in the battle, but was never heard to groan;
If I've done ought to deserve it,' - then the General smiled 'Of course,' -
'Give back to the Tenth their Colonel - the Man on the old White Horse!

'If ever a man bore up, Sir, as a soldier should, with pluck,
And fought with a savage sorrow the demon of cursed ill-luck-
That man he sits beside you! Give us back, with his wounds and scars,
The man who has sorely suffered, and is loved by the Tenth Hussars!'

Then a cheer went up from his comrades, and echoed across the sand,
And was borne on the wings of mercy to the heart of his native land,
Where the Queen in her Throne will hear it, and the Colonel Prince will
    praise
The words of a simple soldier just uttered by Trooper Hayes.
Let the moralist stoop to mercy, that balm of all souls that live;
For better than all forgetting, is the wonderful word 'Forgive!'[24]

The following year, on 13 March 1885, Hayes was personally presented with the Distinguished Conduct Medal by Her Majesty Queen Victoria at Windsor Castle. It was the only DCM awarded to the 10th Hussars for the Battle of El-Teb. Hayes was appointed lance corporal in March 1887 but reverted to private three months later. He was discharged from the 10th Hussars at his own request on 6 August 1887, upon his payment of £21. He joined the Scots Guards shortly afterwards as a musician, for twelve years. He was finally discharged as medically unfit on 21 April 1899, and died sometime in or about 1926.

Another DCM awarded for the Sudan War was granted to Lance Corporal W J Johnstone, 8th Railway Company, Royal Engineers, for his part in the Defence of Ambigol Wells, north of Akasha, from 3 to 4 December 1885. This astonishing action was in the highest tradition of British imperial 'daring-do'; it was real *Boys Own* stuff, and one is struck by the similarities with the action at Rorke's Drift six years earlier. One wonders, had the latter incident inspired this defence? The men involved must surely have been aware of it.

The defences of the post at Ambigol Wells, on the railway line consisted of little more than sandbagged breastworks. Yet it was of great importance because it was one of only two places on the railway to Khartoum (after it diverged from the Nile) where water was obtainable. The lonely outpost was attacked by some 700 dervishes, who shouted:

Railway finish! Telegraph finish! You finish!

at the commanding officer, Captain J A Ferrier RE, and his tiny garrison of fifty men from the Royal Berkshire Regiment. For three days, Ferrier made a most gallant defence, and drove his assailants away before the relieving forces arrived on 4 December 1885. Lance Corporal Johnstone was awarded the DCM for obtaining ammunition from a goods van while under fire.[25]

~ 0 ~

Whilst the war in the Sudan was an unwelcome distraction forced upon the British by circumstance, the continual guarding of the North West Frontier of India was a more serious matter. India was the jewel in Britain's crown, but protecting it from the rebellious pushtun tribes in the tribal territories of the Afghan border area was a matter of permanent patrolling and short sharp skirmish actions. Four DCMs were awarded to the Buffs (East Kent Regiment) for bravery in the night action at Bilot on the North West Frontier in 1897. In addition, Corporal James Smith of the same battalion was awarded the Victoria Cross.

On 5 July 1899 troops of the Nagpore District paraded to witness the presentation of the Victoria Cross to Corporal Smith, and the Distinguished Conduct Medal to Private C Poile. A speech was made by Brigadier-General Sir R Westmacott KCB DSO in which he stated:

Officers, N.C.Os and men of the Nagpore Command. You are paraded here today by order of Her Most Gracious Majesty The Queen to witness the presentation of the VC to Corporal Smith of The Buffs. It is the highest order for valour in the world, is open alike to officers and men, and is the ambition of every soldier. Four men of Corporal Smith's section were awarded the Distinguished Conduct Medal at the same time, a decoration second as regards valour only to the Victoria Cross. Privates Nelthorpe, Lever and Finn have already received their medals at the hand of Her Most Gracious Majesty The Queen, at Windsor, and Private Poile is on parade today. The circumstances under which these brave men won these decorations were as follows:

On the evening of the 16th September, 1897, The Buffs were returning to Camp fighting their way inch by inch in one of those rear guard actions we all know so well, against large forces of an invisible enemy. A call was made on the regiment for an escort for a wounded officer in a dhoolie. Major Moody who was in command of the rear guard, told off the left section of 'G' Company as it happened to be the nearest. This was Corporal Smith's section, consisting of twelve men, all told. They never found the wounded officer, but they came across No. 8 N.M. Battery, with some sappers, to whom they attached themselves. Being very heavily pressed it was decided to bivouac for the night in the village of Bilot. That part of the village not occupied by this little force was held by the enemy who set fire to the village to try to drive our people into the open. Lieutenants Watson, RE, and Colvin, RE, both decorated since with the VC, with Corporal Smith's section and some sappers made two desperate attempts to drive the enemy out of the village. Corporal Smith, who was twice severely wounded, continued to command his section, and only lay down when he received a distinct order to do so, and even then continued to fire on the enemy. Privates Poile, Lever, Finn and Nelthorpe were also awarded Distinguished Conduct Medals for their conspicuous gallantry on this occasion; Privates Poile, Lever and Nelthorpe were all wounded. The little force was relieved from Camp in the early morning, but not until out of the twelve, two were killed and four wounded.

Remember this; this was no selected section, it was no picked body of men, Major Moody took the first section that came to hand, and so I say we may take them as a fair sample of what the other sections throughout the regiment are. Corporal Smith, Privates Poile, Lever, Finn and Nelthorpe, are worthy successors to those pioneers in following Lieutenant Latham who, in spite of losing his arm, saved the King's Colour, and won the gold medal (which was the V.C. in those days) at Albuhera, that battle where The Buffs went into action 750 strong and 65 only answered their names at evening Roll Call.[26]

~ 0 ~

Growing French and Belgian expansion in central Africa, and the need to control the headwaters of the Nile, meant that the British Government could not allow the turmoil in the Sudan to continue indefinitely. Horatio

Herbert Kitchener, later to become famous in the Boer War and the Great War, was appointed Sirdar (or commander) of the Egyptian army and in 1896 he was authorised to commence the reconquest of the Sudan. After the death of the Madhi, his successor the Khalifa had taken control of the region. As Kitchener's forces advanced southwards, the dervishes offered no resistance until the Battle of the Atbara, in April 1898, which the British won decisively. On this occasion Sergeant George Wyeth, Army Service Corps was awarded an unusual posthumous DCM. Indeed, the award to Wyeth up to this point was possibly unique, as the DCM was never ordinarily granted to a deceased recipient. Perhaps the controversy surrounding the award may offer some explanation as to why an exception was made. Under normal circumstances Wyeth was Chief Clerk in the 3rd Brigade office, in the safe surroundings of Aldershot Garrison. However, on the morning of the Atbara battle, General Gatacre, the brigade commander and his staff led from the front. Among them was George Wyeth, carrying Gatacre's personal Union Flag, and at the height of the battle he was shot through the left kneecap. He died some days later, following the amputation of his leg. This led to criticism from some of the officers present at the battle to the effect that Gatacre was personally responsible for this man's entirely avoidable death, by having him carry a quite unnecessary flag and thus making him an obvious target for the enemy.

The next confrontation in the Sudan came at the Battle of Omdurman, outside Khartoum, on 2 September 1898. The Khalifa's estimated 52,000 followers were soundly beaten by Kitchener's forces who were armed with superior weapons. Kitchener's Maxim machine-guns for the most part managed to keep the dervishes, who were mainly armed with swords and shields, at around 200 yards' range. One of the most famous incidents in this battle was the charge of the 21st Lancers; famous partly through its portrayal on film, and also because one of the cavalry officers present was a certain Lieutenant Winston Churchill, who would go on to greater things. Raised originally as the 21st Hussars and later converted to Lancers, the 21st were one of the last British regular cavalry units to be formed. Consequently they had fewer battle honours than many other units, and a popular joke among cavalrymen from rival regiments ran along the lines that the 21st Lancers' motto was 'Thou Shalt Not Kill'! Thus the 21st were keener than most to get into action at Omdurman, and when a party of dervishes appeared on a crest the order was given to charge. Only when the lancers breasted the rise did it become apparent that the dead ground behind sheltered an enormous force of several thousand enemy fighters. It was too late for the charging horses to stop and the lancers ploughed through the mass of dervishes. Many men were unhorsed and were left fighting for their lives. Great bravery was shown by those men whose horses had carried them through the dervish mass, and who at once turned around back into the melee to assist their comrades. Seven DCMs were awarded for this action.

Two soldiers from this regiment who received the award at Omdurman were Trooper Harold Dunstan Penn, and Trooper B Ayton. In the charge Ayton rode with 'C' Squadron whilst Harold Penn rode with 'A' Squadron, that commanded by Major Finn with Lieutenant Winston Churchill as one of its troop commanders. Penn was born at Ootacamund, Madras, in July 1876. He attested for the 21st Hussars as a boy on 1 May 1893, at Secunderabad, being appointed trumpeter four days later, reverting to private in March 1894. He was appointed lance corporal on 11 June 1898, and sergeant on 23 January 1901. His discharge documents state under 'Special instances of gallant conduct':

> At the Battle of Khartoum 2nd September 1898, assisting Private Ayton, 21st Lancers, to bring a wounded man out of action.[27]

Great bravery was also shown by the infantry in this action. One soldier decorated for his actions here was Thomas Burdett, who was born in Bradford, Yorkshire, and enlisted in the Northumberland Fusiliers in May 1883, aged twenty years. A carpenter by trade, he was also at that time a member of the 4th (Militia) Battalion, Derbyshire Regiment. He went on to gain rapid promotion, being advanced to corporal in December 1883 and to sergeant in February 1885, in which latter month he arrived in India. Prior to embarkation he had married Ellen Sadler in Dublin. Burdett was subsequently engaged in the Hazara Expedition of 1888, gained advancement to colour sergeant in September 1889 and returned home in early 1894. Then in January 1898, following a posting to Gibraltar, he participated in the operations leading to the re-conquest of the Sudan, and was awarded his DCM for the action at Omdurman. Near the end of the same year, Burdett returned home to take up an appointment with the 1st Volunteer Battalion, Northumberland Fusiliers. In June 1899, the *St. George's Gazette*, regimental newspaper of the Northumberland Fusiliers reported:

> After the inspection and drill by senior officers of the Regiment, Colonel Garstin presented the Khedive's Medal to Sergeant-Instructor T. Burdett. On presenting the medal Colonel Garstin complimented Sergeant Instructor Burdett on his well-earned honour; and also drew the attention of the Brigade to the fact this NCO was to receive the Medal for Distinguished Conduct in the

Field, which he earned at the Battle of Omdurman, especially remarking to the Volunteers that the medal was the next highest honour to be obtained by a soldier to the Victoria Cross.[28]

In fact, Burdett was to receive his decoration personally from Queen Victoria, at Windsor Castle. In the company of other heroes who were to be decorated that day he was marched up the Grand Corridor into the Queen's presence. There he dropped to one knee, whilst Her Majesty pinned the decoration to his chest. Afterwards she spoke a few words to him, congratulating him on his gallantry. It was a moment that must surely have remained with him for the rest of his life.

Burdett afterwards gave an interview to the *Morning Leader*, which was reproduced in the *St George's Gazette* of December 1899:

Windsor Castle was magnificent and he [Burdett] was particularly interested in the Khalifa's black flag in the Castle, riddled as it is with English bullets. Burdett possesses two other medals – the Black Mountain Expedition and the Khedive's, and is entitled to the English war medal for Khartoum. He is now attached to the 3rd Volunteer Battalion, Northumberland Fusiliers. Hearing that one of the men of his regiment was the present Barrack Warden at Victoria Barracks, Windsor, Burdett paid him a visit, and the old comrades were glad to meet. Sergeant-Major Fowles of the 1st Grenadiers, also warmly welcomed Burdett as an old chum.[29]

More Distinguished Conduct Medals were awarded for gallantry at the same time as the fighting in the Sudan, but for brave conduct in the eastern Mediterranean, during the Muslim riots on Crete. After the Cretan uprising against Turkish rule in 1896, the Greek army had landed on the island to protect the Cretans. As war broke out between Greece and Turkey, an international force was landed to try to keep the peace. A settlement was negotiated, but sectarian violence still flared on the streets. Massacres continued, with a serious one taking place at Heraklion in August 1898. On that occasion, whilst a British Army detachment was leading officials to their accommodation at the tax office building, a Turkish mob attacked them, killing seventeen British soldiers, the British Consul and some hundreds of Christians, and looting and setting fire to many shops. The British reacted immediately. They arrested and hanged seventeen of the ringleaders and jailed or sent to exile a large number of others. Another uprising, by the Bashi-Bazouks, or Turkish militia, took place at Kandia, on 6 September 1898, when many civilians died. After this, the international force demanded the expulsion of all Turkish paramilitaries. All six DCMs were awarded for bravery in this latter incident, and this was a rare instance of gallantry decorations being awarded without an accompanying campaign medal. Three of the six were awarded to soldiers of the Highland Light Infantry, with one also going to each of the RE, ASC and RAMC. The official despatch, published in the *London Gazette* of 24 January 1899, states that:

> The infantry called on to defend themselves, with the assistance of other detachments, against this sudden, general and treacherous attack, all belonged to the 1st Bn., the H.L.I., and behaved in a manner worthy of the traditions of this distinguished corps. [30]

Meanwhile, back in the Sudan, the pursuit of the Khalifa and those of his dervishes who had escaped the defeat at Omdurman continued into 1899. However, the bulk of the troops involved now were Egyptian and Sudanese, with only a few specialist British troops required in this later stage of the campaign. One of these men was Frederick Saddon, a Royal Marines Maxim machine-gunner. He was born in November 1865 at Portsea, near Portsmouth, Hampshire, and gave his occupation as a tailor when enlisting at Eastney on 26 January 1886. On completion of recruit training at the Walmer Depot he was posted as a private to the Royal Marine Artillery on 23 September 1886, and promoted to gunner on 19 December 1886. He embarked aboard his first vessel HMS *Cyclops* in July 1887, returned to the RMA depot (August 1887) and was next afloat aboard Neptune in March 1898 being promoted to bombardier. More ships followed, and he was promoted to sergeant on 14 September 1894. He again served at the depot (1894–98), prior to embarking for service with the Egyptian Army in June 1898, being promoted to colour sergeant on 25 October 1898.

Saddon's service record states that he was mentioned in the despatch published in the *London Gazette* of 30 January 1900 and awarded the Distinguished Conduct Medal in the *London Gazette* of 18 September 1900, 'For services during the final defeat of Khalifa November 1899'. In fact it was the action at Gedid, on 22 November 1899, that witnessed the last stand of the Khalifa and his faithful lieutenant, the Emir Ahmed Fedil, both of whom were killed, and which brought to a close the reconquest of the Sudan. The Maxim battery had played a crucial part in the operations and the Royal Marine machine-gunners, Saddon, Seabright and Sears, all received the DCM for their deadly and decisive work in this battle. A further note on Saddon's service record dated 4 April 1899 states:

Noted by direction of the Lords Commissioners of the Admiralty for excellent service with the Nile Expedition 1898.[31]

~ 0 ~

The Second Boer War was Britain's ultimate imperial conflict. It was the longest and most expensive of Britain's colonial campaigns. Coming as it did at the end of a century almost all of which had witnessed Britain's relentless expansion in Africa and Asia, it represented Britain's imperialist policy in its most naked form. The two Boer republics in southern Africa, the Transvaal and the Orange Free State, were populated by the descendents of Dutch settlers who had arrived almost a hundred years earlier. Devoutly religious, intransigent and often bigoted, the Boers nevertheless sat on some of the greatest mineral wealth in the world. This alone might not have been a catalyst for war. However, the two republics also stood stubbornly in the path of the British imperialists Cecil Rhodes and Joseph Chamberlain. The two men dreamt of building a railway linking Cape Town to Cairo, which passed through British territory all the way from the southern tip of Africa to the shores of the Mediterranean.

Tensions had been simmering for a number of years until finally in October 1899, matters came to a head. The 'Insulting Ultimatum' issued to the British government by the Transvaal's president, Paul Kruger, calling for the withdrawal of British troops from the Transvaal border, was the final trigger for war. The Boers swiftly invaded Natal and the Cape Colony, driving the British back before them at the battles of Elandslaagt and Talana in late 1899. However, instead of pressing on to Cape Town, and sweeping the British Army out of southern Africa, the Boers allowed themselves to become distracted by besieging three towns of middling strategic importance: Mafeking, Kimberley and Ladysmith. The sieges tied up large numbers of Boer fighters, and allowed the British time to regroup, get reinforcements to the Cape, and begin to drive the Boers back into their republics.

Yet the tactics of the British generals were on the whole based on the lessons of the Crimean War fifty years earlier. Whilst they were reasonably competent at moving large columns of infantry around, they took little account of modern weaponry such as the Boer Mauser rifles, with smokeless cartridges, or their Creusot 'Long Tom' field guns, which were highly effective and outranged much of the British artillery. Above all they were perplexed by the enemy's use of small fast-moving bands of mounted infantrymen, able to hit and disappear quickly. The Boers possessed few regular troops. With the exception of the Transvaal Artillery and the Transvaal Police, most of their units were commandos, formed by calling up men of military age who could ride and shoot, and who supplied their own horse. The commandos were fast and mobile, unlike the British who at the start of the war were too reliant on railways for transport and whose ponderous movements signalled their intentions well in advance.

The British relief effort was at first under the command of Sir Redvers Buller VC. Buller divided his force into three columns, one each to follow the railways towards the besieged towns. Buller's main effort was directed towards Ladysmith and he fought a series of battles in late 1899 with the intention of breaking through to the town. His early efforts, however, were not crowned with success. The disastrous 'Black Week' when the British lost three major battles in the space of seven days, earned him the nickname 'Reverse' Buller in some quarters. The most infamous of these defeats was at Colenso, when Buller's attempt to cross the Tugela River was met with submerged barbed wire entanglements in the water, and heavy and accurate Boer rifle fire. During the opening stages of the battle, the guns of 14 and 66 Batteries Royal Field Artillery were deployed by mistake too far forward in a bend of the Tugela River. All of the gunners were killed, wounded or driven off by the ferocity of Boer rifle fire, delivered at close range from three sides.

The precious field guns stood abandoned on the battlefield, a tempting prize for the Boers should they attempt to carry them off. For practical reasons as well as for reasons of honour, Captain Billy Congreve and Lieutenant the Honourable F H Roberts decided to mount an attempt to recover them. Calling for volunteers, they assembled composite teams of horses and drivers and rode out to try to save some of the guns. Of the thirteen men who went out in one attempt, five were wounded and one killed, such was the intensity of the enemy fire. An extraordinary number of nineteen DCMs were awarded to Royal Artillery gunners and drivers, for this single action on 15 December 1899.

Meanwhile, the column under Lord Methuen, which was charged with the relief of Kimberly, had modest success but still rather more than that under Buller's command. At the Battle of the Modder River on 28 November 1899, Methuen's force ran into a combined force of Boers from the Orange Free State and Transvaal. Using then novel tactics, the Boers had dug themselves in in a series of trenches on the banks of the River. The British, having no other plan than simply to try to force their way across, were at first bemused by the non-appearance of the Boers, and were then taken aback by their withering and well-aimed fire. By the end of the day they had managed to secure a toe-hold only across the river. Among the British units engaged that day was the 1st Battalion, Loyal North Lancashire Regiment. *Red Roses on the Veldt*, the story of the Lancashire Regiments in the Boer War, states that:

> The next morning it was found that the Boers had evacuated their positions and retired. It was another victory, but a dear-bought one. Methuen had lost 63 dead, and was himself among the 388 wounded. The Loyal North Lancashires had suffered three killed in action and seventeen wounded, of whom two later died. Corporal Hodgson and Private Caddick were brought to notice for rescuing wounded men, Lance Corporal Smith and Private Smith respectively, and carrying them to a place of safety under fire. Hodgson was awarded the Distinguished Conduct Medal.[32]

Thomas Hodgson, a soldier from Kensington, London, was subsequently promoted to the rank of Lance Sergeant and eventually, by 1908, Colour Sergeant. A gas fitter by trade, he had enlisted in the Army in 1894 aged eighteen. By the time of the First World War he was Regimental Sergeant Major (RSM) of the 1st Battalion, however, his military career was somewhat chequered. Despite a steady climb through the ranks his service papers record a number of brushes with authority. He was tried by court martial for the last time in France in October 1914 for dereliction of duty, in failing to place under arrest an NCO who was drunk. Although initially reduced to the ranks, the sentence was reduced to loss of seniority in his present rank. Hodgson was killed in action in France in January 1915, still holding the rank of RSM.

~ 0 ~

Inside Ladysmith, one of the besieged towns, there were numbers of acts of bravery as the defenders fought stoutly to keep the investing Boer forces occupied. The defenders were equipped with a variety of artillery pieces, notably some of the guns from HMS *Powerful*. They were also bolstered by the arrival in Ladysmith shortly before the siege began of two antiquated 6.3 inch rifled muzzle loader howitzers, together with a quantity of ammunition. Despite their age, 'Castor' and 'Pollox' as the two guns were nicknamed, performed a very useful task in the defence of the town.

On 18 December 1899, 'Castor' was hit by a shell from a Boer 'Long Tom' Creusot field gun, damaging the carriage. A repair was made and the gun was back in action the following day. However, the repair was subsequently found to be inadequate and whilst the gun was in situ, Army Ordnance Corps blacksmiths Staff Sergeant W Ford, Private E Stupple and Private J Armstrong, together with civilian blacksmiths from the Natal Government Railway depot in Ladysmith, began to effect repairs.

Their efforts evidently attracted the attention of the Boers for the gun position came under fire again and several times the small workforce was driven away by Boer shells. Commencing at 6am on 21 December 1899, the team worked for over forty hours non-stop to get the gun back into action. The three Army Ordnance Corps men were each awarded the Distinguished Conduct Medal for their efforts in repairing the gun whilst under fire.

While much of the Boer army was occupied with the sieges of the three towns, there still remained a serious threat to the Cape Colony from a Boer force moving south from the Orange Free State, which had seized Colesberg and threatened further advances. General Sir John French had, before the war, gained a name for himself as a smart and energetic young cavalry officer. To him was entrusted the checking of the Colesberg Boers. French's original force was a mere handful of men, scraped together from anywhere. Naauwpoort was his base, but finding that Arundel was weakly held, French advanced up to it, and established his camp there towards the end of December 1899, within 6 miles of the Boer lines at Rensburg, to the south of Colesberg. His mission, with his existing forces, was to prevent the further advance of the enemy into the Colony, but he was not strong enough yet to make a serious attempt to drive them out. Before the move to Arundel his detachment had increased in size, and consisted largely of mounted men, so that it attained a level of mobility unusual for a British force at that time. With one regiment of infantry (the Berkshires) to hold the centre, his hard-riding Tasmanians, New Zealanders, and Australians, with the Scots Greys, the Inniskillings, and the Carabineers, formed a mobile screen to cover the gateway to the Cape Colony. They were aided by two batteries, O and R, of the Royal Horse Artillery.

On 30 December the enemy abandoned Rensburg, which had been their advanced post, and concentrated at Colesberg, upon which French moved his force up and seized Rensburg. The next day, 31 December, he moved out of Rensburg camp, with R and half of O Batteries RHA, the 10th Hussars, the Inniskillings, and the Berkshires, to take up a position on the west of Colesberg. On 1 January 1900, Colonel Porter, with the half-battery of O, his own regiment (the Carabineers), and the New Zealand Mounted Rifles, left camp and took a position on the enemy's left flank. The

Berkshires drove the Boers off a prominent hill, while the Horse Artillery enfiladed the enemy's right flank. After an artillery duel, O Battery succeeded in silencing the enemy guns, and they began to retire. The Boer advance into the Cape Colony had been halted. Among those decorated for this day's action was Sergeant William H M Dow, O Battery Royal Horse Artillery, his DCM being gazetted on 27 September 1901. Dow was a long-serving regular artillery NCO. Born at Northampton, he had enlisted in 1888 aged just fifteen years. He was, however, exceptionally intelligent for a Victorian enlisted man, gaining not just his army education certificates, but also passing as a qualified army schoolmaster. Promotion through the ranks was rapid and shortly after the Colesberg action, he was made battery quarter mastersergeant, followed rapidly by the rank of battery sergeant major. He served as an officer in the First World War, dying aged ninety-five in 1968.

In the new year of 1900, the British renewed the offensive to relieve the besieged towns of Ladysmith, Kimberley and Mafeking. The one battle whose name has truly entered the English lexicon, via the stands at football grounds is Spion Kop, the name given to a large flat-topped hill whose potential as an observation platform had led the Boers to name it 'Spy's Hill' in Afrikaans. In January 1900, in thick fog the British led by the Lancashire Brigade, attempted to take the hill by scrambling up the steep sides. The Boers at first abandoned the hill, then re-occupied one side. The British dug in, but as the fog lifted they realised too late that they were overlooked by Boer positions. For most of the remainder of the day they were subjected to a withering artillery bombardment by the Boers. It was said that this was the heaviest barrage ever experienced prior to the First World War. Some 350 British soldiers were killed and over 1,000 wounded. Fallen British tommies littered the hastily dug entrenchments afterwards, in an eerie precursor of the carnage that was to come on the Western Front.

Among those who fought here was Private George Charles Sholto MacLeod, a gentleman ranker, born at Sylhet, Assam, on 28 June 1877. At the age of nineteen he had enlisted in the Royal Lancaster Regiment, in which he served for over three and a half years. He served with his regiment during the South African War, and with them gained the award of the Distinguished Conduct Medal (announced in the *London Gazette* of 19 April 1901):

> ... for gallantry at Spion Kop, in the absence of stretcher-bearers he did good work in carrying wounded out of action under hot fire.[33]

MacLeod subsequently took part in the operations on Tugela Heights, where he was severely wounded. He received a commission in the Lancashire Fusiliers in May 1900. Captain MacLeod died in hospital at Bethune in France, after being wounded by shrapnel in May 1915.

Seven posthumous awards of the DCM are known to have been made during the Boer War; as noted previously, this was highly unusual and outside of normal practice for the bestowal of this award. Perhaps the need to offset the sense of national humiliation, following the disaster at Spion Kop, overrode other considerations on this particular occasion. One of the posthumous awards was to Private J Royle of the Lancashire Fusiliers, and was granted for his part in the Spion Kop action. Private Royle's was a very different walk of life from that of MacLeod; he was from the grimy terraced streets of Manchester. Royle was killed in action on 24 January 1900 and a recommendation for the award of the DCM was published in the *London Gazette* on 8 February 1901:

> 4761 Private J. Royle, 24th January, Spion Kop, ammunition carrier – conspicuous gallantry in carrying several wounded men from the firing line.[34]

The campaign to relieve the three towns went on into early 1900, the last to be reached being Mafeking, where the siege dragged out to May 1900. That year would see the British press on relentlessly through the Boer Republics, and though the Boers fought hard in a number of set-piece battles, the weight of the British Empire was against them. Buller was now replaced as overall commander by Field Marshal Frederick Roberts, whose advance on the Boer capitals, Bloemfontain and Pretoria, was slow but relentless.

Serving with the 1st Battalion King's Own Scottish Borderers in the advance on Bloemfontain (capital of the Orange Free State) was Private William Fessey, a midlander. Born at Tysoe in Warwickshire in 1870, he had enlisted in 1888. Fessey was highly literate and kept a diary of his active service; its entries paint a fascinating portrait of the war in this part of South Africa:

> 27th March 1900 Again on the march to a camp 16 miles from Bloemfontain called The Glen where the Guards were camped to guard a large bridge. This bridge was partly blown up by our own men for the purpose of stopping the enemy from taking all the rolling stock away from Bloemfontein ...

> 28th March ... We received information from one of the outposts that the enemy was in sight. Several of our cavalry were surrounded

by the Boers. When our reconnoitring scouts was out on patrol one of them was killed and one of them taken prisoner.

29th March 1900 Received orders from Lord Roberts that General Tucker and General Chermside were to take their brigade and shift the enemy who were holding Karee Siding, a small station between Glen and Brandfort. Paraded at 6.30am and we sat down in the sun till 10am, we then got orders to advance. We got in sight of the enemy about 12 mid-day and the Boers opened a terrific fire on us as soon as we got into the open veldt. Karee Siding Hills is a horseshoe shape and the Boers had occupied this when we had orders to advance. A deadly fire was put into us, but we took the position that day.

We were fighting till dark all day long without water or food. It was the severest fight the Borderers have had to the present. We had 5 men killed with one of the enemy shells. We only had nine pounders with us on this occasion for we thought there was only a small party of them which we could shift easily, but we found the difference, I am sure.

Well I was with the Maxim gun and it was a good target to them as we got into the open veldt they were on the kopjes all round. Well our gun was hit 13 times as we was advancing to get undercover and get into action. Our sergeant got hit in the hand and several others. I was firing the gun [alone]. We got to a small hill on the line, we took cover and got into action proper only 700 yards from them. I fired as long as I could see, then they ceased fire, so did I. We were a long way off the Battalion, do not know where they are.

We was complimented for our brave stand with the Maxim and that is where I was Mentioned in Despatches and got the Distinguished Conduct Medal. We had 86 killed in action that day. I shall not forget it in a hurry. My regiment suffered the most that day, but as long as we drove them out of it and beat them it was alright, but poor chaps we left 86 at Karree Siding - 29th March 1900.

30 March 1900 Up at 4am and went out on duty on the Hills which we had won from the Boers, but we could see a large place in front of us called Brandfort where the enemy supposed to have fled to in large numbers. We stayed at Karree a day or so after the Battle and it was very cold and wet at night, we had no coats or blankets and nothing to eat. We had our emergency rations, but only the Gun Team ate it as they was lost sight of all day and night, and I must say that I am one of the Gun Team and I enjoyed my rations very much,

but could have eaten more if I could have got any but no such thing as that, stuck it out.

31st March 1900. Well next day us chaps went out into the open veldt to try and find our Corps for we wanted some food very bad. I found our baggage guard and soon I got some bully beef and biscuits and a chaff about the previous day's work. I did have a jolly good feed, not having any for about 48 hours and I was ready for some packing. We found the Battalion about mid-day, they thought we was cut up the whole Regiment did, but back alright, then we camped again and had a large funeral party burying our dead.[35]

Fessey's DCM was announced in the *London Gazette* of 27 September 1901. He left the army in 1902, and worked for an engineering firm in Rugby. In 1914, at the age of forty-four and despite having eight children, William Fessey volunteered to serve in the Army once again. He was gassed at the Battle of Loos, and died in 1947 from chest problems resulting from that incident.

During the operations towards Bloemfontain in April 1900, Winston Churchill was in the thick of the action as war correspondent for the *Morning Post*. His account of the incident at Dewetsdorp in the Orange Free State was published on 22 May 1900. In it Churchill writes of accompanying a patrol of Montmorency's Scouts in an attempt to seize a kopje, or piece of high ground. Ambushed by a larger than expected Boer party, the patrol beat a hasty retreat. Churchill wrote of trying to regain his horse in the melee:

> I put my foot in the stirrup. The horse, terrified at the firing, plunged wildly. I tried to spring into the saddle. It turned under the animal's belly. He broke away and galloped madly off.
>
> Most of the Scouts were already 200 yards off. I was alone, dismounted, within the closest range, and a mile at least from cover of any kind.
>
> One consolation I had – my pistol. I could not be hunted down unarmed in the open as I had been before. But a disabling wound was the brightest prospect.
>
> I turned and, for the second time in this war, ran for my life on foot from the Boer marksmen, and I thought to myself, 'Here at last I take it.'
>
> Suddenly, as I ran, I saw a Scout. He came from the left across my front; a tall man, with skull and crossbones, on a pale horse. Death in Revelations, but life for me.

I shouted to him as he passed; 'Give me a stirrup.' To my surprise he stopped at once. 'Yes,' he said shortly. I ran up to him, did not bungle the business mounting, and in a moment found myself behind him on the saddle.

Then we rode. I put my arms round him to catch a grip of the man. My hand had become soaked with blood. The horse was hard hit; but, gallant beast, he extended himself nobly. The pursuing bullets piped and whistled – for the range was growing longer – overhead.

'Don't be frightened,' said my rescuer, 'they won't hit you.' Then, as I did not reply, 'My poor horse, oh, my poor horse; shot with an explosive bullet. The devils! But their hour will come. Oh, my poor horse.'

I said, 'Never mind, you've saved my life.' 'Ah,' he rejoined, 'but it's the horse I'm thinking about.' That was the whole of our conversation.[36]

Churchill's rescuer was a trooper named Clement Roberts. For his actions that day Roberts was awarded a DCM, and Churchill corresponded with him subsequently. On 10 December 1913 Churchill wrote:

I need not say that I have myself very great admiration for the coolness and courage with which you assisted me at Dewetsdorp. I have always felt that unless you had taken me up on your saddle, I should myself certainly have been killed or captured, and I spoke myself very strongly to General Rundle on your behalf.

I was very glad to see you had received the Distinguished Service Medal [sic] – a decoration of very great distinction and honour ... The Victoria Cross is a decoration often very capriciously awarded and there is a great deal of chance in its distribution, but the Distinguished Service Medal [sic] is much prized and respected in the Army, and you will no doubt find it a satisfactory memento of what was, beyond all question, a very faithful and self-sacrificing action on your part.[37]

~ 0 ~

Having annexed the Orange Free State into the British Empire in May, Field Marshal Roberts went on to capture Johannesburg, and finally Pretoria, the capital of the Transvaal, fell to him in June 1900. James Docherty, of the Gordon Highlanders was wounded at Leekoehoek, near

Krugersdorp, north of Johannesburg on 11 July 1900, when he received gunshot wounds in two places on the left thigh. During this action Docherty had carried a wounded artillery officer to safety, and then assisted two others before taking part in an attempt to rescue some abandoned field guns, for which he was awarded the DCM. Docherty, who was born near Thurso in March 1868, the son of a Crimean veteran of the Black Watch, enlisted in the Gordon Highlanders in September 1883. Posted to the 1st Battalion in Egypt in September of the following year, he participated in the Nile Expedition, and went on to serve on garrison duty in Malta and Ceylon before being discharged to the Army Reserve in September 1895.

In December 1899, soon after the outbreak of hostilities in South Africa, Docherty had rejoined the Colours and was posted to the 1st Battalion. In the Gordon Highlanders' regimental history, *The Life of a Regiment*, it is recorded that General Sir Horace Smith-Dorrien visited the wounded in hospital after the action at Leekoehoek and was introduced to Docherty:

'Splendid fellow, has distinguished himself in every action,' said Captain Allan. To Smith-Dorrien's encomiums on the conduct of the troops, Docherty shook a doubtful head: 'Aye, we may hae dune weel eneuch, but I dinna haud wi' yon rinnin' awa.' 'Running away?' exclaimed the startled General, 'We didn't run away, we retired by order of the C.-in-C!' 'Aye, sir, you'll maybe call it retirin' bit I ca' it rinnin' awa!'

The same source credits Docherty with having been 'brought up on porridge and milk' and that he considered the kilt the 'finest fighting dress in the world'![38] Invalided home, he transferred to the Royal Garrison Regiment, but had the unhappy experience of being court-martialled in May 1902 'for making away with a military decoration'. Found guilty, he was sentenced to fourteen days imprisonment with hard labour. Docherty subsequently found his way back to the Gordons and was finally discharged in November 1906. Once again, however, the outbreak of hostilities in 1914 found him re-enlisting in the Gordons, although on this occasion he was quickly discharged as being unfit for overseas service. Undeterred, he then enlisted in the Royal Naval Reserve in August 1915 and served as a deck hand in minesweeping trawlers for the rest of the war.

The Boer War fell into three distinct phases: the first was that of the besieged towns and the relief attempts; the second was one of set–piece battles. The final phase was a guerrilla campaign, conducted by the Boers after their defeat in conventional warfare. The Boers adopted hit and run tactics against British targets, and their guerrilla campaign, against a numerically far stronger but slower and more cumbersome enemy, had the British Army perplexed. By the closing stages of the war, the British had begun to bring the Boers to heel by emulating their tactics. Small, almost irregular units of mounted infantrymen acted in a semi-independent fashion. The Boers were finally defeated by large columns of mounted troops, sweeping the veldt and driving the Boers towards lines of blockhouses.

This was the era in which the Imperial Yeomanry and the mounted infantry really came into their own. Most infantry regiments formed a mounted infantry section, which were then grouped together as battalions. The mounted infantry were not synonymous with cavalrymen; they were not expected to ride into battle with sword and lance, but as mounted troops they possessed far greater mobility than their footsore counterparts. The Royal Irish Regiment raised such a section and its history contains a reference to a soldier of this unit, Colour Sergeant Thomas Connolly whose quick thinking resulted in a DCM award:

> At Reitvlei, on July 15 [1900] a piquet of sixteen men was saved from capture or destruction by the intelligence of Sergeant Connolly who, discovering that a party of two hundred Burghers with three guns was threatening the post, reported so clearly and promptly that his officer was able to signal for reinforcements, which fortunately arrived in time.[39]

Another soldier of the Royal Irish Regiment mounted infantry was Private Sweeney, whose DCM was gazetted posthumously in October 1902:

> Between March and November 1901, the section was in the south of the Free State, occupied in clearing the country and similar uncongenial duties, the monotony of which was relieved by occasional skirmishes. In one of these affairs two soldiers distinguished themselves. Private W. Sweeney found himself surrounded by four mounted Boers who, covering him with their rifles, called upon him to surrender; though they were all within fifty yards of him he refused to do so, and firing at them from the saddle succeeded in making his escape. His name was specially mentioned to the General commanding the column for his gallantry on this occasion. This man's death was a sad one; he fell down a well, 45 feet deep, at Needspan, and his body was not discovered for several days. An officer writes of him: 'he was one of the best soldiers and the

cheeriest of men whom I have ever met; and his behaviour both in camp and field was excellent.'[40]

A typical incident in this type of guerrilla warfare occurred at Bakenlaagte on 30 October 1901, in which Private A Lewis was awarded his DCM for his gallant behaviour. The rear-guard of Colonel Benson's column, which was the object of the enemy's main attack, was composed of two companies of Mounted Infantry, two squadrons of the Scottish Horse, two guns of the 84th Battery, and one company of the 2nd Battalion the Buffs. This force was under the command of Major Anley, 3rd Mounted Infantry. The guns, the company of Buffs, and fifty Mounted Infantry were posted on a ridge, with some Mounted Infantry and Scottish Horse being thrown out as a screen. The cavalry screen was attacked by a strong force of the enemy and compelled to retire. The company of the Buffs that formed the original escort, posted well to the front of the guns, was captured in its entirety by the enemy, as they were completely surrounded and cut off. Two additional companies of the Buffs were ordered to reinforce the ridge, but despite the bravery of men like Lewis, these companies did not succeed in reaching a position from whence their fire could effectively be brought to bear. Only one end of the ridge, occupied by some of the Mounted Infantry, remained in British hands when darkness fell. The two guns were captured by the Boers and removed after dusk. The Buffs casualties in this action amounted to ten killed, and forty-one wounded.

Over thirty years later, Private Lewis wrote to the editor of the regimental journal:

I am taking the pleasure of writing to you to let you know that as I have received *The Dragon* for this month and was reading down the story of the South African War about the Battle of Bakenlaagte when I saw that my name was mentioned in it as having assisted to carry ammunition along the firing line. I am very pleased to say that I am still alive, as it was said that I had nine lives, like a cat, and was recommended for the D.C.M. but did not get it. I am pleased to let you know that I did receive the D.C.M. and also had a watch presented to me by the officers of the regiment. I also received a silver-mounted pipe from Queen Alexandria. So I thought it would be best to let you know, as I thought you would like to. So I must say that I felt quite proud of myself to see my name mentioned in the book. Please give my best respects to all, Sir. I remain, yours truly, A. G. Lewis (No. 4496). One of the old Buffs and proud of it. Good luck to all of them![41]

Often the best mounted units were those raised in parts of the empire where the wild terrain bred men who were able to take on the Boers on their own terms, who could ride and shoot and didn't always play strictly by the rules of conventional warfare. Such units were raised in Australia, New Zealand and Canada as well as in South Africa itself. Some, such as Rimington's Scouts (known as 'The Tigers') gathered a reputation as formidable fighters.

At the same time, towards the end of the war many Boer commandos began to fragment, and some had become little more than bands of brigands, out simply for plunder. Against this background the Bushveldt Carbineers were raised in February 1901, a force of some 300 men, multinational in character but with a strong Australian contingent. The BVC fought a tough war on the Boers, using many of their own tactics against them. However, it was the execution of Boer prisoners of war that was to prove a step too far, and after a complaint by an officer to the military authorities, several of his brother officers were put on trial. This story, which remains controversial to this day, is reasonably accurately portrayed in the film *Breaker Morant* (1980). Two of the officers involved, Australians Harry Morant and Peter Hancock, were tried, convicted and shot by firing squad for their part in the murder of Boer prisoners and a German missionary who was a witness. Another officer, George Witton, was sentenced to life imprisonment.

However, what is less well known is that a fourth officer, Lieutenant H G Picton, although acquitted of murder, was cashiered and forfeited his DCM, which had been awarded to him whilst serving in the ranks. George Witton's book about the affair, *Scapegoats of the Empire*, mentions Picton on numerous occasions:

> Statement by Lieutenant Picton:— 'I have been in South Africa two years on service. I hold my commission in the B.V.C. since last May. Previous to that I was attached to the 8th M.I., and served under Colonel Le Gallais. I have received the Distinguished Conduct Medal, and been mentioned in despatches. I have been three times wounded since the outbreak of the war. I produce three letters from different commanding officers under whom I have served, and could refer the court to Col. Hodgson, commanding 9th Area, Cape Colony. During the month I was in Spelonken under Capt. Hunt I took 37 prisoners, 50 rifles, 15 waggons, and 500 head of cattle, mules, horses, &c.'

> Letter (1) from Captain Savil, O.C. Loch's Horse:— Sergeant Picton came out with Loch's Horse as a corporal in February, 1901. He has

given entire satisfaction to his officers, and I am very pleased to state I have found him not only very plucky when in action, but steady and painstaking in the execution of his duty. He has been recommended for the D.C.M. Having been under my personal command for some time, I cannot speak too highly of his good conduct.

Letter (2):— This is to introduce to you Sergeant Picton, of my corps, Loch's Horse. He is a worthy fellow and well connected, and is seeking a commission. Could you help him in getting such, in your regiment? I understand you have some vacancies.

Letter (3) from Lieut.-Colonel Hickee, O.C. 8th M.I.:— I am sending Sergeant Picton, Loch's Horse, for discharge. He has served with the 8th Corps M.I. for the last eleven months, and has been under my command since 9th November, 1900. I am able to say that he has carried out his duties in a most satisfactory manner. He is a most efficient interpreter and a good man in the field, and was recommended to the C. in C. for his behaviour at Bothaville.[42]

When the sentences were handed down:

Lieutenant Picton was the next called. He soon returned. 'Well, what luck?' I asked. 'Found guilty of manslaughter and cashiered!' was his reply. The appalling injustice of the sentences was a terrible blow to us.[43]

The cancellation of Picton's DCM was notified in the *London Gazette* of 6 May 1902, one of only a handful of such forfeitures ever imposed. Another unusual aspect of the Boer War is the fact that, for the first time, significant numbers of civilians were decorated with the DCM. Some of these recipients were quasi-military in that they were actually guides working for the Field Intelligence Department. Others were locomotive drivers. On 19 April 1901 the *London Gazette* announced the award of the DCM to Civilian Engine Driver G Pickerill, of the Imperial Military Railways, whilst on 31 October 1902 DCM awards were announced to engine driver J Crighton and fireman Sheehan. These latter awards were made in connection with an incident in which Crighton's train was attacked by the Boers and the vacuum braking system pierced by a bullet. The driver and fireman dismounted from the cab, proceeded under fire to the damaged pipe, plugged it, and got the train away into a position of safety. Their engine was later found to have twenty-nine bullet marks on it, testifying to the bravery that they displayed in the incident.

By contrast, a number of Boer War DCM awards, particular those to senior NCOs, appear to have been made to reward good service over a long period of time, rather than for an individual act of bravery. A particularly good example of this is the DCM awarded to Orderly Room Sergeant Herbert Gladstone Cowan of the 2nd Battalion Cheshire Regiment. Cowan's Queen's South Africa medal carried only the bars Cape Colony, Transvaal and Orange Free State, indicating that he had not been involved in any of the major set piece battles of the war. However, the officers of his battalion thought very highly of him, and this seems to have been the basis for the award.

~ 0 ~

Whilst the British Army was heavily committed fighting the Boer republics in South Africa, difficulties broke out on the other side of the world. At Peking in China, the so called 'Boxer Uprising', though not on the same scale as the fighting in South Africa, nevertheless resulted in a number of DCM awards. The uprising grew out of the resentment felt by the Chinese people towards the western powers who had come to dominate Peking, imposing their own laws and customs, and insisting that westerners who committed crimes be tried by their own courts and not by the Chinese. The Society of the Righteous Fist (nicknamed 'Boxers') were at first against the Emperor and the Dowager Empress of China (who was the real power behind the throne). The Empress likewise was suspicious of this grass-roots movement sweeping the country. However, the two sides eventually united to make common cause against the hated British, Italians, Russians and Americans. The foreign embassies, or Legations, in which western civilians and Christian Chinese alike sought refuge from the Boxer mobs, were besieged for fifty-five days. Meanwhile, a relief force, which included marines, Indian troops, and the 2nd Battalion Royal Welsh Fusiliers, fought their way across North China to reach them. Four DCMs were awarded to soldiers of the Royal Welsh, whilst five went to soldiers of the Royal Marines. The Chinese Regiment, also known as the Wei Hai Wei Regiment, took part in the fighting and received three DCMs. This regiment was composed of locally recruited Chinese soldiers with British officers and senior NCOs. Two of the DCMs went to British NCOs on attachment, Colour Sergeant R Ruxdon, Coldstream Guards and Quartermaster Sergeant E Brooke of the Duke of Wellington's (West Riding) Regiment, but interestingly, the third went to a Chinese NCO, Sergeant Gi-Dien Kwee.

The dispatch published in the *London Gazette* on 11 December 1900 contains a vivid description of the fighting at Peking and contains a reference to Sergeant T Murphy Royal Marines, who was awarded a DCM inside the city, in the defence of the Legation buildings. It reads as follows:

> 4th August [1900] Sergeant Murphy did great execution with the five-barrelled Nordenfeldt, mounted at the south–east corner of Imperial Carriage Park, in covering the subsequent occupation of the 'Ruins' behind the Chinese secretary's house, and the holding of the Mongul Market by us.[44]

The dispatch also contains a reference to a marine who was originally recommended for the CGM, the naval equivalent of the DCM:

> I have the honour to bring before your notice the conduct of, and to recommend for the conspicuous gallantry medal, lance Sergeant T.E.Preston, of Her Majesty's ship 'Orlando'. On the 14th July [1900], after the enemy had been driven from their barricade on the Imperial Carriage Park wall near the West Hanlin, by shell fire, this non-commissioned officer climbed on to the wall, some 12 feet high, with the intention of capturing a banner left on the barricade by the enemy. Finding that he could not reach it, he called for his rifle to be given him, and pushing down part of the barricade he kept the enemy, some 50 in number, at bay, while an American gunner, named Michell, was enabled to lay hold of the flag. Sergeant Preston then jumped down and assisted Gunner Michell in drawing the flag over with difficulty, as the enemy had laid hold of the other end. He was struck on the head at the same time by a brick, which partly stunned him.[45]

In fact, as the action had taken place on land, Preston received a DCM, gazetted at the same time as Murphy. An intriguing aspect of the China campaign was reported in *The Times* newspaper in 1964. One of the five marines awarded a DCM for the defence of the Legations was a Private T A Myers. It seems that upon his return to England, Myers had deserted before his DCM could be awarded, and no trace of him had come to light since. In addition to the medal, which had been found languishing in a cupboard at the Ministry of Defence, the newspaper reported that the 6d per day gratuity owing to Myers in respect of the award had been accrued in his absence and Private Myers was owed the astonishing sum of £626 5s!

~ 0 ~

A total of nine DCMs were awarded for the Indian North West Frontier campaign of 1908, a punitive expedition against the troublesome Zakka Khel peoples. Four of these went to soldiers of the Royal Warwickshire Regiment. The following account of the incident that resulted in these awards was published in *The Antelope,* regimental newspaper of the Royal Warwickshire Regiment, in May 1908:

> Following the retirement from 'Green Hill' at Matta on 24 April 1908, the last party had scarcely reached the plain when some thirty of the enemy emerged from a nulla to the left of 'Green Hill'. Lieuts. Waterworth and Martin went back to the aid of a man who was wounded in the foot, Private Gurney, 'G' Company, and the enemy were pressing hard. Word was called to Major Westmorland 'Lieut. Martin is hit' and things looked serious, he was just about to advance his covering party with fixed bayonets when the enemy, who were now within 20 or 30 yards of Martin, were suddenly seized with panic and bolted. Meanwhile, Lance Corporal Moore and Private Stone had both been wounded in assisting the wounded Officer and man. The whole of this time all the above had been under a hot cross fire. During this critical period and throughout the day Sergts. Mitchell and Milledge had been of the greatest assistance in controlling the fire of the men and showing a splendid example by their coolness, steadiness and courage. Second Lieut. Hume-Spry who had retired a party from 'Green Hill' with Major Westmorland was assisting Private Wincup (wounded in the thigh) a short distance from the foot of the hill, when 9101 Private H. Lloyd 'A' Company came to their assistance. Lloyd gallantly covered their retirement and while they were resting proceeded to make head cover for them, when he was shot through the chest, the same bullet, so it is supposed, entered Hume-Spry's back, fortunately just clear of the spine. Hume-Spry however, continued the command of the party and those who came to their assistance until all were in safety. Major P.T. Westmorland and Lieut. G.F. Waterworth were awarded the D.S.O. whilst Sergt. J. Milledge, Lance-Corporal W. Moore and Privates H. Lloyd and A. Stone received the D.C.M.[46]

Private Lloyd was subsequently discharged as a result of his severe wounds. The cat and mouse nature of warfare on the North West Frontier would lead to more decorations and distinction, as well as casualties, before Britain finally relinquished her hold over India.

Chapter 2

The Great War and Beyond

The Western Front

The Great War, because of its very nature, was bound to bring about changes in the way gallantry medals in general - and the DCM in particular - were awarded. The war was fought on an unprecedented scale. Quite rightly it has been described as the world's first industrial war. It was industrial in the sense that all the nation's resources were poured into winning, including factories on the home front, but also industrial in the sense of the war itself being a huge machine, voraciously gobbling up men as they were fed wholesale into its jaws. By the second year of the war, the British Army was no longer a small professional elite, but had expanded to become overwhelmingly a force of civilians in uniform. A conflict on this scale would naturally affect the way gallantry medals were perceived, and we will examine these changes in more detail as this chapter progresses, but let us start by looking at the way the war began.

The First World War, in so far as the British are concerned, commenced on a hot August morning in 1914. The bulk of Britain's army was still deployed on overseas garrisons but that portion that had been earmarked for a potential future European war, the British Expeditionary Force (BEF), was concentrating at its assembly point, Mauberge, in northern France. Operating on the left flank of the French Army, the numerically tiny BEF was to sally forth to meet the Germans as they advanced through Belgium. What no one on the British side had as yet fully appreciated however, was the sheer size of the German Army bearing down upon them. The Germans had mobilized all of their reservists, and had put some six million men into the field.

The first clash came in the outskirts of the Belgian town of Mons. First, the BEF's cavalry screen was driven in, then the Germans began to make wholesale attacks on the British soldiers defending a series of positions along the Conde Canal. All day on 23 August 1914 the Germans broke like waves on rocks against the British positions, and were driven back. As the day wore on, weight of numbers began to tell and the British battalions began to withdraw. To impede the progress of their enemy, sappers began to destroy the lock gates and bridges on the canal. One of the first DCMs of the Great War was earned here, by Private S Heron, of the 1st Battalion, Royal Scots Fusiliers. Late on 23 August, Heron rendered great assistance to the Royal Engineers, who were preparing to destroy the canal bridge at Jemappes whilst under heavy enemy fire. He was awarded the decoration for his conspicuous courage and coolness.

The British, in spite of their superiority man for man, could not hope to hold back the Germans any longer around Mons and on the night of 24 August began their withdrawal - the famous Retreat from Mons. At the same time as Haig's I Corps was retiring to the north of the Forêt de Mormal, Smith Dorrien's II Corps were retreating to the south. Smith Dorrien could see that the only way for his corps to extricate themselves cleanly was to stand and fight. They gave the Germans a bloody nose, but some units did not receive the order to withdraw and were cut off. Others extricated themselves under the nose of the enemy.

On the morning of 26 August 1914, 6th Battery Royal Field Artillery were holding positions on a road junction 200 meters south of Audencourt. Equipped with quick-firing 18-pounder field guns it was their job to keep down the heads of the Germans, and provide coving fire to the British infantry in front of them. During the morning they moved forward to a position just north of Caudry. Later in the day, as enemy pressure began to tell, they moved back again to a position near Audencourt before finally withdrawing. It was for his actions here that Driver H J King of the battery was awarded his DCM. The citation states that:

> ... when the limber was upset, [he] helped to hook into another limber and brought a gun away under heavy fire. [1]

Loss of guns carried great stigma in the Royal Regiment of Artillery - the regiment carries no colours. Instead, its guns are considered to be the equivalent of Colours, the property of the monarch himself, and it is regarded as the greatest dishonour for a battery to allow them to fall into the hands of the enemy. Numerous acts like that of King were performed in 1914, in saving field guns from the enemy.

Many forget that the first months of the Great War witnessed a great deal of movement. In the chaos of the Retreat from Mons it was easy for men to become detached from the main body of their units. Even quite large formations could become separated from the remainder of their brigade or division, and could be surrounded or cut off by fast moving German columns. One DCM awarded for the Retreat went to Sergeant Alfred Charman of the Royal Warwickshire Regiment. Charman's citation reads simply:

> For conspicuous good service, at a critical moment, whereby he was mainly responsible for averting the capture of many men.[2]

This citation sits oddly with many others published in the early part of the Great War that are, on the whole very detailed and often mention both places and dates at which the act for which the award was made occurred. Further light is shed on the matter by a commercial postcard that was produced later in the war showing a portrait of Sergeant Charman. The card adds:

> During the great retreat about 250 men would inevitably have been taken prisoners at St Quentin had Charman not acted promptly, and despite many dangers brought up reinforcements.[3]

There is a very strong possibility that Charman was in some way involved in the 'Colonels' surrender' when stragglers of the Royal Warwickshire Regiment and the Royal Dublin Fusiliers, under their respective colonels, arrived weary and footsore in St Quentin on 27 August. Suffering from hunger, French wine and heat exhaustion, many of the men were at breaking point. The two colonels, equally exhausted, convinced themselves that the Germans were at their heels and the only option was to surrender. They went as far as signing a surrender note, which never reached the Germans. The troops were roused - some reports say by a drummer - and the men began the retreat once more. For their actions the two colonels were cashiered and dismissed from the service, and perhaps Charman's rather vague citation deliberately obscures some of the detail of this embarrassing incident.

The retreat ended at the outskirts of Paris. In the 'miracle of the Marne' the Germans were fought to a standstill. They retreated to the Aisne, where an inconclusive battle saw both sides begin to dig in as protection against artillery and machine-gun fire. Now began the 'race to the sea' as each side tried to find the open flank by attacking further and further north. Heavy fighting took place around La Bassée and Armentières in October, as the men of the BEF, in hastily dug slit trenches, fought off wave after wave of German infantry. A former Metropolitan policeman who was decorated for bravery here was Acting Sergeant William Edwards, previously a PC in J Division (Hackney), who served in France with the 1st Battalion East Surrey Regiment. Like so many of the men who fought in the battles of 1914 he was a reservist, recalled from his civilian occupation to return to the colours when war broke out. His DCM was awarded for heroism on 28 and 29 October in going out under fire near Richebourg to bring in wounded. In 1915, Edwards returned home. His period of reserve service had ended and as conscription was not yet in place, the Army had no grounds upon which to retain him. Edwards returned to the Met, this time to F Division (Paddington), and his DCM was presented to him at a police parade by the commissioner, Sir Edward Henry. Edwards left the police on 1 August 1919, when he was dismissed for going on strike.

The repeated attempts to outflank one another finally brought the BEF and the Germans to battle in the greatest clash of 1914, outside the Belgian city of Ypres. Its name would become hallowed throughout the Empire, such would be the quantity of British and dominion blood spilled to defend it over the next four years. Now, though, the Germans were determined to break through the weak British lines here and reach the channel coast. If it were cut off, the BEF would have been forced to surrender. Yielding ground was not an option, and the old British Regular Army largely found its muddy grave in the sugar beet fields around Ypres in October and November of 1914. Germans in serried ranks marched forward to attack the British lines, making little attempt to use cover, and often singing *Deutschland uber Alles* or other patriotic songs, before being mown down in heaps by concentrated British rifle fire.

Another reservist who had served with the Metropolitan Police prior to the war was Sergeant Alfred Mart, of the 1st battalion Bedfordshire Regiment. He was awarded a DCM at Ypres, the citation reading:

> For gallant conduct on 10th November in assisting to recover one of our abandoned machine guns, killing one German who was watching the gun. Sergeant Mart distinguished himself previously on dangerous services. [4]

The battalion war diary adds further detail to this incident, though it places it one day earlier:

> 9 Nov 1914 Sergt. MART, assisted by Corporal CYSTER succeeded in creeping up to trench occupied by enemy, where 2 machine guns had been previously lost. Found only about 1 German actually with guns, though adjoining trench, a few yards away in prolongation, was occupied. Sergt. MART shot the German & guns were safely brought back. 1 wounded soldier found in trench also. He was

brought back by MART assisted by 2nd Lt. GARROD & others. MART & GARROD in turns facing the enemy to keep their heads down by accurate fire at a few yards range. Battalion thanked in wire from Corps Commander. Sergt.MART wounded. [5]

Mart was from Tottenham, in Middlesex, and had served overseas in India before the Great War. In 1911 he was discharged to Army Reserve Section B, and joined the Metropolitan Police. After he was wounded in France, he was transferred to a garrison battalion of the Suffolk Regiment. The military authorities later tried to draft him into the Military Police but he was unwilling to go, and now only medical category C2, in 1917 he was discharged in order to return to his former occupation as a police constable.

The fighting around Ypres reached its crescendo around 11 November 1914, the Germans broke through the British lines at a number of points and threatened to roll the BEF back into the sea. Any and all reserves the British Army had were thrown into the front line. There were no 'second line' troops that day - all fought as infantry, engineers included. Corporal Arthur Chambers was a member of the 5th Field Company Royal Engineers. His diary for that date records:

The bombardment of our trenches is awful. Having breakfast in dug-outs at 7am an order to turn out at once is given, we all know that something serious has happened. We double across a field and learn from a wounded Jock they have broken through. Sapper Stone falls dead & we know by the crack of bullets that we are under heavy fire. The company is in rather a muddle & no one appears to know what to fire at. Six of us a little apart from the rest under Lieut. Collins spot the Germans right on top of us. We blaze away & many fall at such close range. Lieut Collins falls mortally wounded. The air is humming with bullets. The Germans, who are enormous men enter the wood on our right and we fear a surprise rush from there, a farm in the wood catches fire, and the smoke is blinding us. We continue to fire all day & pick off a great number of them. One big fellow got to very close quarters, but he had to give best to 303 at 20 yards' range. We hang on till 2.30pm & hold up the attack & learn that reinforcements are coming up on the right - the Black Watch, Ox & Bucks and the Irish Guards are advancing in skirmishing order on our right towards us. When they get level with us we all charge. I shall never forget the sensation, but it certainly isn't fear. The Germans broke and ran for it, but we captured a good many. I got on ahead somehow with Lieut Renny-Tailour & six sappers & I fear that the company has been badly knocked about as men were going down all round when we ran on. Am lying in a turnip field with Lieut Tailour & six men & are under the German parapet isolated, as the others have been called off into the wood. We are in a warm shop. The machine guns are sweeping the tops off the potatoes and turnips in which we are lying. Mr Tailour says we will make a bolt to the communication trench on the right but I think it risky to try. He makes the attempt but falls riddled with bullets. I crawl to him and find that he is dead, & I order the sappers to try to wriggle through the turnips back to the wood. French shells begin to burst all around and one of my sappers gets his wrist badly shattered. We all get in eventually & I report that Lieut. Tailour is killed … But we have done a good days work & saved the situation. I am deeply moved at our losing 4 officers & 27 men …. A staff officer has asked me my name. [6]

This last incident undoubtedly led to Chambers' award of the DCM, which was gazetted on 16 January 1915. This citation recorded his:

> Gallant conduct on 11th November. When his officer was killed he took command of a small party engaged in driving the enemy out of a wood, being met with very heavy machine-gun fire.[7]

As the autumn of 1914 turned to winter the casualty rate among Britain's regular forces was so great that it was necessary to call on the part-time volunteers of the Territorial Force for reinforcements. In each territorial battalion, volunteers for overseas service were called for. The first of those battalions that were deemed to be in a high enough state of efficiency reached France in September of 1914. Perhaps the most famous of these Territorial formations was the London Scottish (14th Battalion the London Regiment). Among its members was Harold Leslie Sanderson. Sanderson was born in September 1890 and was educated at Blackheath School. Enlisting in the London Scottish on 6 August 1914, he quickly found himself in France. He served with this unit until early January 1915, when, having sustained a gunshot wound in the arm, he was invalided home.

In October 1914, Sanderson had been present with the regiment when it made its gallant stand at the Battle of Messines, the first time that a Territorial battalion went into action as a unit. He displayed further gallantry later that same year, for which he was awarded the DCM. Unusually, the incident was afterwards depicted on a cigarette card of WD & HO Wills Ltd, as part of a series of fifty commemorating 'War

Incidents'. His DCM, moreover, was the first to be gained by the London Scottish as a regiment, those awarded to its members in the Boer War having been named to the parent regiment, the Gordon Highlanders, or in some cases to the City Imperial Volunteers. The citation for Sanderson's DCM was published in the *London Gazette* on 1 April 1915:

> For conspicuous gallantry at Givenchy on 22 December 1914. Fired upon by two snipers, at a range of 20 yards, he rushed at the men presenting a pair of wire-nippers, which they took to be a revolver, and made prisoners of both - notwithstanding that he was quite unarmed.[8]

Sanderson was subsequently discharged from the Army on 13 June 1915, on account of his being unfit for further military service, being awarded £1 per week conditionally for a year, plus an extra 3/6d a week for his DCM.

A further early Territorial DCM was awarded to another member of the London Regiment, this time the 13th Battalion (Princess Louise's Kensingtons). Frederick William Shepherd was an employee of Messrs. Haigh & Sons Ltd, of Norwood Mill, Southall, in London, at the time of the outbreak of hostilities in 1914. He was keenly interested in the Boy Scout movement and served as Assistant Scoutmaster of the Norwood and Southall Troop. He was amongst the foremost recruits who responded to the call for men to join the Colours and in August 1914, joined the Kensingtons. His DCM citation reads:

> For gallant conduct on several occasions, especially on 19th November 1914, in rescuing a wounded man whilst under fire, and again on 4th December for voluntarily leading a search party over ground exposed to the enemy's fire.[9]

In a letter to his father after the announcement of the DCM, Shepherd wrote:

> You should have seen the meeting between me and the General! I was stripped to the waist, shirt-washing, when he rode into the yard and asked for me. On hearing my name, I stood to attention, and he said, 'Come out as you are,' and, all soap-suds, I went, and shook him by the hand. He had some nice kid gloves on at the time, so you can guess that it spoiled them. The words that he said to me were: 'Well lad, I must congratulate you on winning the DCM, and may you live long to wear it, and also get a bar.' [10]

These were to prove prophetic words as within a few months of that meeting, Shepherd did indeed receive a bar to his DCM, indicating a second award, for gallantry near Rouges Bancs during the Battle of Aubers Ridge on 9 May 1915. The bar was announced in the *London Gazette* of 5 August 1915:

> On the 9th May, 1915, during the operations near Rouges Bancs, he made his way from the firing line for over 400 yards to the enemy's breastwork with a telephone line. Before he reached his destination the line was cut. He crawled on to the Signal Section and started back laying another line, which he eventually got through. He was under a heavy fire the whole time; fourteen men had already been killed and wounded passing over the same ground. He subsequently carried two wounded men to a place of safety under a heavy fire. His conduct throughout the action was magnificent.[11]

Shortly after his acts of gallantry, on 1 July 1915 Frederick Shepherd married Eveline Howarth, and upon the birth of their daughter on 3 July 1916, he decided to commemorate the award of his decoration by christening her Dorothy Celia Marie. Sadly, Eveline died of diabetes in April 1917, leaving baby Dorothy to be brought up by her maternal grandparents. At the end of the war Frederick was transferred into the 17th Battalion, South Lancashire Regiment, a labour battalion used for loading canal barges in the UK. Whilst at home on a month's demobilisation leave, from 17 January 1919, Frederick suffered a seizure and was admitted to the local VAD hospital, where he died from the effects of war service on 4 February 1919. Little Dorothy Celia Marie was brought up in Southall by her family. She remained a spinster and died on 27 October 2000.

In April 1915 the Germans launched an offensive that was to become known as the Second Battle of Ypres. Using poison gas for the first time, the Germans made a breakthrough unexpected even by themselves. Among the troops thrown into the breach were the Indian Corps, made up of the Lahore and Meerut Divisions. This corps had arrived in France in the previous autumn, and comprised both Indian soldiers and British troops who had been stationed in India. Caught up in the fighting around Ypres in the spring of 1915 was a regular soldier of the Lahore Division Signal Company, Private Edward Humphries, from Exeter. Humphries was to be decorated for his part in this battle. On 26 April 1915, his DCM citation records that he was in the thick of the action for the entire day, not fighting with rifle and bayonet but continually attempting to repair breaks in telephone wire connecting divisional headquarters with the front line. Humphries was to survive the war, being later commissioned into the Indian Signal Service. He eventually retired as a lieutenant-colonel and in 1972 he remembered:

> We marched up through Poperinghe ... we went through Ypres. Ypres was devastated. It was a sorry sight. The beautiful cathedral was partly in ruins and there was a smell of carnage with dead horses about the place and the whole place was under shellfire the whole time and one felt oneself lucky if you got through without getting quite a lot of casualties. We were in position a little bit to the north of St Julien ... I walked into the action with my unit ... Well, you see I was [one of the] Divisional signallers. We had telephone lines out to the brigades and those telephone lines were being busted every half hour or so and I spent the whole of one night and part of one day out mending one line continuously... [12]

Much of the line here was held by the Cavalry Corps, fighting dismounted as infantry. On 2 May 1915 they launched a counter-attack to recover lost trenches. Private George Ingle of the 4th Hussars was advancing on foot with his troop under the command of Lieutenant Radclyffe, when he received wounds to his head. At the same time he saw his troop commander Radclyffe fall severely wounded to the ground, where he remained unable to move. Ingle and an NCO at once located a wheelbarrow from a nearby farmyard and returned to the lieutenant. They loaded the now unconscious officer into the wheelbarrow; the two men then crossed open ground, which was under heavy shellfire, returning Radclyffe to the safety of British lines. With his deed completed, Ingle collapsed from loss of blood. For his actions he received the DCM. George Ingle returned to the Western Front, where he fought until he was killed in action, in March 1918.

Another soldier decorated for his bravery in holding the line during the Second Battle of Ypres was Bill Irvine, who was born in County Armagh in 1879. He had enlisted in the Manchester Regiment prior to the Boer War, but by 1911 he had taken his discharge and was living at his aunt's house in the village of Uppermill, on the very edge of Yorkshire. He was employed in an iron foundry, probably the sprawling Soho ironworks in nearby Oldham, which produced machinery for the Lancashire cotton industry. Uppermill was within the recruiting area of the 7th Battalion Duke of Wellington's (West Riding) Regiment, which stretched from Huddersfield in the east, through Holmfirth and Slaithwaite, into

Saddleworth and beyond to the outskirts of Oldham in the west. It was predominantly a hilly country, each village nestled isolated in its valley. This, it was said, bred a hardy independent spirit in its men folk, which was reflected in the battalion. With the coming of the Great War, Irvine volunteered to join the Dukes. With his previous military experience he was soon promoted to sergeant. His DCM was awarded for helping to hold the line at Ypres, and was gazetted on 11 January 1916. In a letter published later in a local newspaper he wrote:

> The camaraderie of this battalion is excellent and goes a great way towards the winning of the glorious record we have earned for ourselves. Unlike many regiments we have never been able to gain honours in one engagement, our reputation has been earned by that fidelity and devotion that comes from duty nobly done. We have, at times without number, held the breach under all conditions. We have suffered losses, 'tis true, but the reinforcements have proved to be of the same sterling quality as the original first-line ... we have passed through some seven months in that position which was too hot for any only the best troops, a memory that is written into our annals with young manhood's lifeblood. ... Looking back on the last twelve months, and on my previous campaign, I arrive at this conclusion that my present unit upholds its country's honour and traditions just the same as the immortal 'boys of the old brigade'. They go into action just as my old regiment did, and with the same cheerful spirit ... I often wonder if one can ever realise the stupendousness of the task which we are so cheerfully upholding ...[13]

Irvine survived the war, and returned home to the neighbouring Saddleworth village of Delph. In later years he was something of a local character, and tried to enlist for his third war in 1939, aged sixty. The local children made up a song about Irvine, which ran:

> He's Sergeant Bill Irvine, the Delph DCM
> He's Sergeant Bill Irvine, he's killed twenty men
> He's Sergeant Bill Irvine, the Delph DCM...

Many years later, Irvine's son recalled that after the war, his father had taken a hacksaw to his DCM, not out of any feeling of anger or resentment, but rather to refashion it into the shape of a cross. This he presented to his wife, who wore it as a pendant around her neck![14]

The German offensive at Ypres was a failure, in spite of the temporary advantage afforded to the Germans by the first use on the Western Front of poison gas. The trench system running from the North Sea to the Swiss border was now firmly in place, and new ways had to be found of breaking this deadlock. On 24 April 1915 the *Daily Mirror* newspaper reported:

> Having discovered German mining operations in the neighbourhood of Le Touquet, near Armentières, we forestalled their efforts this (Thursday) morning by exploding a mine, which we had prepared there.[15]

Among those involved in these operation was a soldier from St Helens, Lance Corporal John Webb Ching. Ching's parent regiment was the South Lancashire Regiment, but when mining operations were in progress the tunnelling companies of the Royal Engineers could and did call for reinforcements from nearby infantry battalions. Ching's DCM citation states that he laboured for many weeks in the flooded workings at Le Touquet, and the award was made for his courage in persevering with his task, with the ever-present danger of an enemy counter-mine destroying the gallery in which he was working.

Mining on the Western Front was a particularly grim and dangerous business, but by 1915 it was a growth industry. It was too dangerous to attack above ground, so troops of both sides decided instead to tunnel under their enemy's positions and to try to destroy them with an explosive charge from below. Sometimes, tunnellers would accidentally encounter enemy miners, and an underground fight would ensue. On other occasions the mining operations were deadly just by themselves. On 28 April 1915, poisonous fumes in a mine gallery at Kemmel overcame three officers and a sergeant. Lance Corporal Victor Gray, of the 4th battalion Middlesex Regiment, attached to the 172nd Tunnelling Company Royal Engineers, ordered four of his men to descend the mine and bring them up. After two officers had been saved, he descended himself to help the third officer and the sergeant. He found the mine gallery full of fumes - probably Carbon Dioxide - and the officer lying helpless. Gray dragged him to the shaft, from which he was taken to the surface. The rescuers were by this time themselves suffering from the effects of the gas, but Gray descended again to help the sergeant, who was brought up, though he could not be saved. Lance Corporal Gray was awarded the DCM for these selfless acts.

On 16 October 1915, not far from the Hulluch quarries, the British discovered an enemy shaft. A sentry reported that he had seen two of the enemy moving along a gallery leading out of it. In company with an officer, Acting Second Corporal Philip O'Brien of the 170th Tunnelling Company Royal Engineers, at once descended the shaft by means of a rope ladder, expecting to find the enemy there. No gallery was found, but for the courage that he had shown, Corporal O'Brien was awarded the DCM.

Often the Germans would use listening devices to detect British miners and would use a charge called a camouflet to cave in their workings. Around the same time, one such countermine was exploded by the enemy at the face of a mine in which Second Corporal G Smith, of the 176th Tunnelling Company, Royal Engineers, was in charge. Several of his men were buried. Second Corporal Smith was thrown about 15 feet down the gallery by the explosion, and was badly bruised and shaken. However, grasping the situation immediately, he ordered his men out of the gallery, into which gas was leaking. When found by his officers he was propping up a dangerous part of the gallery to ensure the rescue of his men. For this gallant conduct he was awarded the DCM.

Again in late 1915, Private John Torrance, of the 1st Battalion, Royal Scots Fusiliers (attached 9th Brigade Mining Section) remained at the head of a mineshaft, after one pump had already been put out of action by heavy shellfire, and another was in danger of failure. Torrance, from Garbeds, Glasgow, refused to take cover and worked the remaining air pump throughout the bombardment. If it had not been for his gallant action the mine would probably have run short of air. He too was awarded the DCM.

~ 0 ~

Near Fromelles in the spring of 1915, the British 1st Army under Sir Douglas Haig planned to drive the Germans off the slightly rising ground of Aubers Ridge. On 9 May 1915 the battle of that name was launched. By nightfall, all of the troops involved who were not dead were back on the start line. It had been a day of disaster and bitter disappointment, in spite of the heroism shown by the men involved. Lance Corporal Richard Starkey of the 1st/13th London Regiment, the Kensingtons, showed great devotion to duty on this day when:

> Near Rouges Bancs, when he continued to work his machine gun with the left blocking party with the greatest coolness and bravery while the enemy's bombs were continually bursting around him. Finally his gun was disabled and himself wounded. [16]

Similar gallantry was shown by Sergeant Alfred Starr of the 2nd Battalion the Rifle Brigade, who showed conspicuous gallantry on 9 and 10 May near Rouges Bancs when he:

fought his machine gun with the greatest bravery for several hours until all the gun team were killed or wounded. He continued working his gun until he was at last bayoneted by the Germans.[17]

Both men were decorated with the DCM, and Starr in fact survived his close encounter with the enemy. Undeterred by the failure the 1st Army launched what was in effect a subsidiary attack at Festubert, less than a week later. Among the leading formations was the 2nd Battalion Border Regiment, part of the 20th Brigade of the 7th Division. Its men scrambled over the sandbag breastworks at 3.10am on 16 May, in order to close up to the German front line before the British preparatory bombardment lifted. Unfortunately, some of the men advanced too far and were cut down by their own shells. Further problems were encountered by the Borders as they came under unsuppressed machine-gun fire from German positions on their flank. Considerable losses were sustained, including the commanding officer, Lieutenant-Colonel Archibald Moffatt, who was killed in action. All was chaos now, but Sergeant Thomas Toner, a member of the special reserve who was serving with the 2nd Borders, rose to the challenge. Born in Carlisle of a Scottish father and an English mother, he had been a cloth measurer in a factory before joining the Border Regiment militia battalion around 1902. The citation for his DCM reads:

> For conspicuous gallantry and ability on the 16th May 1915, at Festubert. Some men were in a captured first line without a leader, and Sergeant Toner, although not belonging to the Company, ran forward under fire, took command, and led, with great courage and coolness, a further advance.[18]

The bravery of men like Toner, however, made little impact on the course of this battle, which despite some early advances achieved scant results, and did not even succeed in drawing German reserves away from a much larger French offensive to the south. Toner himself was killed in action later on the same day as the deed that earned him distinction. He was originally buried in the picturesquely-named Indian Village North Cemetery, immediately behind the British front line at Festubert. However, his grave was later destroyed by shellfire and he is now commemorated on a special memorial stone.

Trench warfare on the Western Front was now taking a heavy toll on the British Army. At this stage of the war much of the burden was now borne once again by territorial soldiers. One such man received a DCM for an outstanding act of bravery: Lance Corporal John Yates of Barnsley, serving with the 1st/5th Battalion York and Lancaster Regiment, received the award:

> For conspicuous gallantry on the 10th July 1915, on the Yser canal. Two men, who had been wounded, were cut off from the rest of the platoon. Lance Corporal Yates, with great bravery, crawled a considerable distance over exposed ground and under heavy fire to their assistance. Ultimately, in order to rejoin his platoon, he was obliged to get over what remained of our parapet in full view of the German lines. He gave a fine example of courage and devotion to duty.[19]

Other rewards followed, for on the day after this incident, Yates was promoted to sergeant. Aged forty at the time of his enlistment in June 1914, Yates had already seen twelve years' service in the regular army as a bandsman, before returning to civil life and to work underground as a miner in one of Barnsley's many pits. Badly wounded by a trench mortar round in August 1915, he was evacuated to England. Despite the fact that he was as a consequence discharged with a pension (to which in August 1918 he was granted an extra 6d per day in respect of his DCM award) he rejoined the Territorial Army in the 1920s as a bandsman, serving until 1930 and earning the Territorial Efficiency Medal.

The Battle of Loos, fought in September 1915 by Haig's First Army, was the earliest large scale attempt at Anglo–French co-operation, with the French army attacking simultaneously in Artois. The battle ultimately was a failure, but it taught the British high command much about the realities of warfare on the Western Front. Another DCM was awarded to a territorial soldier in connection with Loos, specifically for a remarkable act of reconnaissance at Cuinchy immediately prior to the battle. Corporal Reginald Evans was serving with the 1st Battalion Hertfordshire Regiment, and has left a wonderfully vivid account of the action for which the award was made:

> On the afternoon of the 22nd [September 1915], my Company Officer sent for me and explained in some measure, the position, the artillery preparation and the hoped for results in enabling us to reach our objective. He then said that Headquarters wanted a volunteer to go out that night and report what damage had been done to the enemy's wire and front line trenches by the intensive bombardment. The artillery would receive orders to cease fire for an hour whilst the reconnaissance was carried out but so as not to raise suspicions at the lull, machine guns would carry on covering fire

over the German lines. Whoever took the job on would have to go alone. It would probably mean death but would certainly mean glory.

Then after a pause, he came to the point. 'Will you go?' he asked. For a few seconds I hesitated. What could I say? That evening I slipped out through an old sap head into 'No Man's Land'. The din was terrific though the intensity of our bombardment had died away. The enemy was sending up Verey lights, and star shells in reckless profusion and to crown it all, the moon rose early at the full, cloudless and serene. I wormed my way along till I reached the road on my right and proceeded along the side of it until I came to a stupendous barricade of wire and trestles which extended across and for some yards on either side.

Realising the hopelessness of forcing a way through such an entanglement I reluctantly left the friendly edge of the road which had seemed to afford me some protection against the incessant stream of bullets whistling by, and making a detour, after an arduous journey finally came to the barbed wire immediately protecting the enemy's trench. Here sudden movement on my right caused me a few moment's alarm and I lay almost frozen to the ground, eyes and ears more than ever on the alert, thinking I had come across a hostile patrol. Careful watching proved my enemy to be nothing more than some fluttering rags, and I crawled on again until after a bit I found an opening in the wire and once through soon reached the German parapet.

I traversed some distance in this close contact till at last seeing another large gap in the wire I turned to make the return journey. Only just in time. Suddenly as if an inferno was let loose the artillery bombardment burst out anew. All around me fell the shells with tremendous explosions, the earth seemed to rock as I lay stiff and scared on its surface, and the sound of the broken metal was like the rattle of a hailstorm as it pattered to the ground with a noise incessant and penetrating even amid the louder roar. I really thought that my end had come and resumed my awful journey through shell holes and debris though feeling all the time that I should never complete it.

The state I was in when I finally did reach our trenches can be imagined. Challenged by a sentry, I was almost too exhausted to reply. Plastered with mud and clothing literally in shreds I was almost unrecognisable even by men of my own company. After making my report I found an old dug out where I was only too glad to turn in and sleep. I had been out for over an hour longer than was intended and had been given up for lost, hence the recommencement of the bombardment which so nearly caused my death. A personal letter from the General Commanding the brigade was handed to me next morning, thanking me for the reconnaissance made and the report sent in, and when after a few days, news came that I had been awarded the DCM I felt that I should need the attraction of a whole barrow-load of decorations before undertaking another expedition of the same kind.[20]

Following the Battle of Loos, matters once more settled into static trench warfare on the Western Front. In these circumstances, it was felt by the Army high command that it was more important than ever to maintain the aggressive attitude of the troops, in order to prevent the development of a 'live and let live' attitude. This aggressive approach was maintained by constant patrolling and raiding. It was felt that the British Army must dominate no man's land as far as was possible, but of course for every aggressive act, the Germans were likely to retaliate in kind. This constant low-level warfare produced a steady drain of casualties. In a typical example of this tit-for-tat style of fighting, Acting Lance Sergeant John Black of the 8th Battalion, Somerset Light Infantry was decorated for his bravery during an enemy counter-raid. He was seriously wounded in the incident, and his citation read:

> For conspicuous gallantry in an attack near Armentières when in charge of a bombing party on the night of 15th/16th December [1915] he displayed great promptness and courage in repelling a German attack. Again on the night of 20th/21st December, when the enemy made a bombing attack, he set a splendid example of pluck and fortitude. When his leg was blown off he continued to give orders to his men till he was carried away.[21]

Around this time a similar award was made to Private Alfred Bench, of the 10th Battalion Rifle Brigade, who was a member of a raiding party. His citation reads:

> For conspicuous good work near Cordonerie on the night of 15th/16th December 1915. Corporal Hunt and Privates Bench and Higgins remained out over two hours and successfully cut through the enemy's wire although a German sentry was in view all the time.[22]

However, by the end of 1915 this industrial type of war was producing acts of bravery on an industrial scale. The sheer savagery of the fighting, and the unprecedented number of men committed to the war, meant that the DCM was being awarded at a rate never before witnessed. For an award that still carried with it a gratuity, this could have serious implications for the public finances. Thus, in January 1916, a new award, called the Military Medal (MM), was introduced. This junior award ranked below the DCM in the hierarchy of gallantry, and crucially carried no gratuity with it. Front line soldier Frank Richards, in his classic memoir *Old Soldiers Never Die*, commented:

> About this time a new decoration was introduced which could only be won by officers and warrant officers; it was called the Military Cross. I overheard one of our old officers say it had only been introduced to save awarding too many DSOs. All officers thought a lot of the DSO and all men thought a lot of the DCM; both decorations ranking next to the Victoria Cross. In the spring of 1916 another decoration was introduced which was called the Military Medal. It was a decoration for NCOs and men and in order of merit ranked below the DCM. There were no grants or allowances with the Military Medal, which without a shadow of a doubt had been introduced to save awarding too many DCMs. With the DCM went a money grant of twenty pounds, and a man in receipt of a life pension who had won the DCM was entitled to an extra sixpence a day on to his pension. After the new decoration was introduced, for every DCM awarded there were fifty Military Medals. The old regular soldiers thought very little of the new decoration.[23]

Richards himself was to gain the DCM after the introduction of the MM, and so by his own standards the award was well deserved. He has left an account of this action, which is full of his usual eye for detail, also in *Old Soldiers Never Die:*

> On the night of 4th February [1916], C Company, made up to two hundred men, were sent into the line between Cuinchy and Cambrin to capture a large crater which was about sixty yards from our front line trench. In the first place the enemy had exploded a large mine and had rushed and occupied the crater. They had been driven out of it the following night but had recaptured it two nights later. During the last fourteen days three separate attacks had been made on the crater but each one had failed. We could not afford to let the enemy hold the crater that distance from our front line: they would

have been able in a short space of time to have driven mine galleries from there in under our front line and blown up hundreds of yards of our trenches. Four signallers were told off for the attack – two with the attacking party and two to remain with Lieutenant Stanway who was in charge of operations and who would be in the front line trench. We were issued out with steel helmets, the first we ever wore, and arrived in the front line at 10.30pm.

I and a signaller called Paddy were going over with the attacking party, and our orders were to run a reel of wire out and endeavour to keep up communication if the crater was taken. There was to be no bombardment by our artillery, and men were to leave the front line as silently as possible; each man was to carry as many bombs as he could and a number of men were told-off as bomb carriers. The attack would be made at 11pm. The 2nd Worcesters holding the front line thought we had come up to relieve them, and were surprised to learn we had come up for an attack on the crater. There were a few old Expeditionary Force men left in this battalion. One man said: 'I don't envy you your job; only two nights ago two hundred men came up to do the same job and failed, and two hundred didn't get back, not by a big number. And the other night we had a try at it too, but we got more than we bargained for, just look over the parapet and see for yourself.' I got up on the fire-step and although it was very dark I could see little heaps dotted here and there which I knew were dead men. I told him that we were having no artillery bombardment before going over. 'All the better,' he replied, 'you are more likely to surprise them, but you'll surprise me greatly if you do capture that crater: there are good men holding it and they are very wide awake as well.'

He was such a cheery individual that I was delighted when 11pm arrived. We left our trench and dashed silently for the crater, we signallers running our wire out; we could not keep pace with the rest of the company, who were soon ahead of us. They had reached over halfway before they were spotted. Then the enemy opened out with machine-gun and rifle-fire and bullets were now zipping around us. We had made it up before we left the trench that if one of us fell the other would carry on the best way he could; but luck was with us and we got safely across to the lip of the crater. The scrap was well in progress and I covered Paddy whilst he was fixing the lines to the instrument and establishing communication. At 11.30pm the whole of the crater was captured, and we were consolidating our position.

Half of the men were digging in, the other half covering them. The officer in charge now got on the phone to Stanway, reporting the complete success of the attack. But five minutes before that, Paddy had privately sent the news by Morse to our signallers at the end of the line ...

About twelve o'clock the enemy commenced shelling our position and by 12.30am they had put up an intense barrage between us and the front-line trench. It was impossible to get our wounded back, and our lines also went West. Paddy and I decided to try and keep the line going and go back, every other time, when there was a break; and if one did not come back within a reasonable time, the other would go out to look for him. Paddy went first. I didn't expect to see him come back, but he did. I went next. I don't know how many times we repaired that line, but during the whole of the night we managed to keep up communication, which we were afterwards told was of the utmost assistance to our officer and Lieutenant Stanway. About 2.30am the shelling ceased, and we were expecting a counter-attack, but none came. The men in the front line began hurriedly to sap out to us, and at 5.30am we were relieved by a company of our own battalion ... The crater was afterwards named the RWF crater. For our night's work Paddy, I and the two sergeants were awarded the DCM. We had did no more than the other men; we were the lucky ones. In a successful stunt a man who got recommended had far more chance of receiving a decoration than a man who had been recommended for an unsuccessful stunt.[24]

At the end of March 1916 Frank Richards and some of his comrades received warning that they were to be presented with their DCMs by General Sir Charles Monro, commander of the British First Army, that same day in the nearby town of Bethune. They had come straight out of the communication trenches, and there was no time to prepare. Richards remembered:

Troops were lined up on the square and with brasses polished they looked clean enough to have mounted a guard at Buckingham Palace: they had been warned for this show three days before, whilst we who were the principals had only been warned during the last hour. We looked at ourselves: we were in fighting order and I and Paddy were as black as two sweeps. Not one of us had washed or shaved for the last three days and we must have been the four most dirty men in Bethune. We were wondering whether we would have time for a wash and a shave when a sergeant–major approached us and lined us up in the square in front of the troops. A few minutes later General Munro and his staff arrived. He gave a lecture on the spirit of self sacrifice; afterwards each one of us marched up to him and it was read out to him what each man had did to win the DCM. After pinning the ribbon on our breasts he shook each man heartily by the hand and wished him the best of luck to live and wear it. When I was in front of him he asked me where I came from. I replied that only an hour before I had left the Cuinchy trenches. He said it must be very dirty there, I told him it was, and in more ways than one; and a good honest grin swept over his face.[25]

Returning home on leave later in the war, Richards was presented with an inscribed gold watch, marking his distinction in gaining the Distinguished Conduct Medal. Such presentations were a common feature of the First World War, rather more so it seems for awards of the DCM than for the MM. Significant numbers of similar watches are known to exist, and are usually observed to be engraved with the details of a local DCM recipient and the fact that the watch was presented by his own community. Distinguished Conduct Medal recipients were also frequently presented with so–called 'gallantry cards'. These were often produced at battalion, brigade or divisional level, they might be highly decorated or carry an ornately written account of the action for which the decoration was awarded. One of the most frequently encountered types is that produced by XI Corps, which were personally signed by the corps commander, Lieutenant General Sir Richard Haking. Haking had robust views on the importance of morale and offensive spirit in winning battles, and it may be that he felt the gallantry cards that he presented contributed to this.

Another intriguing contemporary account from a First World War DCM recipient – this one actually penned whilst the war was still in progress – was produced by Alexander McClintock. Entitled *Best O'Luck; How a Fighting Kentuckian Won The Thanks of Britain's King*, it was published in New York in 1917 and was to some extent intended to give raw United States troops a flavour of what they might expect in the trenches. Indeed, it is a surprisingly accurate and unvarnished account of the reality of war on the Western Front. McClintock was from Lexington, Kentucky, and in 1915 resolved to himself that whilst the United States was neutral, it was up to individual American citizens to fight for the side they felt to be in the right. He travelled to Montreal, and enlisted in the 87th Battalion Canadian Expeditionary Force (Canadian Grenadier Guards). He was quickly made a sergeant, on the basis of his previous experience in the Virginia Military Institute. He arrived in France in 1916, and his DCM was awarded for his bravery in a trench raid in the Ypres Salient in September of that year (*London Gazette*, 13 February 1917). He wrote of the hour leading up to the raid:

> The inaction was driving us all into a state of funk. I could actually feel my nerve oozing out at my finger tips, and if we had had to wait fifteen minutes longer, I shouldn't have been able to climb out of the trench.
>
> About half an hour before we were to go over, every man had his eye up the trench for we knew 'the rummies' were coming that way. The rum gang serves out a stiff shot of Jamaica just before an attack, and it would be a real exhibition of temperance to see a man refuse. There were no prohibitionists in our set ...
>
> There were two things which made it possible for our raiding party to get started 'over the top and give 'em hell' across No Man's Land. One was the momentary quickening of the blood which follows a big and unaccustomed dose of rum, and the other was a sort of subconscious, mechanical confidence in our undertaking, which was a result of the scores of times we had gone through every pre-arranged movement in the duplicate German trenches behind our lines. Without either of those influences, we simply could not have left shelter and faced what was before us.
>
> An intensified bombardment from our guns began just as soon as we had climbed 'over the top' and were lining up for the journey across. 'Lining up' is not just a suitable term. We were crawling about on all fours, just far enough out in 'No Mans Land' to be under the edge of the German shell-fire, and taking what shelter we could in shell holes while our leaders picked the way to start across. The extra heavy bombardment warned the Germans that something was about to happen. They sent up star shells and 'S.O.S.' signals, until there was a glare over the torn earth like that which you see at the grand finish of a Pain's fire-works display, and meanwhile they sprayed 'No Mans Land' with streams of machine-gun fire. In the face of that, we started.
>
> It would be absurd to say we were not frightened. Thinking men could not help but be afraid. If we were pallid which we undoubtedly were the black upon our faces hid it, but our fear-struck voices were not disguised. They trembled and our teeth chattered. [26]

As the raiding party crossed no man's land, they were sprayed with machine-gun bullets by the Germans and men fell to the left and right of McClintock, but true to his orders he pressed on and left them for stretcher-bearers. He reached the German front line:

> I heard directions given, and I gave some myself. My voice was firm, and I felt almost calm. Our artillery had so torn up the German barbed wire that it gave us no trouble at all ... When we reached the low, sand-bag parapet of the enemy trench, we tossed in a few bombs and followed them right over as soon as they had exploded. There wasn't a German in sight. They were all in their dug-outs. But we knew pretty well where every dug-out was located, and we rushed for the entrances with our bombs. Everything seemed to be going just as we expected it to go ... I was just thinking that the only tough part of the job remaining would be getting back across 'No Mans Land', when it seemed that the whole earth behind me, rose in the air. For a moment I was stunned, and half blinded by dirt blown into my face. When I was able to see, I discovered that all that lay back of me was a mass of upturned earth and rock, with here and there a man shaking himself or scrambling out of it or lying still.
>
> Just two minutes after we went into their trench, the Germans had exploded a mine under their parapet ... That mine blew our organization, as we would say in Kentucky, 'plumb to Hell.' And it killed or disabled more than half our party.
>
> There was much confusion among those of us who remained on our feet. Someone gave an order to retire and someone countermanded it. More Germans came out of their dug-outs, but, instead of surrendering as per our original schedule, they threw bombs amongst us. [27]

Whistles blew and the survivors made their way back as best they could, helping the wounded. McClintock subsequently volunteered to go back out to look for more injured. The raiding party were then withdrawn from the front line, to billets in the rear. He recalled:

> I was so dead tired that I soon fell asleep, but not for long. I never slept more than an hour at a time for several days and nights. I would doze off from sheer exhaustion, and then suddenly find myself sitting straight up, scared half to death, all over again. There may be soldiers who don't get scared when they know they are in danger or even when people are being killed right around them, but I'm not one of them. [28]

In fact, McClintock was to display further bravery later that year in the Canadian attack on Regina Trench near Courcelette, France. Here he was so badly wounded, that after prolonged treatment he was finally discharged from the Canadian Army. He was subsequently commissioned into the US Army, and desperately wanted to be posted back to France. However, his poor physical condition precluded this, and in 1918, in a state of depression, he took his own life.

~ 0 ~

In July 1916 the British Army launched its Somme offensive, the biggest operation so far mounted on the Western Front and for the first time the BEF was beginning to take on the lion's share of the fighting, the French Army having been woefully mauled in the battles around Verdun earlier that year. The first day of the Battle of the Somme has gone down in history as a day of disaster, with the British Army suffering some 60,000 casualties of whom around 20,000 were killed. This, however, has tended to overshadow the fact that the battle continued for a further four and a half months. Exploiting what success had been achieved on the first day, the British pushed on to try to breach the German second line. The Germans had entrenched and fortified a series of woods, and clearing the Germans out of these positions would take the second half of July and on into August.

On 14 July the 9th Scottish Division was allotted the task of taking the village of Longueval and the associated positions in Delville Wood. The wood was to be cleared by the division's South African Brigade, comprising four battalions raised in the Union of South Africa. It was to become one of the most gruelling struggles in a battle of bloody encounters. For six days the South African Brigade hung on grimly in the shattered remains of Delville Wood, pounded by artillery, fighting off local German counter-attacks, short of rations and drinking water which, - when it arrived at all - was foul tasting as it had been carried in petrol cans. Sergeant Jack Naisby, a forty-five-year old veteran, formerly a Royal Engineer but now serving with 'D' Company of the 3rd Battalion South African Infantry, was originally recommended for the Victoria Cross for his part in the fighting. In the event he received a DCM for his efforts, but the full recommendation read:

> For conspicuous bravery under fire at Delville Wood during July 15–18 1916, when he constantly fearlessly exposed himself under a

heavy artillery, machine-gun and rifle fire to assist the wounded, fetch water and ammunition, etc from Longueval and in the wood. When himself wounded (severely) refusing help to the dressing station and when wounded helping another wounded man away. His cheery fearlessness and conspicuous bravery under heavy fire for ten days was an outstanding example of heroism.[29]

Another South African of distinguished years was Private Nicholas Vlok of Bloemfontain, aged forty-nine at the time of the Delville Wood battle, who was serving with 'B' Company of the 2nd Battalion South African Infantry. He had previously served as a Boer officer during the 1899-1902 conflict. Vlok was an early casualty of the Delville Wood fighting, being wounded on the morning of Saturday 15 July. He wrote afterwards:

At 11 o'clock I was wounded in the right knee, but felt I must still fight on. A little later I received the wound in my back, and for some time no assistance was able to come near us. I lost a fearful amount of blood, and I learnt afterwards it was a marvel that I did not bleed to death.

While I was sitting up against a tree in an almost unconscious state, a huge black-bearded Hun came up to me and said in Dutch, 'Come here, you swine-hound.' By some means or other they knew the South Africans were fighting them.

I was too ill to move, and without saying another word he drew his revolver and fired point-blank at my head. Although my helmet was blown off he fortunately did not hit me, but I shammed dead in case he should have another try.

However, he left me, evidently in search of other helpless men that he could shoot, but before he had gone far one of our fellows rushed at him, sending his bayonet right through him. Before he went down I heard the miserable fellow shout: 'Mercy, Kamerad!'[30]

Vlok's DCM was gazetted alongside that of Naisby on 22 September 1916. The citation reads:

For conspicuous gallantry in action. He displayed great coolness under heavy fire, and did fine work throughout the operations.[31]

The third phase of the Battle of the Somme focussed upon the attempts to throw the Germans off a series of ridges. One of the best known of these attacks is the Battle of Flers-Courcelette, which saw the first use of tanks in battle. The tanks supported an attack by the New Zealand Division and the Guards Division. Dawn on the morning of 15 September 1916 found the men of the 1st Guards Brigade on the edge of Delville Wood, about to participate in this historic action. The early chill was still in the air that late summer morning as the men waited in shell holes or abandoned trenches for zero hour. The 1st battalion Irish Guards, in one of the secondary waves, followed up behind as the leading waves advanced into the crash and roar of the enemy artillery, raked by machine-guns from the direction of Ginchy. Private James Boyd of this battalion, from Kirkaldy in Scotland, received the DCM for:

> Conspicuous gallantry in action when he advanced single-handed and took an enemy machine gun in flank, shooting one of the team and bayoneting another, while the officer bolted after receiving a blow on the head from Private Boyd's fist. He brought back the gun complete. [32]

Boyd's action subsequently appeared as an illustration in *Deeds That Thrill The Empire*, a patriotic periodical that featured illustrated stories of the heroism of VC, DCM and Indian Distinguished Service Medal holders. Whilst there can be no questioning Boyd's bravery in the circumstances of such a dreadful battle, the naïvety of the artist brings a wry smile to the face of the informed observer. Boyd carries his rifle single-handed, in a way that anyone familiar with the weight of the Short Magazine Lee Enfield and its bayonet would agree would be difficult. The German machine-gun is positioned incongruously in the open, exposed to enemy fire, rather than in the shelter of a shell hole or even the trench located closely behind it.

Some of the most breathtaking acts of bravery are not those carried out in the heat of battle, when the blood is up and when soldiers' perception of danger is clouded by adrenaline, anger or hatred for the enemy, but rather those when danger is faced coolly, by those whose role means they cannot in fact bear arms: stretcher-bearers and medics. The Distinguished Conduct Medal of Private H B Brett of the King's Royal Rifles was gazetted on 14 November 1916, for an action on the Somme. The citation reads:

> For conspicuous gallantry and devotion to duty. While his company was attacking across the open under such intense machine gunfire that it seemed impossible for any human being to stand up under it, this man, employed as a stretcher bearer, utterly regardless of his personal safety, and at a time when it appeared to be madness to attempt to leave our trenches, repeatedly went out and brought in wounded, handing over most of them to other stretcher-bearers to dress, in order that he might go and fetch in more men, until he

himself was badly wounded. Even then he wished to go on helping, and did in fact dress his platoon officer in the open. [33]

~ 0 ~

More changes to the system of gallantry awards were made in 1917. Up to this date, the DCM was also available as a reward for distinguished conduct that did not always involve action in the face of the enemy, for example the DCM citation of Staff Sergeant A J Steele of the Army Service Corps seems almost bizarre when set against some of the other acts of breathtaking heroism described in this book:

> For great zeal and devotion to duty as Master Baker during the early part of the campaign at Boulogne, when, working under the greatest difficulties in the open, and exposed to all weathers, he successfully carried out the work of the First Bakery, never failing to turn out the maximum output from the ovens. [34]

A number of awards to the Royal Field Artillery were also made, not for combat in the face of the enemy, but instead for consistent good work in maintaining the supply of ammunition and for administrative work at depots many miles behind the front line. In order to better reward services of this nature, in 1917 the Immediate award of the Meritorious Service Medal (MSM) was introduced. This grew out of the pre-existing Gratuity award of the MSM, which had reflected consistent good service over a number of years. The new award allowed the DCM to function henceforth as a medal granted purely for gallantry in the face of the enemy. In accordance with this change of practice, orders were passed to all commanders on 1 January 1917 that the DCM (and DSO and MC) were henceforth to be restricted as far as possible to the 'fighting services'.

~ 0 ~

The Third Battle of Ypres (popularly known as Passchendaele) was one of the grimmest battles of the First World War in terms of fighting conditions. The battlefield east of Ypres had, by the late summer of 1917, been turned into a cratered wilderness by the impact of over a million shells. Yet it was here that Haig believed he could force a decisive defeat upon the Germans, for if they yielded ground in Belgium, they would have to concede their important submarine bases on the Belgian coast. It was from these bases (the British Government believed) that the Germans were conducting their U-boat war against shipping in the Atlantic. It was widely held at the highest level that if the submarine menace was not neutralized by late 1917, then Britain might well be starved into submission. If instead of withdrawing the Germans stood and fought, then Haig believed that the German army would be destroyed. However, if the enemy has only two options open to him, he invariably chooses a third, and the Germans instead developed the tactic of defence in depth. Rather than hold their front lines with trenches densely packed with men, they had instead constructed hundreds of concrete pillboxes. Each pillbox needed only a small garrison, and they could offer mutual support with their machine-guns. Meanwhile, most of the German reserves were kept back, out of artillery range, ready to launch a counter-attack.

A typical Passchendaele DCM was awarded to Company Sergeant Major Charles Miller, of the 12th Battalion, Durham Light Infantry. Miller, a native of Spennymoor, was a veteran of the Boer War. He had re-enlisted upon the outbreak of the First World War and had been posted as a sergeant to one of the newly raised service battalions of the DLI. He was quickly promoted to warrant rank. After fighting on the Somme in 1916, the battalion was moved north in late 1917 and on 20 September the 23rd Division, of which the Durhams were a part, was to fight what its divisional historian called its greatest battle: the fight for the Menin Road ridge, east of Ypres. Pushing forward over the shell-cratered ground, the Durhams were supposedly in reserve but were quickly in action as they came under machine-gun fire from Dumbarton Wood. Having reached their final objective, the Green Line, as it was shown on maps, the Durhams began to consolidate, digging in and reversing the parapets of captured trenches. Now they began to receive the inevitable German counter-attacks; a German shell hit and collapsed a dug-out, burying a number of men alive. Thinking quickly, Miller was first on the scene digging the men out. His swift actions, though exposing him to danger, undoubtedly saved the lives of his men, and earned him a DCM award.

It will be noted that early awards of the DCM, those in 1914 and 1915, carry very detailed citations. Quite often both the date and the place at which the act of gallantry occurred are recorded. From around 1916, citations became much more vague. Few dates or places were given, and it often now becomes a matter of educated guesswork to try to establish the action for which an award was made. This was clearly because the citations were publicly available, being published in the *London Gazette*, and there was simply too much chance of giving military information to the enemy in this way. Sometimes, however, it is fairly easy to work out when and where an award was made, even if this is not explicitly stated in the citation. The DCM of 21-year-old Private Harry Mason, a young soldier of the 171st Company Machine Gun Corps, from Stockton Heath, near Warrington, was gazetted in May 1918. The citation for the award reads:

> For conspicuous gallantry and devotion to duty. When a gun was blown up, one man being killed and another wounded, this man stayed with his wounded comrade for twelve hours under heavy fire. He then in full view of the enemy assisted in carrying the stretcher back, though weak from exposure.[35]

It is usually fairly safe to assume the actual award occurred four to six months prior to the citation, which suggests an incident in late 1917. Mason's service papers show that he did not join 171 Company until August of 1917. The Company was part of the 57th (2nd West Lancashire) Division, and this unit as a whole did not see a great deal of heavy fighting in late 1917 or early 1918, apart from its involvement in the latter stages of the Third Battle of Ypres. Here again, reading between the lines of the citation gives tell-tale clues. If the twelve hours Mason spent with his wounded comrade left him weak from exposure, this suggests the weather conditions were cold and wet. On the Ypres battlefield, by late autumn 1917 the ground had been so utterly destroyed by shellfire that there was no choice but to take cover from enemy fire in flooded craters. The grim weather of October and November and the cloying mud in which wounded men drowned have become synonymous with the horror of the First World War. This would probably have been Mason's first introduction to the reality of warfare on the Western Front. Distinguished Conduct Medals by this stage in the war were particularly hard earned, with the Military Medal being available for most acts of gallantry. Taken together with his tender age, this makes Mason's bravery on this occasion particularly remarkable.

~ 0 ~

The spring of 1918 witnessed Imperial Germany's last throw of the dice in the Great War. With the ranks of her army on the Western Front swelled by troops released from the Eastern Front following Russia's collapse, she gambled on a knockout blow delivered before American troops could arrive in Europe in sizeable numbers. The Germans also employed new tactics developed in the years of trench warfare: lightly armed storm troops would smash their way through weak points in the Allied lines, whilst counter-battery fire would suppress their artillery. Without artillery support, strong points would be left to wither on the vine.

The first blow fell on 21 March 1918, when the Germans launched Operation Michael along a front stretching from Vimy in the north to St Quentin in the south. Looking over the parapets of their trenches, the British could see nothing but advancing field grey figures in every direction. The British Third and Fifth armies were driven back in disarray by the offensive. Thousands were killed and many thousands more were captured. Others fought a desperate defensive action holding on as best they could. Sergeant James Gerrard of the 9th Battalion Cheshire Regiment received a well-deserved DCM for an action in March 1918. The citation, as is typical for later war awards is somewhat vague giving no date or location and only stating that at a critical moment Gerrard had rushed forward to kill the crew of a machine-gun threatening his battalion. However, in old age Gerrard wrote a detailed account of the incident in his memoirs:

Then I saw a machine gun, placed on top of a 7 or 8 feet high bank of soil which were on the side of a light railway which came down to the cross roads, I were waiting & when a head appeared to sight the gun I fired and down it went, a gun had also been placed a few yards on the left of the 1st gun and a head appeared to sight this one. I were waiting and fired again with the same result they were about 70 yards from me. Then another head appeared at the right gun, I fired and down he went. Two gunners never came up at the same time, which gave me every advantage. I came to the conclusion an officer were forcing them up with a revolver ...

Then as I saw my company advancing up the incline - extended - to about 100 paces I jumped out of the hole and ran for the gun jumping down into the road. I landed just in the rear of one [German] ... lied flat on his face in the gutter, he were alive, he lifted his left arm & shoulder only and said, 'Mercy' ... his dark Prussian eyes said 'murder' and my bayonet went into the back of his heart. He collapsed with a grunt, I withdrew the bayonet and pressed the trigger. You can't trust Germans and live ...

The officer were in the middle of the road dead, the 1st man to reach me were named Mellor from Stockport, he turned the German over I had bayoneted, and said he had a lovely revolver. I have often wondered if the last man killed the officer because the officer were not beside the gun but at least a couple of yards away. Mellor got the revolver for a souvenir, so I went to the officer and took the Zeiss field glasses he had on a strap round his neck and the watch off his wrist ... this gun were between me & the gunners, and although it were only about ½ the distance of the other 2 guns of which I had a frontal view. As my company came up the field on my right I saw 2 Germans who had been lied flat jump up with their hands above their heads and run through the gaps in the extended order towards the rear. When I got to the cross-roads the guns were still on the top of the embankment, with a pile of dead beneath each gun 4 or 5 feet high. On the other side of the cross roads, were Delsaux Farm which were battered buildings ...[36]

On demobilisation, James Gerrard took a general store in Hollingworth, Cheshire, which he ran successfully until his retirement. He died in March 1976. Although he suffered no physical after-effects from his war wounds, his experiences haunted him mentally for the rest of his life, and his conversation invariably returned to them. In his final illness, he returned in his mind completely to the trenches and urged other patients on his hospital ward to keep their heads below the parapet.

Also decorated for bravery in the March 1918 offensive was Corporal John Henry Harvey of the 1st battalion Leicestershire Regiment. Harvey had served overseas with his Battalion since 1914, going through most of the campaigns on the Western Front. By March 1918 he was a trench mortar gunner, operating a 3 inch Stokes gun with the 71st Trench Mortar Battery. These versatile weapons gave infantry commanders on the ground a degree of local control over artillery and were capable of putting down a smoke or explosive barrage, of a very high rate of fire. To fire the weapon the gunner simply pulled a pin on the top of the round (akin to the pin on a hand grenade) and dropped the bomb down the tube, where a striker would set off a sporting cartridge in the base, propelling the round out of the barrel. It was possible to get three rounds into the air at the same time, and greater range could be achieved by adding extra propellant to the base.

Harvey's citation describes his bravery:

... during an enemy attack when in charge of a light trench mortar. He kept up a steady fire until surrounded by the enemy, when he made his way across the open with his mortar. Later, he occupied a forward position, holding up the enemy's advance and destroying a machine gun and team. During the whole operation he proved himself invaluable to the officers of his battery, and showed great courage, determination and devotion to duty.[37]

In an act reminiscent of that of Bill Irvine mentioned previously, after the war Harvey had the suspension removed from his DCM by a jeweller, and a chain mounted upon the medal, so that his wife could wear it around her neck as a pendant.

~ 0 ~

In April 1918, as their attack on the Somme ran out of steam, the Germans opened a new front further north on the Lys, using the same smash and grab tactics. It was here, at Festubert, that Acting Corporal Harry Holcroft of the 1st/5th Battalion South Lancashire Regiment earned his DCM, the citation reading:

> For conspicuous gallantry and devotion to duty. While a platoon of his company was moving forward to counter-attack a party of the enemy on the right flank this man rushed out of a trench on his own initiative and single-handed attacked a machine gun and its crew which was checking the advance. He killed two, capturing the gun and four prisoners. He afterwards went out several times under heavy fire bringing in wounded. [38]

Harry 'Mad Ginger' Holcroft was born in Crawford Village, near Rainford, Lancashire. A miner by occupation, he volunteered for service in the Army at the outbreak of the Great War, giving a false date of birth, being just seventeen years of age at the time. He joined the 5th Battalion South Lancashire Regiment, a St Helens-based battalion that followed rifle volunteer traditions with black buttons and badges. He proceeded to the Western Front in October 1915. It was on 10 April 1918 that the incident in question occurred, and in fact Holcroft was originally recommended for the Victoria Cross for his actions that day. This was subsequently downgraded to the DCM, but the original VC recommendation adds more detail:

> Rifleman Holcroft, H. is strongly recommended for reward for excellent work and devotion to duty throughout the last tour of duty in the line and particularly for his epic gallantry when during an enemy attack on Loisne Central Keep on 10th inst. he attacked single handed and on his own initiative an enemy machine gun and crew which was holding up and inflicting losses on our counter-attacking platoon. He killed two and captured four others and the machine gun thereby facilitating the operations of the counter-attack. Afterwards he repeatedly patrolled up to the enemy trench clearing our own dead and wounded and securing documents and

identifications from the enemy dead. Also at great personal risk, locating the body of Lt. Dymond who was killed on the enemy wire whilst exploiting the success of the counter-attack and securing from his person very valuable company documents. [39]

Holcroft was discharged on 30 January 1919 and was awarded the Silver War Badge. After the war he was for some time the landlord of the Colliers' Arms at Kings Moss, St Helens, and was for a number of years employed by Pilkington Glass. He died in St Helens, at the age of ninety-two.

By the summer of 1918, both sides had fought themselves to a standstill and June passed relatively quietly before in July and August British, Australian, Canadian and American troops began driving the Germans back. 4 July saw the Battle of Hamel, an Australian victory, but 8 August 1918 was described by German supreme commander Erich Ludendorf as 'the Black Day of the German Army'. Its divisions were pushed back along a wide front, and for the first time there were widespread desertions among the German soldiers and open defeatism. By now the Allies were fighting over some of the old Somme battlegrounds from 1916. Sergeant A Wignall, of the 1st/6th Battalion Manchester Regiment received a DCM for bravery in the final advance of the war, the 'Battles of the 100 days'. His citation in the *London Gazette* simply states:

> For bravery and initiative as Scout Sergeant during operations East of Colincamps from 14th to 18th August 1918.[40]

However, in addition to his medal he received a hand-painted card, containing a more detailed account of his action:

> On the 14th inst., as soon as information was received that the enemy was withdrawing, this N.C.O. led out a reconnoitring patrol about 2,500 yds. in advance of our line to just West of Serre and brought back invaluable information as to the enemy's movements. Later he was employed particularly to get in touch with troops on the flanks where others were unable to do so. This he succeeded in doing on every occasion and his information was invariably accurate and most valuable. His work entailed his moving about in the most exposed positions, over difficult country not previously reconnoitered and he was subjected to heavy m.g. fire and accurate sniping throughout.[41]

Finally, it seems that unlike the situation following the Boer War, after the Great War the authorities took the view that subsequent misdemeanours were not sufficient to make acts of bravery carried out during the war null and void. Sergeant John Curran was a resident of Sale, in Cheshire, though

Sergeant Major John Breeze, 11th Hussars. Awarded the DCM for his actions at the Battle of Inkerman on 5 November 1854, in which a cannon ball took off his right arm. (© Dix Noonan Webb Ltd - www.dnw.co.uk)

Private Michael McNamarra, 5th Dragoon Guards. Recommended for the DCM in January 1855, after attacking and killing a Russian lancer who was about to run through a helpless comrade. (Courtesy of the National Army Museum)

Corporal John Allen, 13th Light Dragoons, who rode in the third line at the Charge of the Light Brigade, 25 October 1854. His horse was killed beneath him, but he survived unscathed. Note that he wears the DCM after the Crimea Medal, the correct order of wear at this time. (© Dix Noonan Webb Ltd - www.dnw.co.uk)

Colour Sergeant Frank Bourne OBE DCM, 24th Regiment, later South Wales Borderers. Decorated for his part in the defence of Rorke's Drift, January 1879. (Courtesy of the Regimental Museum of The Royal Welsh, Brecon)

Sergeant Thomas Burdett, 1st Battalion Northumberland Fusiliers. Awarded the DCM for his part in the Battle of Omdurman, September 1898. (Courtesy of Paul Williams)

Colour Sergeant Frederick Evan Saddon, Royal Marine Artillery. Decorated with the DCM for services as a machine-gunner at the Battle of Gedid, in the Sudan, November 1899. (Courtesy of Alastair Jack)

Sergeant Thomas Hodgson DCM, Loyal North Lancashire Regiment. Hodgson was awarded the DCM for rescuing a wounded man at the Battle of Modder River, on 28 November 1899. (Courtesy of Steve Rosbotham)

Private William Fessey, King's Own Scottish Borderers. A Maxim machine-gunner, he was awarded the DCM for keeping his gun in action on 29 March 1900 in the face of heavy Boer fire. (Courtesy of Heather Wilson)

Battery Sergeant Major William H M Dow, O Battery Royal Horse Artillery. DCM gazetted 27 September 1901, awarded for the action at Colesburg on 1 January 1900. (Private collection)

Sergeant Thomas Connolly, Royal Irish Regiment (attached Mounted Infantry), awarded a DCM for an incident at Reitvlei, on 15 July 1900 when he saved a piquet of sixteen men from capture by Boer forces. (Author's collection)

Sergeant Herbert Gladstone Cowan, of Birkenhead, with his wife Gertrude. Cowan was awarded the DCM during the Boer War, as Orderly Room Sergeant with the Cheshire Regiment, for continuous valuable service rather than a single act of bravery. (Author's collection)

Driver H J King, 6th Battery Royal Field Artillery. He was awarded the DCM for an action at Le Cateau in 1914, the citation reading, *'At Audencourt, on 26th August, when the limber was upset, he helped to hook into another limber and brought a gun away under heavy fire.'* (Courtesy of Patrick Gariepy)

HERO OF MONS RETREAT.

SGT. A. CHARMAN, D.C.M.
(ROYAL WARWICKSHIRE REGIMENT).
The official description of the act of bravery was: "For conspicuous good service at a critical moment, whereby he was mainly responsible for averting the capture of many men."
With "THREE CHEERS."

Sergeant Alfred Charman, Royal Warwickshire Regiment. Charman was awarded the DCM for an incident at St Quentin during the Retreat from Mons. According to his citation, he saved 250 men from capture by the enemy. (Author's collection)

BRITISH HEROES.

SERGEANT A. J. MART (Distinguished Conduct Medal), 1st Bedfordshires.
For gallant conduct on November 10 in assisting to recover one of our abandoned machine guns, killing one German, who was watching the gun. He distinguished himself previously on dangerous services.

A contemporary postcard features an artist's impression of the deed of Sergeant A.J. Mart, 1st Battalion Bedfordshire Regiment, awarded the DCM for gallantry near Ypres on 10 November 1914. He killed a German sentry and recovered a captured British machine-gun. Inset: A portrait of Mart. (Author's collection)

Sergeant A G Chambers DCM 5th Field Company Royal Engineers, decorated for bravery near Ypres on 11 November 1914. (Reproduced with the permission of Leeds University Library)

A cigarette card from Wills' *War Incidents* series shows Lance Corporal Sanderson, London Scottish, capturing two Germans armed with nothing more than a pair of wire cutters. (Author's collection)

Sergeant Bill Irvine, 1st/7th Battalion West Riding Regiment, of Delph in Saddleworth, who was decorated for bravery near Ypres. Something of a local character, after the war Irvine cut up his DCM to form a brooch for his wife. (Author's collection)

Lance Corporal John Yates 1st/5th battalion York & Lancaster Regiment. On 10 July 1915, near the Yser Canal in Belgium, he crawled out into No Man's Land to assist two wounded men. (Author's collection)

Sergeant Edward Humphries, Lahore Division Signal Company. He was awarded the DCM for repairing telephone lines during the Second Battle of Ypres, April 1915. (Reproduced with the permission of Leeds University Library)

Sergeant Thomas Toner, of Carlisle, 2nd Battalion Border Regiment. He was awarded the DCM for bravery at Festubert on 16 May 1915. He was killed in action later that same day. (Author's collection)

Corporal John Ching, of the South Lancashire Regiment. Awarded the DCM for tunnelling operations near Le Touquet in the spring of 1915. (Courtesy of Manx National Heritage)

Sergeant Charles Williams DCM, East Lancashire Divisional Signals Company RE. Williams was decorated for his bravery at Gallipoli in June 1915, when under heavy fire he repeatedly repaired broken telephone wires. (Author's collection)

Commissioner Sir Edward Henry decorates PC William Edwards, Metropolitan Police, with the DCM in 1915. The award was for services in France with the East Surrey Regiment the previous year. (Author's collection)

Sergeant John Black DCM, 8th Battalion Somerset Light Infantry. Black lost part of his leg in the action for which he was awarded the decoration, repelling an enemy bombing attack in December 1915. (Author's collection).

Private Alfred Bench, 10th Battalion the Rifle Brigade. He received the DCM for bravery near Cordonerie on the night of 15/16 December 1915 whilst out in No Man's Land. (Courtesy of Patrick Gariépy)

The engraved watch presented to Private Frank Richards by the Blaina Penny Fund, upon his gaining the DCM. (Courtesy of Dr John Krijnan)

Private Frank Richards DCM MM, 2nd Battalion Royal Welsh Fusiliers. Richards was awarded the DCM for his part in maintaining telephone cables in the open under fire during the capture of RWF crater, in the Bethune sector, on the night of 4 February 1916. (Courtesy of Mrs M.Holmes)

Private J Boyd, Irish Guards, of Kirkcaldy in Scotland, captures a German machine-gun single-handed, during the Battle of the Somme. An illustration from *Deeds that Thrill the Empire*. (Author's collection)

Private James Bryan, of Longton near Stoke-on-Trent in Staffordshire. Prior to the First World War he worked in the local potteries, but enlisted into the 7th (Service) Battalion of the North Staffordshire Regiment. He received the DCM for his part in the capture of Baghdad in December 1917. (Courtesy of Mark Simner)

Bandsman Peter McGarry, 1st Battalion Connaught Rangers (seen here after the war in the band of the Princess Patricia's Canadian Light Infantry). In January 1916, in Mesopotamia, he was awarded the DCM for spotting enemy targets. McGarry was from Liverpool. (Courtesy of Captain Michael W Clare, CD Ret.)

Private Nicholas Vlok DCM, of Bloemfontain, who served with B Company of the 2nd Battalion South African Infantry. Aged forty-nine at the time of the Delville Wood battle, he had previously served as a Boer officer during the 1899-1902 conflict. (Courtesy of Ian Uys)

Company Sergeant Major Charles Miller DCM, 12th Battalion Durham Light Infantry. Miller received the award for quick thinking during the Third Battle of Ypres, September 1917. (Author's collection) he was born in Salford. Called up for military service in 1916, he had a chequered military career to say the least. Convicted of desertion whilst still in England, when he was sent to France he was nonetheless promoted rapidly, reaching the rank of sergeant. By 1918 he was serving with the 17th Battalion Manchester Regiment and the *London Gazette* of 3 October 1918 carried a citation for his DCM:

> For conspicuous gallantry and devotion to duty. He went forward with two men and surprised and captured an enemy post of one officer and six men in broad daylight. Later, he assumed command of his platoon, and under a very heavy barrage held an isolated position until relieved. His conduct throughout was splendid, and inspired his men.[42]

Curran seems to have had a hard war; in one document he states:

> I am always coughing and spitting phlegm and short of breath. I consider this is the result of hardships in the trenches and being gassed on several dates, 31 July 1916 at Ypres, 1 May 1918 at Ypres, and 15 May 1918 at Ypres.[43]

Nevertheless he chose to re-enlist for Regular service at the end of the war. Sergeant Curran's service papers have survived, and they reveal that once more his conduct was far from ideal. On 24 June 1920 he was awarded fourteen days detention for absence from 2200 on 12 June 1920 to 0050 on 13 June 1920, resisting an escort, and stating a falsehood to his commanding officer. On 7 July 1920 he was declared a deserter by Court of Inquiry held at Kinmel Park Camp, and on 4 August 1920 he was arrested by the Civil Power at Manchester and rejoined at Kinmel Park on 5 August 1920. He was also in 1920 treated in hospital for syphilis.

On 7 August 1920 the military authorities discovered that Curran had in his absence been awarded three months' hard labour, at Chester Castle Sessions on 19 June 1920, for aggravated assault on a female. He was arrested at Kinmel Park and committed to Liverpool Prison to serve his sentence. On 4 October 1920 he was discharged from the Army in consequence of having been convicted by the Civil Power, his character at the time of discharge was recorded as 'bad'.

It is clear from the documents that the military authorities originally intended to deprive Curran of both his gallantry awards and his campaign medals. However, on 29 April 1922 a letter from the War Office to Infantry Record Office Preston countermanded this:

> I am commanded to inform you that the Distinguished Conduct

Medal awarded to No. 90232, Private J. Curran, Manchester Regiment, for service as No. 38544 Sergeant J. Curran, MM, 19th Battalion, Manchester Regiment, vide the *London Gazette* dated 3 October 1918, and forfeited by him in consequence of his discharge on the 4th October 1920 (on conviction by the Civil Power) under Article 1236 of the Royal Warrant for pay, etc., of the Army which was in force on that date has been restored by the Army Council under Article 1240 of the above mentioned Royal Warrant ... I am to add however that the commemorative war medals earned by this man are forfeited under Article 1236(b) of the Royal Warrant.[44]

John Curran resurfaced again in London in the summer of 1927. By now he was going by the name of John Ryan, and was being held by the Metropolitan Police at Albany Street Police Station awaiting sentence, having been convicted of housebreaking. A letter received by Manchester Regiment records, Preston, from a police sergeant, sheds some light on this:

When arrested on 2 May 1927, prisoner refused to give any particulars of himself. He now states that he served in the 17th Manchesters under Colonel MacDonald from 5 March 1916 till the end of the war when he was discharged as a Sergeant. He also states that he was awarded the DCM and MM, and that his Army character was very good. [Please] furnish us with full particulars of this man ... for the information of the Learned Judge.[45]

A letter written by Curran to the same office from Brixton Prison two weeks later, requesting details of his service, states:

Dear Sir, I am in some trouble and should thank you ever so mutch [sic] if you can kindly let me have the deeds that I got my DCM and MM for.[46]

It appears that in response to these requests a copy of the 1922 letter was furnished, to show that Curran, in spite of his bad character, was indeed a legitimate holder of the DCM. It is not, however, known if this was enough to influence the presiding judge!

Minor Fronts and Foreign Awards
In the spring of 1915 the British Army faced a shells crisis. The shortage of artillery ammunition was so desperate that some batteries on the Western Front were limited to firing only two or three rounds a day. At the same time the cabinet was split between the 'westerners', chief of which was Lord Kitchener, who maintained that the war could only be won in the

west, and the 'easterners', led by Winston Churchill, who advocated taking on Germany's weaker allies in the eastern Mediterranean. Yet such was the weakness of Prime Minister Herbert Asquith's leadership that despite not having sufficient artillery ammunition for one major offensive in the spring of 1915, the British Army actually launched two, one in the west, at Aubers Ridge, and another in the east, at Gallipoli. However, even if they were short of ammunition, neither theatre was short of heroism.

The British Army landed at Cape Helles, Gallipoli, on 25 April 1915. A few miles further up the coast, at Anzac Cove, the fledgling Australian and New Zealand Army Corps made its first assault on the Turkish positions. Both forces failed to make sufficient headway in the first few hours, and would become bogged down in trench warfare as paralysing as that on the Western Front. For the British, their corps commander, Hunter-Weston, had become fixated with the battle raging at one beach in particular: Lancashire Landing in the Cape Helles sector, and failed to capitalise on weak Turkish opposition elsewhere.

The Australians meanwhile displayed extraordinary tenacity on that first day. Being rowed ashore north of their intended landing area and facing in some places sheer cliffs, they nonetheless pressed inland, in the face of strong Turkish opposition. Private Horrie Martyr of the 8th Battalion Australian Imperial Force (AIF) crawled through the scrub on the afternoon of that first day to rescue a badly wounded sergeant. His deed, which would earn him the DCM, was later described by Lieutenant Hunter Bolton, an officer in the battalion:

> You could not lift a finger above the trench without being in danger of having it shot off. We lay in this trench for 20 minutes or half an hour, when things began to get a bit quieter, and on looking out I saw a man about 150 yards away carrying a wounded officer [sic] on his back. Shells were falling all around and when the man was near our trench with his burden he got a bullet right through the back. We in the trench pulled them both inside and … sent them to the boat en route for the hospital … I recommended Private Martyr to the commanding officer for recognition of his bravery. [47]

Horrie Martyr DCM had a long and distinguished military career. He served with the 6th Battalion, the Royal Melbourne Regiment between the wars, and with the 2/6th Battalion of the AIF in the Second World War. When the Citizen Military Forces were reformed in 1948, Horrie became the RSM of the Royal Melbourne Regiment.

~ 0 ~

Meanwhile, the fighting at Gallipoli raged on into June 1915, with the third Battle of Krithia. The British forces holding the southern tip of the peninsula tried to force a breach in the Turkish lines, and thus effect a breakthrough to link up with the Australians and New Zealanders. In the heat and dust of a Turkish summer, bedevilled by flies, with drinking water in short supply and precious little opportunity for rest or leave, one of the toughest battles of the First World War was fought.

On 3 June 1915, whilst overhauling lines and extensions for the assault on the Turkish trenches planned for the following day, Sergeant Charles Williams was awarded the first Distinguished Conduct Medal gained by the 42nd Division's Royal Engineers Signal Company. He was in charge of two strong parties laying cables along the Krithia Nullah, which was a main communication route in a ravine. All day long the enemy had shelled the route, which was congested with all kinds of traffic. One of the working parties was caught by two salvoes, which killed two men, wounded another, smashed up cable-barrows and wounded a horse. Sergeant Williams, with splendid courage and determination, re-organized his men, and by force of personal example carried on and finished the job. The citation for the award reads:

> For conspicuous gallantry and coolness in action on the Gallipoli Peninsula during 1915. He has frequently laid wires under heavy rifle and shrapnel fire and has consistently shown great bravery and resource.[48]

Private W Stanton, a territorial of the 1st/8th (Ardwick) Battalion of the Manchester Regiment, again part of the 42nd Division, was also awarded the DCM for an action in this battle:

> For gallant conduct on 4th June 1915, south of Krithia (Dardanelles). He advanced across the open under heavy fire with a rope to one of the enemy's abandoned machine guns, which was by this means dragged in and captured.[49]

The 42nd Division consisted entirely of pre-war territorial soldiers (the so-called 'Saturday Night Soldiers') supplemented by this stage with a few wartime volunteers. Its battalions were raised across the mill towns of Lancashire (Accrington, Burnley and Blackburn) and in the working class districts of Manchester. Clearly these men were more than a match in terms of physical courage for the soldiers of the Regular Army.

In August of 1915 a new front was opened at Gallipoli, further north at Suvla Bay. This time the attack was undertaken by New Army troops, as well as yeomanry and territorials. On 21 August 1915 these men launched an attack on the Turkish position known as Hill 70. The attack was a disaster, as Turkish troops were able to mow down the attackers on their long approach march. The heavy firing set the tinder-dry undergrowth alight, and many of the British wounded were burned to death. Many yeomanry regiments fought on foot here, including the Queen's Own Dorset Yeomanry. Squadron Sergeant Major Phillip Finlay, a draper's assistant from Mere in Wiltshire, had mobilised with the Regiment in 1914. At Chocolate Hill he was one of the few survivors of his regiment who assembled in a rocky shelter, before launching a dashing attack on the Turkish trenches, an action that earned him a DCM.

The Great War was also the first conflict for which DCM awards were made to the soldiers of other nations. Inter-allied awards were common, and in the same way that British soldiers who received the DCM often received the Russian Cross of St George in the early part of the war, so the soldiers of the French, Belgian, American and other armies received awards of the DCM from time to time. *Statistics of the Military Effort of the British Empire during the Great War 1914-1920* (published by the War Office in 1922) states that 4,957 DCMs and one bar were awarded to foreign troops in the conflict. Recent research by Howard Williamson indicates that the figure may well actually be higher, at 5,024 awards. However, these were not recorded in the *London Gazette*, and there is often only anecdotal evidence as to the basis on which the awards were made. War Office lists of foreign recipients are held by The National Archives, an example of an entry being 'SERGENT MARCEL GREUILLET 167e REGT d'INFANTERIE'; however, there are no citations recorded in these documents. Around a quarter of awards to foreign troops were made to those attached to British units. The best-known example of such a Distinguished Conduct Medal to a French soldier is that awarded to Paul Maze. Maze volunteered to act as interpreter to General Gough in the first weeks of the war. The two became friends and Maze survived a number of incidents during the course of the war. He wrote about his experiences in *Frenchman in Khaki,* but the book does not indicate the particular action or incident for which the award was made. Another French DCM award was made to James Armand 'Jimmy' de Rothschild. A member of the French branch of the famous banking family, he was privately educated, yet nonetheless served in the ranks of the French army. He received a DCM in 1915 as a French '*poilu*' (ordinary soldier) but was commissioned into the British Army in 1918. Again, the circumstances behind his award of the DCM are unknown.

At least two United States Army recipients of the Congressional Medal of Honor were also awarded DCMs by the British government. Their deeds were in the highest traditions of the medal: Corporal Thomas A Pope of the 131st Infantry single-handedly attacked a machine-gun post near Hamel on 4 July 1918, whilst Corporal Jake Allex of Chicago, Illinois, also of the 131st Infantry, took command of his platoon after all the officers had been killed or wounded and single-handedly captured a machine-gun nest on Chipily Ridge during the advance of 8 August 1918. Some DCM awards were also made to members of the Czech Legion. One of these went to Antonin Stepan, who was born in Prague in November 1888. At that time Prague was within the Hapsburg Empire and on the outbreak of war Stepan was conscripted into the Austro-Hungarian Army. He was sent to the Eastern Front in the autumn of 1916, but he deserted to the Russian lines in March 1917. Entering the Czech Legions on 23 July of that year, he joined the 3rd Regiment. He was present at the Battle of Bachmac in mid-March 1918, when his unit reinforced the hard-pressed 1st, 6th and 7th Regiments, and it was most likely as a result of his deeds in these operations that he was awarded his Russian St George Cross for bravery.

In July 1918, he joined the newly formed 10th Shooters' Regiment at Samara, in which capacity he was present in several engagements of the Volga Front, among them Simbirsk and Bulgama, and the defence of the Trans-Siberian Railway in the Atchinsk, Kansk and Krasnojarsk sectors. His unit was also charged with guarding Russian gold at Irkutsk. Returning to Czechoslovakia as a warrant officer in April 1920 - via Japan, Ceylon, Egypt and Italy - Stepan was demobilised in August of the same year, but remained an active member of the Army reserve and Czech Legionnaire Veterans' Association. It is probable that his DCM award was connected with his Russian decoration.

~ 0 ~

Considerable effort was expended by the British Army in the Great War in theatres outside of France, in Mesopotamia, Palestine and Salonika. Some old soldiers thought that it was harder to qualify for a gallantry award in these theatres, because they were 'forgotten fronts', out of the public eye. Whether this is true or not would be debatable. Numbers of awards certainly were made for gallantry in these theatres, one such being that of James Bryan, who was born in Longton, near Stoke-on-Trent, in Staffordshire. Prior to the First World War he worked in the local potteries but enlisted into the 7th (Service) Battalion of the North Staffordshire Regiment in September 1914. He was to serve with the 7th Battalion throughout the Gallipoli and Mesopotamia campaigns, gaining his Distinguished Conduct Medal sometime shortly after the capture of Baghdad in late 1917. His citation was published in the *London Gazette* on 1 May 1918 and reads:

> For conspicuous gallantry and devotion to duty. When acting as runner, he carried messages repeatedly under heavy fire, and displayed an energy and ability which were of great value on several occasions. His gallantry throughout was of the highest order.[50]

His DCM was awarded to him by the Mayor of Stoke-on-Trent, Alderman Robinson, in a ceremony honouring a number of local men for their gallantry during the war. After he was demobilised in March 1919, James Bryan returned to the pottery industry and it is known that his DCM was in and out of a local pawnbrokers a number of times in the 1930s. Like so many other decorated veterans, he clearly fell on hard times, and it is thought that he died around 1935, being buried in Stoke's Longton Cemetery.

Also in Mesopotamia, First-Class Air Mechanic Samuel Hall, of Newton Heath, Manchester, was awarded a DCM for work in September 1917 as a wireless operator with 31 Wing Royal Flying Corps, directing aircraft onto their targets in an interesting early example of ground to air co-operation. The citation reads:

> For conspicuous gallantry and devotion to duty. When his wireless station came under heavy shellfire, and though the aerial was shot down on three occasions, he re-erected it on each occasion, displaying great courage and coolness. Still under heavy fire, he eventually succeeded in obtaining communication with his aeroplane, thus enabling two of the enemy guns to be silenced.[51]

Photographic evidence suggests that Hall was presented with the DCM, or possibly just the ribbon, at a ceremony carried out on the airfield at which he was based.

It should also be remembered that for most of the First World War, even after the creation of the Royal Air Force in 1918 and the provision of gallantry awards specifically for that service, the DCM could be (and frequently was) awarded for bravery in the air, to the NCOs and men of the Royal Flying Corps and RAF. One such award went on 15 March 1916 to Corporal C H Nott of No 15 Squadron, operating Royal Aircraft Factory BE2c and RE8 aircraft in the highly dangerous reconnaissance role:

> For conspicuous gallantry on escort duty when acting as gunner. During an attack in the air he was hit in the eye and rendered unconscious, the machine being also considerably shot about, and the engine damaged. On recovering consciousness, he at once made use of his gun with such good effect that he drove off the enemy's aeroplane, which had pressed the attack. Without his fine pluck it is almost certain that the machine and personnel would have been lost. This gallant N.C.O is likely to lose his eye.[52]

Corporal J H Waller of No 25 Squadron was awarded a DCM on 27 July 1916:

> For conspicuous gallantry and skill. On one occasion, as a passenger on an aeroplane, he dived onto an enemy biplane and shot it down. It was seen to crash to the ground. On another occasion, as passenger, he shot down a Fokker, which was also seen to crash to the ground.[53]

Another award went to 2nd class Air Mechanic H W Sutcliffe, on 5 August 1915:

> For great gallantry and zeal while employed as a gunner with an Officer Pilot. On the 9th May 1915, over Wytchaete, they engaged a German aeroplane at a height of about 4,000 feet. After a sharp fight, the hostile machine turned on its side and finally fell to the ground nose first and was wrecked.[54]

The Inter-War Years

As the First World War ground a halt in the mists of November 1918, fighting stuttered on in far-away places around the world, and British troops continued to gain gallantry awards even as the news of the Armistice with Germany was being received at home. Some of these flashpoints were new, for example, North Russia, where fighting against the Bolshevik revolutionaries had threatened to escalate into a major new war, even before the Great War had really drawn to a close. Then there were the familiar trouble spots, known to generations of British soldiers, such as the North West Frontier of India, where sporadic skirmishing developed into a third war with Afghanistan in 1919.

The citations for the DCMs awarded during these conflicts paint an often revealing picture of the nature of the fighting in these far-flung places. Sergeant Ernest Harrison of the 6th battalion Green Howards gained the award near Archangel, in North Russia:

For gallantry and able leadership during the attack on Zemstovo on 25th March 1919. When the attacking platoon was held up by deep snow and heavy machine gun fire, he led his platoon forward with great skill to support the attack. He took up a position close to the village and succeeded in covering the withdrawal of the attacking platoon and the evacuation of the wounded, and finally extricated his platoon from a difficult position without casualties. The determination and resourcefulness displayed by him were admirable. [55]

Company Sergeant-Major William Rutter of the same battalion was awarded the decoration for bravery in a second attack on the village the following day:

During the attack on Zemstovo on 26th March 1919, and the subsequent operations he displayed marked gallantry and determination. When the flank on the village was held up by machine gun fire, he forced his way through deep snow and heavy rifle fire, to the outskirts of the village, acting as a guide to one platoon of his company, which endeavoured to carry the village by a frontal attack. When this platoon was held up by very heavy machine gun fire and deep snow, and ordered to withdraw, he supervised the evacuation of all the wounded. He set a fine example to all.[56]

A miner from South Hetton, County Durham, Rutter had enlisted in the 7th Green Howards in 1914. He was wounded on the first day of the Battle of the Somme, but returned to active service. He had been demobilized and returned to his former occupation by the time his DCM was gazetted in the summer of 1919, and elected to have the award sent to him by post rather than awarded in a public presentation. Nevertheless, he felt compelled to write to the War Office in October 1919 stating:

Thinking my name has been lost from the book I find I must write asking why the bounty has not been sent to me for earning the DCM for which I was honoured. [57]

These citations and others like them paint a graphic picture of a force locked in bitter combat with a determined enemy where terrain and weather were as much against them as anything else. No wonder that the British public after four gruelling years of warfare on the Western Front were in no mood for an escalation of this conflict. Later that year, guns, stores and equipment were dumped into the River Dvina and the North Russian Expeditionary Force was withdrawn.

Far away in India there was more fighting on the North West Frontier.

In 1921, in the Malabar region of the rebellious border country, there were more local difficulties. Unrest among the lawless frontier tribes turned into open revolt. The town of Calicut was garrisoned by about half of the 1st Battalion Leinster Regiment, and when a detachment of this garrison set out to accompany the local British administrator to collect taxes in nearby Tirur Augadi, they were met with a hostile mob. Soon the whole district was aflame, and under threat of violence the party retired on the village of Malappuram. The remainder of the Leinsters set off at once to their assistance, expecting to meet the rebels en route. They were not mistaken for 20 miles further on they were confronted by a thousand-strong mob, and outnumbered about ten to one. Nevertheless, the Leinsters stood their ground, whilst the fanatical mob hurled themselves at their bayonets for some five hours. Ultimately the rebels were repulsed, with considerable losses, and the party at Malapuram was relieved. For their efforts this day, Private James Cahill MM of Kilnaganny, and Private George Ryan of Clonmel, County Tipperary, both of the 1st Leinsters, received the Distinguished Conduct Medal.

After the First World War, at the Versailles peace conference, Britain had been given a mandate over the former Turkish territory of Palestine. Although the British were unpopular, as a result of unfulfilled promises of Arab independence made during the war, the area was relatively quiet until the Arab revolt of the 1930s. One of the main causes of tension was immigration into the area of Jews fleeing persecution in Europe. The resulting pressures on land brought an armed response from the Arab population, and as the British Army tried to keep the peace, Palestine became one of the main trouble spots for British soldiers in the 1930s. One DCM was awarded to Sergeant Lyle Gasson of the Cheshire Regiment for an incident that took place on the night of 21/22 June 1936. The citation was published in the *London Gazette* on 6 November 1936. Part of it read:

> [Sergeant Gasson] was in command of the Railway Patrol Train from Jerusalem to Artuf, with a party of one Corporal and eight other ranks. On arrival at Kilo 64, the line was found to be blocked, and when the party started to remove the block, Arabs opened fire on them at close range, Sgt. Gasson being wounded in the eye. The Arabs then commenced to block the line to the rear of the Patrol Train. Sgt. Gasson engaged the Arabs with Lewis guns, under cover of which the blocks on the line were removed. The Arabs, who were in strength and had surrounded the train, were eventually driven off, after five of their number had been killed or wounded. Sgt. Gasson then took the Patrol Train to Deir-es-Sheikh Station, which he

placed in a state of defence, and at dawn, in spite of his wound and the reluctance of the native engine driver and fireman, continued the patrol to Artuf and back to Jerusalem. [58]

The ambush was typical of Arab tactics during the uprising, as illustrated by the DCM citation of Lance Sergeant James Allen, 1st Battalion Loyal Regiment. Allen, who was born in 1900, enlisted in the Loyal Regiment in 1919, and served variously in Constantinople, Malta, China and India from 1921 to 1936. He was posted to Palestine in February 1936 with the 1st Battalion of his regiment.

On 20 August 1936, Sergeant Allen, with half a platoon, reconnoitred Ara and Arara, two Arab villages near Megiddo. Allen and a police constable were in the leading car when they were fired upon by some Arabs from about 700 yards range. Accompanied by ten men from the half platoon they quickly advanced about half a mile in pursuit of the Arabs who were noticed on a parallel ridge. Allen led his detachment across the intervening valley but on reaching the top he found himself isolated except for the constable and two others. For over three-quarters of an hour they maintained their position on the hilltop, which was completely surrounded. Just as their ammunition was running out Lieutenant Price, commanding 'A' Company's detachment at Karkur, arrived with his own platoon and the other half, who had been pinned down by enemy fire, and forced the Arabs to break off the fight. After two and a half years' home service, Allen was posted to France in September 1939. He was wounded at Dunkirk, where he lost an eye, and made it back to England on 2 June 1940. He was finally discharged in 1951, after nearly thirty years with the Colours.

In India in the 1930s, the British Army returned to a style of warfare similar to that of the late nineteenth century. Its role was very much imperial policing, with skirmishes with tribesmen on the North West Frontier still commonplace. New weapons such as armoured cars and aeroplanes were now frequently used to keep the hostile tribes in check, but often it fell to soldiers on foot to bear the brunt of the dangerous patrol work. The action fought by the 1st Battalion Northamptonshire Regiment at Marai Narai piquet, on 9 September 1937, is typical. The night of 8 September was one of heavy sniping by the enemy tribesmen. In the morning the 1st Battalion Northamptonshire Regiment as advanced guard of a column moved off for Ladha. The usual practice when moving in tribal territory was for the leading troops to make temporary piquets or posts on the high ground either side of the column to prevent snipers firing down at them. Number 6 platoon of 'B' Company, piquetting the Marai Narai, a permanent piquet site from the 1919-21 campaign, soon came under continuous and damaging sniper fire. Lance Corporal Jarvis, commanding the Lewis Gun section, received a wound from which he subsequently died. Private Clarke took over the Lewis Gun, and with Private Lee, kept it in action through out the day, often in an exposed position, despite the fact that both had been wounded early on in the engagement.

The soldiers managed to return an effective fire on the snipers in the surrounding thick scrub and broken ground, and to direct artillery fire onto them from the accompanying mountain batteries, but in the ensuing six hours more men were hit, including Private Nind and the artillery forward observation officer who was with the patrol. In total four of the platoon were wounded. Private John Aubers Ridge Letts, who had declared upon enlistment that he was born in 1913 but who as his name suggests was actually born in 1915, earned a DCM during the course of the day. Although wounded seriously enough to require subsequent hospital treatment, he had insisted on staying with the piquet, frequently exposing himself to danger in order to try and locate the enemy. When the forward observation officer fell wounded in an exposed position, Letts ran out and brought him back to safety.

The platoon had a desperate time withdrawing when their time came. They were to withdraw at 1430 hours but as the rear guard from the 1st/9th Gurkha Rifles reached them, a heavy storm blew up and completely blotted out the usual visual signals. The platoon had to be called in by lamp, and as fast as they left the Marai Narai, the Pathans quickly occupied the now empty posts, even though two light tanks had joined in giving covering fire. It was a party of Gurkhas, acting as a lay back, that effectively stopped the further progress of the tribesmen.

Private Letts was in Razmak hospital undergoing treatment when news came through of his award. The remainder of the battalion was still out on the column at the time, and it fell to Captain Metcalf, who commanded the regimental rear details, to tell him of his award. Metcalf was often given to conveying even light-hearted news in a mock serious manner, and Letts entirely misunderstood him when Metcalf came to his bedside and stated in sombre tones:

It is my duty to inform you, that you have been awarded a DCM. [59]

Letts immediately jumped to the wrong conclusion, that Metcalf had used DCM in the sense of its other Army meaning - District Court Martial - and at once replied:

Why Sir, what have I done wrong? [60]

Another award of the DCM was gained by Lance Sergeant H Blake in similar circumstances on the North West Frontier near Razmak. Blake was serving with the 1st Battalion the Leicestershire Regiment, and the account of his action from the regimental newspaper the *Green Tiger* is worth quoting in full:

> On August 21 [1938] seven casualties were received as a result of a heavy attack on one of the picquets of the 1st battalion The Leicestershire Regiment. Three of the men were missing in the thick scrub when the piquet withdrew behind the crest of Bodari Sar, where our forward troops were in position.
>
> At this time considerable numbers of the enemy had crept up in the scrub on the forward slope of Bodari Sar. They were covered by riflemen posted on a ridge some 300 yards away.
>
> Lance Sergeant Blake volunteered to go forward and search for the missing men. He went out at once and brought in a dead soldier and his rifle. He went out a second time with four men and remained in an exposed position, searching the scrub for the two missing soldiers. He was under fire at close range at the time and there were considerable numbers of the enemy near him in the scrub. He delayed his withdrawal to go forward and bomb a party of the enemy seen below him.
>
> His complete disregard for his personal safety and his coolness and bravery under fire, was a fine example to all ranks. [61]

Both Blake and Letts were of that breed of men who, in the hungry thirties in Britain, refused to sign on the dole when work was short. They chose instead to keep their pride intact by joining the Army, even though this was no soft option. Even in so-called peacetime, the threat of death or wounding by a fanatical enemy were serious possibilities.

Chapter 3

The World in Flames

1939–1945

The Campaigns of 1939-40

With the outbreak of the Second World War in September 1939, a new British Expeditionary Force was assembled and sent to France the following month. However, the first shots fired in anger by the British Army in the Second World War were not heard on the Western Front but in Norway, which at the time was not even a British ally.

Early spring 1940 found the government of Neville Chamberlain anxiously concerned with the menacing position Adolf Hitler was adopting towards Scandinavia. Norway was nominally neutral, but possessed great mineral wealth and of course dominated the North Sea. A British force was hastily put together to bolster the Norwegians, but even as these men were embarking in Scotland, Hitler stole a march by invading Norway and seizing most of the important strategic points. The British force was sent anyway, and two under-strength brigades that had originally been intended only to give moral support were now tasked with liberating a country already occupied by the enemy.

Part of this formation was the 1st/5th Battalion of the Leicestershire Regiment, among them a soldier by the name of Platoon Sergeant-Major John Sheppard, who was destined to knock out the first German tanks of the conflict and gain one of the first DCMs of the Second World War. 23 April 1940 found the 1st/5th Leicesters holding the village of Tretten. It was St George's day, not a date that the Leicesters would forget in a hurry. The village stands at the head of a wide valley through which run the River Laagen, and parallel to this, a railway line. If any single place in Norway offered the chance to hold up the German advance, this was it. John Sheppard was in command of a small force covering the front and right flank of the Leicesters' positions. He takes up the story in his own words:

Enemy scouts were working their way around the edge of a wood some one thousand yards away. They were followed by troops at section, platoon and company strength. We were having a grandstand view of a textbook battalion attack. There had been spasmodic shelling during the afternoon, but now it intensified. Fire was directed at the village and crossroads behind us, and was controlled from a spotter plane which flew backwards and forwards across the valley in front of us.

Four light tanks appeared at a flimsy road block some 600 yards down the road; pushed the spruce poles from which it was constructed to one side and nosed up the road. I sent a man to warn the section on my left flank. He returned with a box of Bren magazines to say there was no one there. We also retrieved the anti-tank rifle and four magazines - 20 rounds.

We could now see a section of 12 pounder guns getting into action directly in front of us and two more light tanks moving up the railway line. The reason for this was soon apparent. A platoon of Sherwood Foresters was marching down the road on the other side of the valley towards the river bridge. The tanks took up positions to ambush it as it came under the railway bridge. None of us had ever fired the Boys [anti-tank rifle] so, together with a private from A company as a number two, I took the gun round behind our building. To get an uninterrupted view we had to lay in the snow in the open. I estimated the range to be 300 yards and fired at the first tank. We clearly heard the strike of the shot. They opened up at us with their machine guns but were aiming too high and we were enveloped by telephone wires which were being shot down from overhead. I put three rounds into each tank and the firing ceased. I sent a runner back to warn battalion HQ of the tanks approaching up the road and he came back with a message warning me to look out for tanks![1]

Sheppard was captured shortly afterwards, and spent the next five years in German captivity. His DCM was gazetted upon his repatriation in 1945.

Meanwhile, the situation in France had, since October 1939, remained a stalemate, or so it seemed to the ordinary British Tommies at any rate. The term '*Sitzkrieg*' was coined to describe the lack of movement on the western front. The new British Expeditionary Force consisted of some twelve divisions, and the Secretary of State for War, Leslie Hore-Belisha, was able to tell the House of Commons that Britain had fulfilled her military commitment to France. However, many of these divisions were poorly equipped, with obsolete equipment. Some of the territorial divisions sent to France were only equipped for labouring duties, having no artillery or signals. Field Marshal Bernard Montgomery, at that time a major-general commanding the British 3rd Division, is reported to have stated that in 1940 the British Army was not in a fit state to take part in a realistic exercise, let alone take on a first-class enemy.

More worrying than the out of date equipment were out of date tactics. The BEF began at once building elaborate earthworks and trenches. For those who remembered the First World War it was all eerily reminiscent of 1918. That, however, was all about to change, as on 10 May 1940, the German offensive in Belgium erupted out of the blue with a ferocity that would sweep all before it. The British Army left its defensive works, which had been constructed with so much effort the previous winter, and in spite of the protests of Belgium that she was neutral, sallied forth to confront the Germans (the French were keen that as much of this war as possible should be fought on Belgian soil). Probably the best equipped of the British troops who were in France in May 1940 were the Guards, and they quickly found themselves holding positions east of Brussels, attempting to hold back the German advance. A British plan to hold the line of the River Dyle was put into effect; the 1st Battalion Coldstream Guards, part of the 7th Guards Brigade of Montgomery's 3rd Division, were holding positions in the outskirts of Louvain. They were initially ordered to take over defences from the Belgians, but found the Belgians initially reluctant to hand over their positions. By 14 May the 1st Coldstreams were in position on the west bank of the Dyle railway and canal, with outposts on the east side. By now a mixture of Belgian soldiers and civilians were streaming back across temporary bridges laid over the canal. This made an excellent target for German aircraft. Later that day German motorised infantry launched an attack on the Dyle positions and the Belgians suddenly withdrew without warning, causing confusion for the Coldstreams. It was only with the greatest difficulty that the outposts over the canal were withdrawn. Nevertheless, the Guards held on, making a series of counter-attacks, and for three days held up the Germans, in spite of facing vastly superior numbers.

During the fighting here 26-year-old Corporal Percy Meredith from Trench, in Shropshire, was to display marked heroism. Meredith had served with the Guards in Palestine prior to the outbreak of the Second World War. In the fighting in Belgium in May 1940 he left a position of cover and ran towards a house across open ground, whilst under enemy fire, in order to deal single-handedly with a sniper who was causing problems for his battalion. Meredith was awarded the Distinguished Conduct Medal for his actions here.

However, the German advance into Belgium was a ruse and the real German offensive came further south in the poorly defended Ardennes, which military dogma had it were so densely wooded as to be impassable by armour. Nevertheless, German panzers rolled through the weak French divisions ahead of them, while the Luftwaffe, with its fearsome Stukas, bombed any opposition that lay in their path. By 26 May 1940 they had driven a wedge between the French and British armies and had encircled the latter in a huge pocket. The sole time that Germans had really been unsettled was at Arras, the only point at which the BEF had managed to hit back hard at the invaders. A local counter-attack here had threatened to cut the line of communications of the wheeling Panzer arm, causing temporary alarm.

Warrant Officer Class III Joseph Hughes Scanlon of the 8th Battalion Royal Northumberland Fusiliers was awarded the DCM for his part in the fighting at Arras in late May 1940, the official recommendation reading:

> As Platoon Commander, he showed unquestionable courage, bravery and leadership during operations from Deval to Dunkirk, and particularly in the defence of Arras, where, by his own conduct, he set his men an example and encouraged them under enemy fire and aerial bombardment.[2]

The 8th Battalion's war diary describes in detail the desperate battle to hold the town. Scanlon and 'A' Company were allocated to the defence of the east perimeter of Arras, where they underwent severe dive-bombing and machine-gun attacks from the air during the hours of daylight. By 22 May the town was completely surrounded, and orders were received for the battalion to make a breakout, Scanlon joining 'Group III' - luckily, as a result of a thick morning mist, most were able to escape the attention of enemy machine-gun posts. In a brief halt, it would appear that Scanlon's group stopped in order to demolish a bridge before continuing the retreat to the beaches of Dunkirk, where the survivors were embarked on the last day of May 1940.

Back in England on 22 June, battalion orders stated that Scanlon had been awarded an immediate DCM, and the following day at church parade, he received the ribbon of his decoration from the hands of Major-General Herbert, the divisional commander. Scanlon subsequently received a letter from a former commanding officer, Captain W F H Cox, now of the Rifle Brigade, stating:

A few lines to send you my heartiest congratulations on your magnificent work when over in France with the B.E.F. I was delighted to read of your decoration with the D.C.M. in today's papers, and the report in The Times was fine. In view of the lack of leadership by certain others, which to us was not at all surprising, 'A' Company of the 8th R.N.F. are, I am sure, very proud of you and I am mighty glad you were with them. I am very distressed at the loss of my old C.O. and Adjutant, Colonel Clarke, and Major Seth-Smith, both of whom were fine and gallant gentlemen ... If not before, I shall look forward to meeting you again in the victory march through Berlin ...[3]

As the Belgian army on its flank began to crumble in the face of the German onslaught, it was now imperative that those units of the BEF holding ground in Belgium, close to the Great War battlefields around Ypres, stood firm. During this desperate fighting in May 1940, the 2nd Battalion Lancashire Fusiliers were under great pressure from the advancing Germans. Corporal John Lymer was in command of a section on the banks of the Escaut canal, when the German attack developed in strength at daybreak on 22 May, and his section being within a few yards of the bank, was subjected to intense artillery and mortar concentrations throughout the hours of daylight. When the order came for the battalion to fall back, unable to leave their cover due to intense fire, the party stayed behind and gave covering fire while the remainder of the Battalion withdrew to safer ground. It was largely due to Corporal Lymer and his section that no enemy broke through on the Company front in spite of the fact that one by one each man of the section was hit and put out of action. Seven men of his section of ten were killed and three wounded before the Germans finally overran the position. Corporal Lymer himself received a bayonet wound to the shoulder, and when his commanding officer witnessed the position finally being overrun, he recommended Corporal Lymer for a posthumous Victoria Cross. It was, however, confirmed by the Red Cross, over a year later, that Lymer was alive and being held in Stalag 357. When released at the end of the war, Corporal Lymer was repatriated to the United Kingdom. On his return to the Lancashire Fusiliers headquarters at Bury, he was saluted by all the officers of the regiment who were present. He was decorated with the DCM by His Majesty King George VI on 29 July 1947, at an investiture at Buckingham Palace.

Sergeant T Williams of the 2nd Battalion Royal Scots Fusiliers was also awarded a DCM for his part in attempting to hold back the advancing Germans in Belgium. The DCM was announced in the *London Gazette* of 27 August 1940. The recommendation states:

> No. 3129046 Sergeant T. Williams, is recommended for the D.C.M., in recognition for his services during May 27th and 28th on the Ypres-Comines Canal. This Sergeant was under my personal observation on many occasions under heavy enemy fire and was always noted to keep cool and use his brains. At about 9 a.m. on the morning of May 28th I took this N.C.O. in a carrier from Brigade H.Q. to try and establish contact with my Battalion H.Q., we were unable to get nearer than the St Eloi cross roads on account of an enemy anti-tank weapon. At this point we found troops in the ditch unable to move as small arms fire was coming from three sides. I ordered Sergeant Williams to drive the carrier to a covered position and dismount the Bren gun and engage the enemy on one front. He carried out my orders with perfect coolness and courage. On engaging the enemy with Bren gun fire the enemy fire from the rear ceased and the troops in the ditch managed to retire. It is for this action in conjunction with continuous reports of coolness and courage that I recommend this N.C.O. for the D.C.M.[4]

The battalion War Diary for 28 May 1940 contains the following account:

> 09:00 hours: The Battalion I.O. and Sergeant Williams of the Carrier Platoon tried to contact Battalion H.Q. in a carrier but were unable to get within two miles of it as the enemy had installed a form of anti-tank weapon in a house at St Eloi cross roads. The enemy infantry had passed right through the battalion area. About 160 men were found in the ditch near the St Eloi cross roads, unable to proceed, owing to the heavy enemy fire from three sides. The carrier was taken into action and a couple of magazines fired at the most visible of the enemy. For some unknown reason enemy fire ceased and the 160 men in the ditch were enabled to make a dash out of their ditch into the cover of some woods from where they were able to withdraw.[5]

Once the soldiers of the BEF reached Dunkirk they were still at the mercy of marauding Luftwaffe aircraft. Many queued patiently in the dunes, but others fought back with whatever weapons they had with them. Some scraped pits in the sand, lay on their backs and took pot shots at enemy planes. Other men manned anti-aircraft machine-guns. The only DCM awards ever made for fighting at sea were granted in connection with the Dunkirk evacuation. Sadly, no original recommendations for these awards appear to have survived. However, it is known that Sergeant J T Carr, Royal Artillery received his for bravery as an anti-aircraft gunner aboard HMS *Grafton*, and Corporal L W Goddard, Royal Engineers for gallantry as commander of an anti-aircraft light machine-gun detachment aboard HMS *Crested Eagle*. Both vessels were sunk during the evacuation. *Crested Eagle* was a requisitioned Thames paddle steamer, famous before the war for her day trips to Margate.

Papers from the Military Secretary's Department, Ministry of Defence, contain references to the deliberations that accompanied these decorations. They refer also to another interesting and unusual group of awards, those made for service against the enemy whilst on home soil. It would appear that there was some debate in 1940 as to whether bravery during air raids for example should be considered 'in the face of the enemy'. At some point in the early months of 1941 a decision was taken that such bravery would be recognised by civilian awards (George Cross, George Medal etc). However, one DCM award and several MM awards were made before the convention was established. The DCM went to Warrant Officer Class 2 J McDonald, 9th Green Howards, the recommendation reading:

> This warrant officer led a rescue party to an emplacement at Dover which had received a direct hit by an enemy bomb. Notwithstanding the blinding and acrid fumes and the fact that bombs were still falling, he was instrumental in digging out two men, one of whom was dead. On another occasion, when Dover harbour was being heavily shelled, his officer was fatally wounded. Disregarding is own safety, he assisted the officer onto a stretcher and superintended his removal while other shells were falling nearby.[6]

~ 0 ~

POW Awards

A whole raft of DCMs were awarded during and after the Second World War for services as prisoners of war and for going beyond the call of duty in escaping from enemy hands, many of which went to men who had been captured in the 1940 campaign in France. One of the most enthralling stories is that of Quartermaster Sergeant John Henry Owen Brown of the Royal Artillery. Brown was captured near Dunkirk on 29 May 1940, but remarkably before the war had been trained in espionage work behind enemy lines as a POW; an extraordinary piece of foresight on the part of his superiors. A Cambridge graduate, Brown had also been a member of the British Union of Fascists before the war (though it is not inconceivable that this was also a smokescreen) and he immediately volunteered his services to the Germans as a collaborator, his BUF membership giving him credibility in this role.

In the summer of 1942 he became actively involved in the German plans to establish a British Free Corps: a division of pro-German sympathisers to fight alongside them as part of the SS. At Stalag IIID at Berlin, a special camp with luxury facilities intended to 'turn' wavering British POWs in favour of the Germans, Brown met up with a British officer who had links to MI9. The officer passed Brown the codes necessary to get messages back and forth on a secret radio, and he began transmitting vital information back to London, reporting on the activities of true turncoats, men like Lord Haw Haw and John Amery. At the same time, he was sending information about targets around Berlin to be used by Bomber Command in planning raids. Most other British prisoners of war in Germany who knew of Brown reviled him, believing him to be genuinely pro-German and a traitor. He was, however, actively subverting the British Free Corps and helped to ensure that it never amounted to anything. Eventually, Heinrich Himmler himself became suspicious of Brown and ordered his arrest.

As the Allies closed in on Berlin at the end of the war, Brown managed to reach American lines but when handed to the British, he was initially arrested as a traitor. It was only when information about the vital role that he had played was revealed that he was released. He was subsequently awarded the DCM, and after the war appeared as a witness at numerous treason trials.

Other British POWs would be decorated for their courage and resourcefulness in escaping from German hands. Robert Dunbar, an Aberdeen man who was a regular soldier in the Gordons before the war, was captured at St Valery-en-Caux on 12 June 1940, while serving in the 1st Battalion. Many POWs were debriefed by MI9 and Dunbar's report takes up the story:

> I was captured at St. Valery on 12 June 1940 and was marched via St. Pol to Bethune. We reached Bethune on 20 June and I escaped in company with Privates A. Harper and S. Westland.
>
> We fell out on the road and hid behind some houses until the column was past. The inhabitants then gave us civilian clothes, and

we walked back eight miles to Auchel. We all separated in Auchel but I used often to see Harper and Westland until I was recaptured.

I spent three months at Auchel as the guest of a café proprietor, but a Polish girl, whose name I do not know, told a German Officer that I was English. I was arrested about 20 September and taken to Lille where I was tried for attempted sabotage. I was acquitted on this charge, but was sentenced to undergo four months solitary confinement for having escaped. I was taken to Stuttgart in a cattle-truck and driven to a camp a few miles outside the city. I never knew its name. I was in solitary confinement until the end of January 1941 and had no chance to escape. When my sentence expired, I found that the camp was full of French prisoners and that the only other Englishman was a Private R. Herring, Royal Signals (escape recorded from Stalag 190; date unknown). He had a French wife, a school teacher, living near Lille and she had been arrested by the Germans.

The camp was so well guarded by wire and M.G. posts that we planned to escape while we were working outside it. We made a dash for it on 14 February, during the afternoon, while we were shovelling coal in a railway siding and ran along a short curving tunnel to avoid the fire of our guards. We were fired at, but, at the far end of the tunnel we hid in an air-raid shelter until dark. We boarded a goods train, having no idea where it was going, and hid in a truck. In the morning we slipped off and found ourselves in Holland. I cannot remember where we left the train, but we spent some three weeks wandering around Holland and Belgium. We reached Lille on 12 April and Herring left me to look for his wife.

I went on alone to Auchel where I found my host and hostess of the previous year had been sentenced to seven years imprisonment each for harbouring me. I returned to Bethune, where another café proprietress, who knew about this, nevertheless gave me shelter and clothes and procured false identity papers for me. I stayed with her for some days. On 20 April I left by train for Paris assisted by a French guide. I do not know his name. I stayed 12 days in Paris and then went down to Dompiere, where I crossed the demarcation line on 2 May with the aid of a butcher's assistant. After crossing the line I was directed to Montlucon, where I was arrested and sent to St. Hippolyte.

I escaped from St. Hippolyte on 7 May but was recaptured three days later and given 14 days imprisonment. Early in June I escaped again and got as far as Narbonne, where I was recaptured at the beginning of July. This time I was given 30 days imprisonment.

On 17 August I escaped with Gunner A. V. Badman by sawing through the bars of a room near the dining-hall. We were directed to Nines, Perpignan and Banyuls. From Banyuls we crossed the Pyrenees in a party of seven, not including a Spanish guide. It took three days and two nights to cross because the guide missed the way twice. The others who were guided across were: Lance-Corporal H. J. Warnett; Driver J. Dulan; Corporal H. Monaghan; Driver D. Owen; Private W. Winslade and Gunner A. V. Badman.

On 27 August we were arrested at Figueras and sent to a concentration camp at Miranda. I was released on 14 October and taken to Gibraltar.[7]

Dunbar was subsequently awarded the DCM for his persistent efforts to escape. Private J Waller of the Green Howards earned his award in similar circumstances. He gave the following account of his experiences to MI9 upon his repatriation:

I was captured on 22 May 40, South of Arras. I was searched and my paybook taken from me. I was taken to Cambrai and then by train, arriving at Thorn on 9 June 40, where I was put in Fort 11. I was not interrogated and personal property was not taken away. From Thorn I was sent to Konitz on 15 July, a working camp. I had one letter. There was one Red Cross parcel between 20 men, containing food but no cigarettes, although 'cigarettes' was written on the parcel. Letters were censored. At Fort 17 there was an RSM called Davidson who was very friendly with the Germans. He made NCOs salute an English private because he could speak German. We were punished if we stole raw materials, he reported us to the Germans and we got 7 days in the cells with no blankets. At Thorn there was also a P/W who acted as interpreter. He spoke German perfectly and used to go out with the Commandant and could go in and out of the camp without being stopped. Once a German General and a high Air Force officer came and questioned a Welsh P/W about the chances of landing paratroops in Wales. The Welshman said that the only way to get there is to swim. They said he ought to be ashamed of wearing English uniform. The Camp Leader at Konitz was Sgt. Nursery appointed by seniority. I escaped on the night of 21 Sept. by forcing a window. Other Privates were with me. We then forced the barbed wire with an axe. The sentries were partly drunk, it being Saturday night. They were mostly elderly men. We travelled South by night for seven days to Tuchel and were nearly caught in a haystack. A German spotted us in a wood and called the Police, who surrounded us, but we got away. We then split into two parties of 3, and have not heard of the other 3 since then. We got civilian clothes and a compass from an American Pole at Schwetz, who also got us a boat to cross the Vistula. We journeyed through Wabreszno to Rypin, where we came in contact with an organisation with Headquarters at Biezun. We lived at different houses and the Poles gave us food, clothing and collected 200 Marks for us. We subsequently had to get off on our own and ran into the organisation again later on. We went through Mlawa and Makow and crossed the frontier near Ostrow on 24 Feb 41 at night. We were captured by about 20 Russian guards, with dogs and night flares, when we were 200 yards across the frontier. They thought we were Poles and treated us very badly. We were in prison at Lomza for a month, five weeks at Minsk and were then taken to the internment camp where we met the rest of the party and our subsequent story is the same as theirs, being released on 8 July [1941].[8]

Waller's DCM was announced in the *London Gazette of* 4 November 1941. The most remarkable story of escape from German captivity through Russia, however, undoubtedly belongs to Lance Corporal James Allen DCM, Corps of Military Police, who published his memoir in 1955 as *No Citation*. This was a reference to the fact that for political motives, no official account of the deeds for which Allen was decorated was ever published. For reasons of diplomatic expediency it was no doubt felt to be wise not to antagonise the USSR, for the bulk of Allen's hardships in his escape journey were inflicted on him not by the Germans but by the Russians, who were convinced he was a spy. Allen's grasp of languages was better than average, and the few memorised sentences in Russian that he learned from friendly Poles convinced the Soviet secret police that there was more to him than met the eye. The DCMs of both Allen and a Canadian, Gunner George Clark, who escaped with him into Russia, were announced in the *London Gazette* of 2 December 1941. For the background to Allen's DCM award it is necessary to consult his statement given to MI9 upon repatriation:

I received a head wound near Lille on 18 May 40 and was taken to the hospital at Camiers, which on 20 May was taken over by the Germans. On 1 July, with other wounded, I was moved, in a lorry through Hesdin, Lille (2 July) and Renaix (4 July) to Loekeren (6 July), where we were packed like sardines in barges and, after 3 days reached Emmerich. We were then taken on to Dortmund. While I was there 7 Irishmen and 4 Welshmen were interviewed by a German official in the presence of an individual who bore, on the lapel of his coat, a badge with the letters IRA. None of the men interviewed subscribed to these efforts to win him over and all of them rejoined us. By this time I was convalescent and on about 16 July was taken by rail, a 4 days' journey, to Thorn (Poland), Stalag XXA. After a fortnight I was transferred to a working camp (No354) at Pischnitz (Popolaska) also known as Hoch Stublau. This camp was about 50km south east of Danzig and prisoners were employed on roadwork on a new road which is to run from Berlin to Danzig … The first requisite for escaping is a large scale map of the vicinity of the camp. I was able to make a copy of a map, which had been brought into the camp by some white Russians who were awaiting repatriation. Poles came into the camp and worked alongside us on the road. They did not give us any escape materials but were practically to a man, willing to help escapers.[9]

On 17 September 1940, in the company of Clark, Allan made his escape whilst out working under the supervision of only one guard. In his memoirs he wrote:

I had decided what to do and there was no time to consult Clark. My nerve was at breaking point, and though I did not like to do it even to a German, I gripped my spade, took one bound forward, and felled him with a single blow from the shovel …[10]

After killing the guard, the pair ran for all they were worth:

Across fields and through plantations we went, avoiding all buildings. Finally, I pitched myself full length in a clearing among the trees and Clark dropped beside me. For about five minutes we could not speak. We lay there gasping and wheezing and taking great gulps of air. My heart raced like a trip hammer and the stitch in my side throbbed painfully. When I got my breath back I sat up and looked round. 'Well, we made it,' I said, 'but I don't know where the hell we are.' Clark propped himself up on his elbows. 'They're sure to have a search party out by now,' he said in his Canadian drawl, 'Reckon we'll have to keep movin' even if we don't know where we're going.'[11]

Climbing a tall tree revealed nothing but fields and woods in every direction. Eventually they encountered a young Polish girl:

'English,' I said. 'British Army. Escaped. Free. From Torun prison.'
I pointed in the direction of the camp. At first she seemed baffled.[12]

After making contact with friendly Poles the two parted and Allen crossed the River Bug in a boat, while Polish scouts kept a watch for any German patrols. Having climbed over the barbed wire fence into Russia he handed himself over to the authorities within five minutes of crossing the frontier. His trials in Russia were only just beginning. Constantly shifted from one prison to another, the only common factors were the relentless questions about who had sent him and why he was spying, and the appalling conditions in which he was held. Finally he reached Moscow, but his hardships continued. When the explosion of bombs indicated the Soviet Union and Germany were at war, he was moved out of Moscow. Herded in with Russian political prisoners, his account of the train journey is particularly harrowing:

When we reached the single-track railway line we were halted beside the train, and thirty at a time loaded into the trucks. The double doors were slammed shut and fixed with bars on the outside. I knew none of the other men in the truck with me. They were all Russians.

The trucks were nearly dark inside, except for a little sunlight that filtered through the cracks in the boards. There were no seats – and, in truth, little enough room to sit down – except for two shelves about 6 feet wide and 4 feet deep at each end. The trucks were not filthy, but seemed grimy and fetid from long use. Two grilled in the sides had been boarded up. In the floor was a hole about 6 inches across, which plainly served as the lavatory. I was not impressed by my first survey of this mobile cell.[13]

Eventually, following the British mutual aid agreement signed with Russia in June 1941, British prisoners held in that country were released into the care of the British Mission in Moscow, and returned home. Allen, and Clarke, who had escaped with him, were finally reunited in England. Two more 'escaper' DCM awards were gained by Battery Sergeant-Major A Paton Royal Artillery and Pte L Green Royal Army Service Corps. The original recommendation for this joint award reads:

RSM Paton was captured in June 1940 at St Valery en Caux, and sent to Stalag XXA (Thorn), and later to a satellite camp at Graudenz, where he was senior Warrant Officer. Private Green was captured in May 1940 between Wissernes and Boulogne, and sent to Stalag XXA. From where he went to various satellite working camps and in October 1942 to Graudenz where he met BSM Paton.

They escaped from here on the 7th June 1943 after much careful preparation. They received some help from Poles (unorganised) but between the 8th and 17th June 1943 were continually on the move travelling by train to Gdynia, Danzig, Lodz, Brombert, Zoppot and other places. On 17th June they boarded a Spanish ship at Gdynia arriving at Stockholm on 22 June 1943. Private Green speaks fluent German, the knowledge of which was an important factor in this successful escape.

This Warrant Officer and Private showed the greatest courage, initiative and ingenuity.[14]

As 1940 led into 1941, the only method Britain possessed of striking directly at the heart of Nazi Germany was through the Royal Air Force. Even though they lacked effective long range fighter cover, and the bombers of the first half of the war - the Stirlings, Wellingtons and Hampdens - were under powered and under armed, the RAF began hitting German cities as often as it could. The rate of attrition was appalling and the Germans for their part were simply not prepared for the massive influx of shot-down RAF aircrew prisoners who were about to come their way. Many of the airmen who found themselves in Germany in the early years of the war were as anxious to escape and rejoin the fight as their army compatriots. Risking life and limb on the ground, they were not eligible for the RAF's own decorations, the Air Force Medal and the Distinguished Flying Medal, which could only be awarded for bravery in the air. They were, however, eligible for the Distinguished Conduct Medal. The first RAF non-commissioned officer to receive the DCM in the Second World War was Sergeant Derrick Nabarro, the second pilot of a No 10 Squadron Whitley bomber, shot down over the north German coast in June 1941. Nabarro wrote of his experiences in *Wait For The Dawn*, published in 1952. Caught in a searchlight during a bombing raid, his aircraft was hit in both engines by flak:

I sat down in the second-pilot's seat. The gauges told their own story, zero oil pressure on the port gauge and falling pressure on the starboard gauge. It was only a matter of time. We sat there and waited, not able to think, not able to grasp the full import of the situation, not able to do anything ... the bottom dropped out of the starboard oil pressure gauge. The engine roared on for a minute, unaware that its death warrant had been signed, then, with a rattle, it failed. Silence whistled with the wind through the feathered propellers, over the ragged wings and down the battered fuselage ...

Fear had been my close companion for a long time, but he had deserted me when the danger was greatest. Like a coward he had whispered in my ear when I was facing up to the prospect. He was nowhere to be seen, nor had I time to look for him when the battle was thickest. Now the tension was relaxing, I was dimly aware that a great weight had lifted from my mind ...[15]

Nabarro was about to become part of the German Stalag system. For many British soldiers and airmen, escape was almost an obsession. They swapped notes and advice, and learned from the experiences of others. Nabarro was recaptured after his first escape attempt, but was wiser when he made his second bid in the company of a Belgian POW:

Tomorrow was the big day. The fears of the night crowded in on me. From experience I knew that the still hours of darkness threw distorting shadows on my thoughts. Wait for the dawn, I thought, sanity returns with light ... Early the next morning I awoke. I felt a tingling expectancy in my chest, a strange fluttering around my ribs. Snores were issuing from most beds and everyone appeared to be sleeping. I crept from my warm blankets, slipped into my civilian clothes and put on an army greatcoat in case any snooping guard burst into the room. I then prepared breakfast - an unorthodox meal, but substantial in calories. It began with porridge, into which went one large tin of Nestles sweetened milk and a quarter of a pound or so of Canadian Maple Leaf butter ...[16]

Having convinced a guard that they had orders to clean the commandant's office, the two slipped quietly behind the hut and scaled the barbed wire fence out of sight. Their plan was to avoid the local railway station (Bad Sulza) but catch a train at the next station heading for Coblenz and the Belgian frontier. At Naumberg they changed trains, trying hard not to attract attention from the German civilian population:

I was [dressed as] a mechanic. I wore my black RAF shoes, threadbare black and grey check flannels, an RAF shirt, a tie cut from a coloured handkerchief, a black leather jacket and a slouch cap. The grease stains on my trousers showed that I was a mechanic.[17]

However, the pair had not gone far when they aroused the suspicions of a sharp-eyed railway policeman. A few telephone calls established that they were not foreign workers returning home from Germany as they claimed and they were taken to a local police station. The following day before dawn, the two escaped again, Nabarro injuring a policeman in the struggle. This raised the odds considerably:

> Scarcely had we reached the road … when pandemonium broke loose. Every church bell in the neighbourhood started chiming. A moment later we had barely time to throw ourselves face down in the gutter before three men on cycles rode furiously past … We were still within two hundred yards of the prison. Unwittingly we had worked a flanker. The searchers were deploying in front of us to the west. We were behind them. To fool them, we headed south, travelling parallel to their lines guarding the direct route to the frontier. We scattered some pepper behind us. One hour or so later we heard dogs barking but did not worry.[18]

Miraculously, Nabarro made his way to occupied France. He attempted to cross the border into unoccupied Vichy territory through a wood, but was picked up by a German patrol. He was able to convince them that he was actually a Frenchman, trying to cross the border *out* of the unoccupied zone. The Germans were taken in by the story, and escorted him over the border themselves. Nabarro was then interned by the Vichy French. After escaping captivity for the final time, from Fort de la Rivère on 25 August 1942, he made contact with the Pat Line, which was smuggling escapers and evaders out of France via Marseilles. Nabarro stayed for two weeks with Pat Line organiser Dr Georges Rodocanachi at his apartment in Marseilles. He was subsequently picked up as part of Operation Titania, a Special Operations Executive mission. The *Seawolf*, a narrow, lateen-rigged SOE vessel operating out of Gibraltar, was on its way to collect him and others. It was half-past midnight on Monday 21 September 1942 when *Seawolf* sent her dinghy and three-man crew into the beach at Canet Plage. In total, twenty-four Pat Line escapers and evaders were picked up that night.

More RAF aircrew were to receive the DCM for successful escapes in the early part of the war. One went to Sergeant Philip Wareing RAFVR, the pilot of a Spitfire from No 616 (South Yorkshire) Squadron stationed at Kenley, who was shot down over Calais in August 1940. His was one of seven Spitfires engaging thirty Me109s. He shot down at least one enemy fighter but soon, as he described it,

> My lovely Spitfire was riddled like a sieve, on fire and the propeller was not turning.[19]

Despite the radiator being hit and enemy bullets rattling on the armour plate protecting his back, Wareing continued to fire at four 109s in line ahead. Then, as another enemy fighter poured fire into his Spitfire, the petrol tank exploded and the blast blew him clear of the cockpit. Fearing that he might be shot at as he descended, Wareing delayed opening his parachute until enemy aircraft had moved away, and landed in a ploughed field. Before an enemy motorcyclist with sidecar arrived to take him prisoner, he remembered to wipe the scribbled recognition signal letters of the day from one of his hands, using his own blood. At a nearby Luftwaffe base he was treated as a comrade, the German pilots apologising that all the captured NAAFI Scotch and beer was finished, and they could offer only cognac. His membership of the German Alpine Club before the war added to the camaraderie, and he was presented with cigarettes and chocolate.

He was taken to Brussels by the Germans and incarcerated at Schubin in Poland. In the late afternoon of 16 December 1942, Sergeant Wareing was detailed with other inmates to collect bread from a railway siding. When one of the working party dropped a loaf on the line, Wareing, on the pretext of picking it up, made his getaway in the gathering darkness. Well prepared, he had food, maps, a compass and was wearing grubby army trousers, a cloth cap and a RAF tunic that he had altered to pass as a civilian jacket. Reaching Bromberg, some 20 miles north of Schubin, he found a rickety bicycle, which he half pedalled and half walked to Graudenz. At the railway station there, he swapped this bicycle for a new one that a German had just left propped against a wall and set out for Danzig. There was a heart-stopping moment as he crossed a heavily guarded bridge over the Vistula. While guards were questioning two Germans in uniform, Wareing cycled past them. Arriving in Danzig, he was dismayed to find he had forgotten to bring the money he had kept ready for an escape. However, it was not long before he saw some Swedish ships whose Blue Peter pennants indicated imminent departure. After hiding among timber piles, he walked up the gangway of one of the ships, which was loading coal. Later that day he was spotted by a party of Russians working in the coal hole but after whispering tersely, 'Angliski pilot' the Russians left him alone. Late that night when they had gone, he concealed himself amid the coal. The ship sailed the next morning. Two days later a member of the crew saw him, but the ship was now close to Halmstad, where the Swedish police collected him. Shortly afterwards the British Legation in Stockholm arranged his repatriation. He finally returned to the UK in January 1943.

Flight Sergeant James Patrick Dowd was the wireless operator of an Avro Manchester of No 83 Squadron, RAF Bomber Command. Based at

Scampton, in Lincolnshire, he was shot down on 13 March 1942 over the Dutch-German frontier, whilst on a mission to bomb Cologne. He was taken by Luftwaffe guards to Dulag Luft, the transit camp for Allied aircrew prisoners. In April he was moved to Stalag VIIIB at Lamsdorf, from which he escaped whilst on a working party. He was, however, recaptured near Freiwaldau in the Sudetenland. A second escape attempt was also unsuccessful. Undeterred, on his third attempt he escaped from a working party at a sawmill at Grottkau and managed to get to Stettin, on the Baltic. In his MI9 escaped POW debrief, he gives the following account of his final break for freedom:

> I went to a pub in Fischerstrasse and stayed there from about 1600 hrs till 1800 hrs. I then decided it was 'do or die' and started to go back to the end of the Kaiser Wilhelm Kai. At the Hansabrucke five Danish seamen stopped and asked me the way to the nearest restaurant. I took them into a pub nearby and told them who I was. One of them spoke English. They agreed to take me back to their ship the *Margarete* (2,000 tons) which was lying in the River Oder on the East side of the Oder-Danzig Insel and which was sailing at 0930 hours next day. The ship was moored in the river because her sailing had been delayed on account of the riots in Denmark.
>
> We went along the Bollwerk until we were opposite the ship, and the Danes signalled for a small boat. The Danish watchman from the ship came over in the boat and said that the German watchman was still on the ship. The Danes had half a bottle of Schnaps left and we decided to get the German watchman drunk.
>
> We all went to the ship in the rowing boat. On board I found that the German watchman was already half drunk, and gave him the Schnaps. When his relief came on board about an hour later the German watchman left without counting the number of seamen on board …[20]

Dowd remained a stowaway whilst the vessel docked at Riga, carrying stone chips for the construction of Luftwaffe runways in Russia. After a week the ship headed for Sweden, where he handed himself in to the police. A Swedish air force officer tried to interrogate him, but Dowd gave him only the code letters of his aircraft to pass on to the British authorities, in order to identify him. He too was eventually repatriated via the British legation and received the DCM.

~ 0 ~

Private Harry Mason, 171 Company Machine Gun Corps, of Warrington. Aged only twenty-one and in his first major action, he stayed with a wounded comrade in the cold autumn mud of the Passchendaele battlefield for twelve hours under heavy fire. He then helped to evacuate him. (Author's collection)

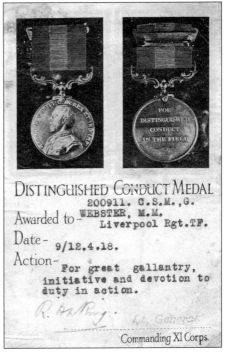

DISTINGUISHED CONDUCT MEDAL

200911. C.S.M.,G.

Awarded to – WEBSTER, M.M.
Liverpool Rgt.TF.

Date – 9/12.4.18.

Action – For great gallantry, initiative and devotion to duty in action.

R. Hacking.
Lt. General

Commanding XI Corps.

An XI Corps DCM award card, personally signed by the Corps commander, Lieutenant General Hacking. These award cards (which have also been noted for the MM and MC) seem to have been exclusive to this corps. (Courtesy of Derek Bird)

Corporal J Harvey DCM, of the 1st Battalion Leicestershire Regiment Stokes mortar battery. During the German advance in March 1918 he kept up a steady fire until the last minute, when he withdrew across open ground, bringing his mortar with him. (Author's collection)

The presentation of the DCM to First Class Air Mechanic Samuel Hall, 31 Wing Royal Flying Corps, at an aerodrome in Mesopotamia in 1917. The award was for maintaining radio communication with an aircraft whilst under fire. (Courtesy of Stuart Brown)

Warrant Officer A Stepan, a member of the Czech Legion, awarded the DCM in 1918. (Dix Noonan Webb Ltd – www.dnw.co.uk)

Private George Ryan, 1st Battalion Leinster Regiment, awarded the DCM for bravery during the 1921 Malabar uprising, on the North West Frontier of India. (Dix Noonan Webb Ltd – www.dnw.co.uk)

Lance Sergeant H. Blake, 1st Battalion Leicestershire Regiment, awarded the DCM for an action with enemy tribesmen at Bodari Sar, on the North West Frontier, in August 1938. Blake volunteered to go out onto a scrub-covered hillside to look for wounded comrades. (Courtesy of the Trustees of the Royal Leicestershire Regiment).

PSM John Sheppard, 1st/5th Battalion Leicestershire Regiment. Awarded the DCM for destroying the first German tank of the Second World War, in Norway on 23 April 1940. (Courtesy of John Sheppard)

Sergeant Tom Richardson DCM, 2nd Battalion Leicestershire Regiment. Richardson single-handedly neutralised an Italian machine gun post at Sidi Barrani in December 1940, killing ten of the enemy. (Author's collection)

Lance Sergeant Percy Meredith, of the 1st Battalion Coldstream Guards. He was awarded the DCM for an action on the Dyle Canal, on 15 May 1940, as Hitler's Blitzkrieg ripped through Belgium. (Author's collection)

Gunner George Clarke, Royal Artillery. With James Allen he escaped from German hands into Russian Poland. He wears the DCM subsequently awarded for his escape. (Courtesy of HarperCollins Australia)

Corporal James Allen, Corps of Military Police. Captured in France in the summer of 1940 he escaped from German hands into Russian-occupied Poland. He returned home after a gruelling period in Russian captivity in the summer of 1941. (Courtesy of HarperCollins Australia)

Sergeant Philip Wareing DCM RAFVR. Shot down over Calais in August 1940, he escaped from German captivity and returned via Sweden to the UK. (Courtesy of Peter Sharpe)

Sergeant Derrick Nabarro DCM, 10 Squadron RAF. The second pilot of a Whitley bomber, he was shot down in June 1941, and escaped from German captivity. (Courtesy of Peter Sharpe)

Sergeant George Brown, 2nd Battalion the Black Watch. On 21 November 1941 at Tobruk, his battalion was part of an attack on the German-held position known as 'Tiger'. When all of his officers and most of his men became casualties he led the remainder on to the objective, routing the Germans. (Author's collection)

T/Sgt Sidney Adcock, South African Forces, awarded the DCM for an action near the Gazala Line, in the Western Desert, in April 1942. (Courtesy of Jeff Ritsick)

Sergeant Marcus Bauer, Royal Artillery. Bauer received a DCM for an action in Tunisia, but was to die in a mental institution after the war. (Courtesy of Leslie Guy)

'Kit' Colfach DCM KM, formerly of the Danish Resistance and MI5, photographed at a muster of the DCM League in 1995. (Courtesy of Julian Burdett)

Sergeant Augie Herchenratter, Highland Light Infantry of Canada, and his wife, after his DCM investiture. The award was made for his part in the attack on Buron, Normandy, on 8 July 1944. (Courtesy of Owen Lackenbauer)

Field Marshal Montgomery decorates Squadron Sergeant Major Bob Macgregor, 1st Royal Tank Regiment, who was awarded the DCM for an action in Holland in September 1944.
(Dix Noonan Webb Ltd - www.dnw.co.uk)

Sergeant Jack Wong Sue (second left), Royal Australian Air Force and Z Special Force, awarded the DCM for his 'cold-blooded courage' during special operations in Borneo in 1945. He had volunteered to go ashore and reconnoitre Japanese positions on the island. (Inset) Jack Wong Sue photographed on Anzac Day 2009. (Courtesy of Barry Sue and Steve Danaher)

A youthful Sergeant Jack Morrison, Royal Australian Regiment. This photograph was taken during the Second World War but Morrison would go on to receive a DCM for bravery in Korea in 1953. He was subsequently awarded a bar to his DCM for an action in Vietnam. (Courtesy of Mike Downey)

Regimental Sergeant Major John Meredith, British Battalion, with his wife outside Buckingham Palace, in 1946. Mrs Meredith holds the DCM awarded to her husband after three and a half years of Japanese captivity. (Courtesy of the Trustees of the Royal Leicestershire Regiment)

Warrant Officer Class 2 Reg Jones DCM, 2nd Battalion Royal Australian Regiment, meeting HRH Prince Philip at Lavarack Barracks, Townsville, in the early 1970s. His DCM was awarded for bravery during Operation Coburg in Vietnam, in January 1968. (Courtesy of John Meyers)

Sergeant Ron Allan, Royal Australian Regiment. Recommended for an MM for action on 27 November 1967 in Vietnam, which was subsequently upgraded to a DCM. (Courtesy of Mike Downey)

Private Denis Horrigan, Royal Australian Regiment, awarded the DCM in 1971. It was quite extraordinary for a National Serviceman to receive the DCM in Vietnam, and a private soldier at that. (Courtesy of Mike Downey)

Corporal Mick Rattigan, Royal Green Jackets. Awarded the DCM for a number of incidents whilst serving as a patrol leader on the streets of Belfast in 1972. (Courtesy of Karen Rattigan)

Corporal Julian Burdett, 45 Commando Royal Marines, (second from right) was awarded the DCM for the attack on Two Sisters - the only Royal Marines DCM for the Falklands conflict. Here he is seen wearing the medal for a major general's inspection in 1985. (Courtesy of Julian Burdett)

Corporal R B Duncan, King's Own Scottish Borderers, decorated with the DCM after the action at Derryard, Northern Ireland, in 1989. (Courtesy of Gerry O'Neill)

Corporal I B Harvey King's Own Scottish Borderers, decorated with the DCM after the action at Derryard, Northern Ireland, in 1989. (Courtesy of Gerry O'Neill)

Regimental Sergeant Major Peter 'Billy' Ratcliffe SAS. Ratcliffe was awarded the DCM in 1991, for his role in leading a team to knock out an Iraqi missile command centre during the Gulf War. (Courtesy of Michael O'Mara Books Ltd)

North Africa and Crete

The first real British success of the Second World War was a now almost forgotten battle in the Egyptian desert. The British General Wavell's 'Hundred Thousand', were all that guarded Egypt from the 'might' of the Italian Empire in North Africa. Mussolini had boasted to Hitler that he would sweep the British out of Egypt, but instead when in December 1940 his forces tried to invade, they were repulsed with heavy loss. The British counter-attack at Sidi Barrani in the Western Desert was a masterstroke that caused the virtual collapse of the Italian armed forces in the region. The 2nd Battalion Leicestershire Regiment were carried into the battle in lorries, and many of them later remembered how ready the Italians were to surrender, with only a few offering resistance. Corporal (later Sergeant) Tom Richardson of this battalion was awarded the DCM for his part in the action at Sidi Barrani. The original recommendation reads:

> On 10 December Corporal Richardson was a Sub-section Commander in the Carrier Platoon. In the attack on the enemy position near Sidi Barrani he led his carrier with great courage in the face of heavy fire. He went straight for an enemy M.G. post and destroyed it totally with grenades. Throughout the battle he behaved with great determination.[21]

We are fortunate in that in addition to the official recommendation, we have a first-hand description of the action for which Richardson was awarded his decoration, in the form of a letter written some years after the war. This sheds light on the grim reality behind the bare facts of the citation. The language and tone will not sit well with some in today's politically correct climate, but it is nonetheless a valuable document. In it he states:

> I remember that day only too well … I killed 10 wops in a machine gun post that had decimated a lot of the regiment, I threw 2 grenades into their fort without the slightest compunction after I saw Tommy Carlin (my carrier driver) get his head blown off with a shell that cut through both tracks of his carrier, and saw that HQ truck and a 30 cwt Morris go up and [a] huge lump of shrapnel just miss Captain Anderson. How I know I killed them was because after we had moved on from there I was with Captain Nicholls [collecting] hundreds of wops in the sand dunes, eventually we rounded up a 100 or so and marched them back. On my way I stopped at the MG post I was allotted and counted my victims, funny thing was we were told not to take any prisoners, some of the poor beggars were lined up with suit cases, ready to go …[22]

However, in 1940 the war in the North African desert was only just beginning. For the next two years this would become Britain's main theatre of operations. After the British captured Tobruk, Italy's main supply port in Libya, the German Afrika Korps under General (later Field Marshal) Erwin Rommel was drawn in and the campaign escalated. The theatre was in many ways critical to the outcome of the war; the great prizes at stake were the Libyan oilfields, but more crucially also control of Egypt. The sea route through the Mediterranean to the Indian Ocean, via the Suez Canal, was the lifeline that held the British Empire together. If the Germans and Italians could sever this then Britain's contact with India and her possessions in the Far East would be lost. Combat in the desert was like no other; it was in many respects warfare in its purest form. There was little in the way of a civilian population to get in the way, and scarcely any fighting in built-up areas. The flat billiard table of the Western Desert was the field upon which this war was fought. Natural obstacles - mountain ranges, marshes and wadis (dry river beds) - formed the boundaries within which it was conducted.

Prime Minister Winston Churchill was fascinated by special forces and irregular troops, of whatever nature. Under his patronage, during the war myriad small elite units came into being. Most of these were swept away at the end of the conflict by an army establishment that wanted to get back to 'normal' soldiering, but in the meantime the North African desert was a particularly fertile place for these *corps d'elite* to grow. One of them was the Long Range Desert Group, a forerunner of the SAS.

Among its ranks was Lawrence Hamilton 'Tony' Browne. Born in England in July 1908, he emigrated to New Zealand whilst an undergraduate at Cambridge. Originally joining the civil service, he went on to spend twelve years with the New Zealand Broadcasting Organisation before enlisting in the New Zealand Military Forces at Wellington in September 1939. He embarked for Egypt early in the following year where, at Cairo in July 1940, he joined the ranks of the fledgling Long Range Desert Group (LRDG) as a corporal. Hardy New Zealanders, who were used to the outdoor life, proliferated in the special forces operating in the desert during the war. Browne's amateur interest in astronomy and a flair for mathematics made him an ideal candidate for the study of desert navigation, an art in which he swiftly excelled.

Browne's exploits in the actions at Murzuk and Gebel Sherif in Libya in January 1941, which were to be rewarded with the DCM, were part of the LRDG's first serious attempt at operating behind enemy lines in force. The two actions were the highlights of an extraordinary five-week long journey, covering 4,500 miles. At Murzuk, the Italian-held fort (and nearby airfield with three resident aircraft), were pretty much laid waste. The LRDG suffered two fatalities and three wounded, including Browne, who was hit in the foot. The Italians suffered ten killed and fifteen wounded. Ten days later, however, the patrol encountered serious opposition at Gebel Sherif, when attacked by an Italian Auto-Saharan force on the ground, and by supporting enemy aircraft. Within a short period of time several LRDG trucks had been damaged or destroyed, the patrol's commanding officer taken prisoner and other men wounded. Remarkably, there was only one fatality, and the remaining vehicles were sufficient for the patrol members to beat a hasty retreat to Cairo. Browne was wounded for a second time in the same action.

Further patrols followed, including a 600 mile excursion to Jalo Oasis in March 1941, and Browne's first outing as patrol leader during a 1600 mile excursion to navigate the first supply convoy from Wadi Halfa to Kufra that May. After this, he was commissioned. Tony Browne's DCM was announced in the *London Gazette* of 8 July 1941. The original recommendation states:

> This N.C.O. displayed exceptional gallantry and resource during the raid on Murzuk on 11 January 1941. He commanded his vehicle most efficiently and maintained his Lewis gun in action with coolness and telling effect on the enemy. His example did much to keep the patrol steady at a critical time when enemy fire was causing casualties. Although wounded in the foot he remained at his post.
>
> In the action at Gebel Sherif, south-west of Kufra on 31 January his coolness was instrumental in saving his vehicle and crew when subjected to a determined low-flying bombing and M.G. attack by an enemy aircraft. Throughout all the L.R.D.G. operations in Libya this N.C.O. has held the responsible post of patrol navigator, and has shown the utmost devotion to duty.[23]

David Stirling, founder of the SAS, wrote after the war that:

> The LRDG had a much larger than minute part in the forming and growth of the early SAS. I always state, when asked, that the LRDG and not the SAS, were the 'Masters of the Desert'. Although we had a different role, it was the LRDG which taught us about the Desert.[24]

It seems likely that Browne was also involved with the SAS in its early stages, as LRDG members, particularly those with navigational skills, were often borrowed by their sister organisation to lead them onto their targets. Tony Browne remained employed as an intelligence officer with the

LRDG until the end of hostilities, having also picked up a Military Cross along the way for his exploits. He joined the British administration in Libya in 1946, in which capacity he remained employed until the independent kingdom of Libya was established in 1951. His connection with that country was prolonged by his next joining Mobil Oil of Canada, which had obtained one of the original oil concessions in Libya, and he was serving as manager of the company's northern operations in Cyrenaica on his retirement in 1965, the year in which he was gazetted for his OBE. He died in September 1970.

~ 0 ~

When the Germans attacked Greece, Churchill had diverted forces that could ill be spared from the desert campaign to go to her assistance. In May 1941, having already driven the Allies off the Greek mainland, the Germans now invaded Crete. Churchill had wanted to turn Crete into another Malta, a thorn in the side of Axis forces in the eastern Mediterranean, but Hitler also had plans for the island. He saw it as the springboard for further advances in the Middle East. The British had been preparing the defences of Crete since January of 1941, but when the German attack came it was in overwhelming strength, including the largest combat parachute drop up to that time. The Crete campaign was the backdrop for a remarkable DCM action: the award going to Private Harry Richards of the Australian Imperial Force (AIF). Harry Richards was born in Normanville, South Australia, on 24 December 1903. He had worked variously as a stockman, policeman and a general labourer before the war, and had been unemployed for a long spell during the Great Depression of the 1930s. He enlisted in the AIF at Subiaco on 26 March 1940, lowering his age by five years in order to do so. He was taken on the strength of the 2/11th Infantry Battalion, the first Western Australian battalion raised for overseas service for the Second World War.

He had already seen service in North Africa when in early April 1941, the 2/11th were deployed to defend Greece. The Allied forces were ultimately unable to stop the German advance, but the 2/11th withdrew from Kalabaka to the Brallos Pass, where they managed to delay the German advance on 24 April, before withdrawing again to Megara, where the Battalion was evacuated by sea on the night of 25 April. Harry landed with the 2/11th on Crete the following day. The battalion was subsequently deployed with the 2/1st Battalion to defend Retimo airfield, which was held for ten days following the landing of German paratroops on 20 May. During the withdrawal from Crete, Harry carried a casualty over the mountains to Sfakia, then declined evacuation himself in order to look for other casualties. Whilst most of the 2/11th were captured or surrendered, Harry swam at night to commandeer and provision an abandoned naval barge. This he used to ferry lost and wounded men across the Mediterranean to North Africa and safety. He christened the vessel 'MV *Leaving*', and as if this were not extraordinary enough in itself, Richards also kept a log of his remarkable journey.

After all fuel and food ran out, he rigged up a crude sail. Surviving German machine-gun fire, and navigating the craft across the Mediterranean Sea, he arrived at Sidi Barrani, Egypt, on 9 June 1941. His care for the men with him was described as 'beyond description' and his command 'masterly'. His actions enabled fifty-two men to evade capture, and he received the immediate award of the DCM. His citation read:

> On 29 May 41, at Crete, Pte Richards assisted and half carried Sgt Kilpatrick, a hospital patient, across the island to the beach at Sfakia. When invited by the Beach staff to go off with Kilpatrick and evacuated, he refused, saying that he would go back and get someone else who could not walk.
>
> On 1 June, having been left behind after the evacuation, Pte Richards recovered an invasion barge which had been abandoned by the Navy, collected a party of 50, including two Marine Officers, took charge (with the concurrence of the officers), laid in supplies of food and water at Gávdhos island, effected repairs after the barge had been damaged on a reef, travelled 80 miles until the petrol gave out, rigged a sail with blankets, navigated to Sidi Barrani and landed the whole party in good heart and condition on 9 June. Pte Richards is a farmer.[25]

The last sentence seems to have been added quite deliberately, in order to emphasise the fact that Richards had no professional background in maritime navigation. Part of Richards' log reads:

> 1 Jun 1941 2120hrs Darkness has fallen and enemy air activity has ceased; I have the motor running now and have cast off ropes; as we go slowly out from the cliffs Jerry opens fire with two machine guns. I was standing at the wheel with my head and shoulders exposed but was lucky not to be hit. I put on full speed - 16 knots and hour - and we kept to this for about three quarters of an hour. We were then well out to sea, having run Jerry's gauntlet without a casualty.[26]

The following day they reached Gávdhos Island:

> Mon 2 Jun 1500hrs I have checked up on our petrol and of the 81 gals that we had when we started from Crete, I am astounded to find out that we only have 55 gals left. The position is so grave that I decided to call the men together and tell them just what the situation is like. After explaining the whole thing to them I called for volunteers to remain on the island, so as to enable those that went on, to obtain extra rations.

> Tue 3 June 0200hrs Have discovered that through grounding on rocks the barge has loosened a plate in the starboard ballast tank and is making water very fast. I awakened all hands and set them to furious baling which was carried on till daylight. The engineer and I located the exact plate where she was making water and we made a tom [sic] pressing the plate firmly down, thereafter we had no more trouble with leaks.

> Tue 3 June 1730hrs Here is where we want a lot of luck as our petrol is all used up, and still have over 100 miles to go.

> Wed 4 June 1030hrs We have been drifting all night under fairly strong breeze. I have made a sail out of 4 blankets and we are now moving along at a fair speed – the wind is dead behind.

> Thur 5 Jun 1000hrs Still making slow progress – SSE. The food question is very low now and water has still to be further restricted, oh what would I do now for a square meal and a cigarette.

> Fri 6 June 1200hrs   Light breeze from the North and once more are making slow progress South. Have made another rudder by nailing a big flooring board to a paddle – this is helping our steerage. I have just given the men an issue of water – half bully beef tin.[27]

By now the food situation was becoming desperate. There also seems to have been some discord that Richards firmly suppressed:

> Sun 8 Jun 0900hrs   Flat calm – more cocoa and margarine. All hands very weak and conditions becoming worse hourly. At this stage I have had to address some of the members in words I cannot write – just the same moaning few.

> Sun 8 Jun 1030hrs   Still making progress South. I have sighted land but am afraid for the time being to announce this as it might be a trick of the imagination, but no – as I creep nearer I distinguish land clearly.

I then tell the crew, and it is now obvious that we have kept a fairly good course. Everybody is jubilant, excitement prevails everywhere. 5 members decide to make a raft and go ashore - I strongly advise against this as their condition is so weak, but they won't take any notice of me. I am thankful to say the raft is not a success.

Mon 9 Jun 0900hrs We have grounded on the beach south of Sidi Barani having safely traversed the whole of the sea journey under our own power - every member of the crew has disembarked and to our starved bodies and delight we have discovered that we have landed at the cook-house of an RASC camp. Here the Tommies turned out in grand style and gave us food, hot tea, cigs, beer and shelter. What a treat we had![28]

~ 0 ~

Throughout 1941, Tobruk remained critical to the war in North Africa. Its deep water harbour was of vital strategic importance in bringing in supplies. Rommel laid siege to the port, and it was robustly defended by Allied troops from a range of nations including Britain, South Africa, Poland and New Zealand. Among the defenders was Sergeant George Meldrum Brown, of the 2nd Battalion the Black Watch, who was awarded a DCM here. On 21 November 1941, his battalion was part of an attack on the German-held position known as 'Tiger'. When all of his officers and most of his men became casualties he led the remainder onto the objective, routing the Germans and capturing it. In 1945, Brown was commissioned into the Black Watch as a second lieutenant.

In 1942, the desert war approached its conclusion; in 1941 the war in North Africa had swung back and forth like a pendulum, neither side had the resources necessary to follow up a victory and each had allowed the enemy time to fall back and regroup. In June 1942, Rommel, on the offensive, had recaptured Tobruk. Now, in July 1942 near an obscure railway halt in the Egyptian desert called El Alamein, the Eighth Army managed to stop his drive eastwards towards Egypt. A few weeks later at this same spot, after an enormous artillery barrage, Montgomery's forces began to push the Afrika Korps back. It was very much a tank crews' war, though the British tanks in this early part of the war were no match either in terms of armour or firepower for their German counterparts.

During the First Battle of El Alamein, one DCM recipient who received the award for a tank action was originally recommended for an immediate

George Cross. At Tel-El-Eisa on 17 July 1942, Corporal Sam Raistrick of 44th Royal Tank Regiment was the driver of one of three Valentine tanks ordered to carry out a reconnaissance. They came under very heavy and accurate anti-tank fire and his tank was knocked out and set ablaze. Seriously wounded, Sam Raistrick had his lower left leg practically severed (the amputation was later surgically completed as the leg was hanging on by only part of the muscle). He climbed from the driver's compartment, losing a huge amount of blood, onto the turret where he struggled to free the commander and the gunner who were both also wounded and were in danger of being burned to death. The commander had almost lost both legs and the gunner's clothes were on fire. Sam Raistrick beat out the flames with his hands. He helped both of his mates down onto the ground and into shelter. This act had been carried out under continuous heavy shell and machine-gun fire. The recommendation ends:

> But for his magnificent courage and his complete disregard for his own life, the gunner and commander must have been burnt to death in the tank.[29]

Corporal Geordie Reay was a member of 3rd Battalion Royal Tank Regiment. On 29 October 1942, during the Second Battle of El Alamein, he was sent on a reconnaissance in a Crusader tank near Tel el Aqqaqir, a long ridge overlooking the German positions. Scattered all over it were the wrecks of tanks destroyed in earlier fighting. Previous attempts to survey the area had been frustrated by a German Panzer III tank hunkered down and protected by a number of anti-tank guns. Reay remembered:

> We crept forward in the early morning when the light was bad and got among the derelicts. This Mark III didn't notice as he was too busy knocking hell out of troops in front of us and we managed to get slightly behind him. As we got near I told the gunner, 'Enemy tank to your left front ... line up on him.' I ordered him to open fire at 1,500 yards but the shell dropped short. 'Up 200' and it went in, so he fired again. The Mark III was broadside onto us, otherwise our 2-pounder wouldn't have done much harm. Anyway, it caught fire and the crew came scrambling out. The gunner, who was new to the desert, got carried away and started to fire the Besa until I told him to leave them alone. Of course, once the Mark III was knocked out they realised I was there and the Jerry anti-tank guns joined in.[30]

Reay continued to observe the enemy positions until he was ordered to withdraw by his troop commander. It had been an exhausting day's work, but one that earned Reay the DCM. A year later, when the desert war was over, Reay was present at the Victory Parade in Tunis representing the 3rd Royal Tanks. He remembered:

> There were a whole lot of lads who'd won medals lined up. I'd actually got my ribbon from Montgomery earlier and the RSM who inspected us said I was the scruffiest on parade and sent me off to smarten up. I had to borrow some shorts and other bits and pieces. Churchill and the rest came down the line but it was General Alexander I remember. He pointed to my ribbon and said, 'Always be proud of that, my lad.' Then he turned to some general who was with him and said, 'There are more VCs awarded than DCMs.'[31]

Later that year, Reay received the medal itself from HM King George VI at Buckingham Palace:

> I was given free travel warrants for my mother and father to come down from Ashington, as I didn't have a girlfriend at the time, and we had to be at Buckingham Palace for 9.45am. There were crowds of folk and all the relatives took their seats in a big hall while someone sorted out all the various decorations in order of seniority. As there weren't any VCs there that day, but there was another DCM, I was the second one to go up and receive my medal according to the drill: 'Walk up three steps, stop at the white line, turn smartly to your left, take two paces forward and stop at another white line just in front of the king and don't shake his hand too hard as there are 300 other people here to get their medals.' The king was smaller than I'd imagined and looked ill. He said: 'Good show. Keep it up,' and I marched off to a big hall where there were lots of policemen. Later I asked several people what the king had told them and it was just the same.[32]

South African forces were to play a major role in the desert war, and South African soldiers had a key part in a number of the Eighth Army's greatest victories. Sergeant Sidney Adcock was serving with1st/2nd South African Field Force Battalion in the Western Desert when he was awarded the Distinguished Conduct Medal. He was originally recommended for the MM, but this was upgraded to a DCM on the authority of General Harold Alexander, Commander-in-Chief of Middle East Forces. Adcock's original recommendation reads:

> For conspicuous and distinguished services in action, and outstanding devotion to duty continuously over a period of the past twelve months to the end of July 42.

When the outpost at Temrad was attacked and forced to withdraw on the 6th April, Sgt Adcock through his initiative and quickness in bringing his section of machine guns into action enabled the troop of field guns which he covered to withdraw unscathed. Several enemy detachments had advanced to within a few hundred yards of the guns and were in the process of erecting mortars, when with great presence of mind he swung his section of machine-guns into position and effectively engaged the enemy, inflicting heavy casualties and causing them to abandon their mortars.

On the 13th April he was in command of a section of armoured cars acting as a screen to a column of all arms operating against the enemy defences at Temrad. In spite of intense artillery and machine-gun fire he led his section to within a few hundred yards of the enemy positions and effectively engaged enemy OPs which were putting down heavy artillery fire on the column, causing them to withdraw. He only withdrew under orders when the column was being threatened by an enemy tank attack.

He was in command of numerous foot patrols which successfully penetrated the enemy defences forward of the Gazala line, gaining valuable information.

He was badly wounded when our position south of the El Alamein box was being consolidated, but in spite of his wounds he insisted on returning to duty within a few days. He has consistently borne himself with the utmost efficiency and fearlessness in the execution of his duties in action.[33]

~ 0 ~

Late in 1942 the Allies landed in Tunisia, nominally Vichy French territory and therefore neutral. This invasion had two objectives, firstly to prevent the French North African territories from falling under direct Axis control, and secondly to attack the Germans and Italians in Libya from the rear. They responded by moving tanks and troops into Tunisia to counter the Allied threat. Tentative American and British advances were met by heavy German counter-attacks in Tunisia early in 1943. One soldier decorated for his bravery here was Sergeant Marcus Bauer, from Stornoway, on the Isle of Lewis. He was serving with the 72nd Anti-Tank Regiment of the Royal Artillery. His citation for the award of the DCM states that:

On 31 Jan 43, this NCO was in command of a 6-pounder gun covering the Pont du Fahs-Robaa road. When the enemy tanks moved down the road in front of his position, Sjt Bauer was the first to open fire at a range of about 650 yards. This brought considerable fire from 88mm, 75mm, and small arms from the following tanks, which wounded the layers. Sjt. Bauer promptly took over and laid and fired the gun himself. His gun became exposed to the following tank, but he continued to fire and after firing another 15 rounds the four following Mk IIIs were all disabled. On the commander's instruction, Sjt Bauer continued to fire at the leading Mk VI, in an attempt to set it on fire, but every round was replied to by the rear Mk VI which was hull down on his right flank. That night the infantry covering the position withdrew, leaving Sjt. Bauer unprotected from covering infiltration. Although the enemy surrounded him, and at one point came within 15 feet of the gun, Sjt. Bauer remained in action until the situation was restored by the arrival of more infantry. The platoon commander (A Coy 5 Buffs) states that every round fired from Sjt Bauer's gun scored a hit on an enemy tank.[34]

Unquestionably a very brave man, Bauer was later commissioned into the airborne forces. However, his later life story was far from happy. He spent the last ten years of his life in Craig House Hospital, Edinburgh, suffering from mental health problems. He died in 1957, aged just thirty-eight. Having no previous history of mental illness, it seems that this undoubtedly courageous man had great difficulty in coming to terms with his experiences in the Second World War, and although he was regarded by many as a decorated war hero, perhaps the stress of repeated exposure to danger was too much for him. As Winston Churchill once said, a medal shines but it also casts a shadow.

During the advance in Tunisia, New Zealand troops were frequently to the fore. One of them, Albert Ronald George Lock, was born at Masterton, New Zealand, on 6 January 1916. He embarked with the 2nd New Zealand Expeditionary Force on 27 August 1940. Sergeant Lock was with the 26th New Zealand battalion from its inception, taking part in all campaigns in which the Battalion was involved. In every action he showed outstanding coolness under fire and devotion to duty. At the time of his award of the DCM he had already been wounded in the face during the Battle of El Alamein (when a captured enemy gunner threw a grenade at him) and also awarded the Military Medal for his actions in that battle. In 1943 he was promoted to warrant officer second class, and awarded the DCM, which was announced in the *London Gazette* of 22 July 1943. The official recommendation reads:

> In the vicinity of Enfidaville, Tunisia, on the night of 24th/25th April, 1943, Warrant Officer Lock was Company Sergeant Major of a Company which attacked and captured Terhouna Ridge. During the consolidation the Company Commander was mortally wounded and Warrant Officer Lock took over temporary command. As the main route to the Company was under fire he reconnoitred an alternative route back to the Battalion, advised them the Company was consolidating on their objective and then guided the supporting arms to the Company area where he handed over to the senior Platoon Commander, who had reported to Company Headquarters at the request of Warrant Officer Lock. The following morning as one of the forward platoons had not reported their consolidation he set out on his own initiative to try and locate them. He had proceeded some distance forward over open ground when he was fired on by an enemy machine-gun post. He successfully withdrew and later, in a Bren carrier, again went forward and contacted the missing platoon which had been isolated in their area by enemy fire. Throughout the whole operation this non-commissioned officer's personal courage and coolness were an example to everyone and his initiative and determination were largely responsible for the successful consolidation and defence of Terhouna Ridge. During all operations in which the Battalion has taken part Warrant Officer Lock has performed with outstanding ability and courage, carrying out his duties without regard for his personal safety and often assisting others where the firing was heaviest.[35]

Lock was also mentioned in despatches and commissioned as second lieutenant on 30 August 1944. Promoted to Lieutenant one year later, during the war he was to serve in the Middle East, North Africa, Italy, the UK and Japan. Only four DCM and MM combinations were awarded to members of the New Zealand forces for the Second World War, Lock being the only one also to be mentioned in despatches.

~ 0 ~

Another product of Churchill's fascination with irregular and covert forces were the commando units. In the Second World War the Army, Navy and

Royal Marines all raised commandos, though only the Royal Marines retained theirs afterwards. A number of awards were made to men of these units for hazardous clandestine operations, including raids on enemy-held coasts from Norway to France, and also in the Mediterranean. Their bravery was all the more impressive when one considers the fact that Hitler regarded them as little more than brigands, and ordered all British commandos captured alive to be executed as war criminals. Squadron Sergeant Major Cyril Feebery was one young man who, like many others, was drawn to this cloak and dagger work. Feebery had first enlisted in the Grenadier Guards before the Second World War. Wounded on the retreat to Dunkirk, he had after recovery back in England volunteered to join the fledgling commandos, then in training in the Scottish Highlands. He quickly rose to the rank of squadron sergeant major in the Special Boat section of the SAS, and it was in this capacity that in June 1943 he was landed secretly by submarine on the Sardinian coast, in order to take part in a raid on Italian positions. The official statement made in support of Feebery's DCM award, made by Major J Verney MC of the 1st Special Air Service Regiment, reads:

> Two parties landed together at night on the coast within a short distance of an Italian port. They had not been seen, but found themselves at the foot of a high and very steep cliff, with only two hours of darkness left. Five out of the ten including Lt Duggin were in a weak state, thought at first to be the effects of the submarine trip, but which turned out to be malaria. Both officers told me afterwards that without SSM Feebery's great strength and courage they would not have climbed the cliff. He scaled it first with a rope, a hazardous task in the dark, and then made several trips up and down hauling the others and their packs to the top. They were all safely up before dawn and remained concealed the next day. The two parties split up then to march to their respective airfield targets.[36]

The submarine commander after making the drop off realised that the remaining SAS patrols still on board were very ill with malaria. The whole operation was abandoned and fresh troops were parachuted in to raid the airfields. There was, however, no way of recalling the men already landed. Feebery himself takes up the story, as recounted in his biography, *Guardsman and Commando*:

> We came in sight of the airfield after three days and found a place to hide where we could observe it. By now the Lieutenant was in a bad way. He had malaria - I was becoming an expert in diagnosing it -

and had been dragging himself up and down the mountains by sheer strength of will. Even so we had made good time and still had a full day in hand before the night of the raid, according to the original timetable we were still following. Noriega and I put the Lieutenant to bed and started the long process of studying the target.

It was a busy aerodrome with aircraft of all sorts taking off and landing. Large fuel and ammunition dumps were dotted around the perimeter and we identified vehicle parks, workshops and barracks. There were few patrol movements as far as we could tell and only a flimsy wire fence between us and all those lovely aircraft. We ate the last of our food and bedded down in the bushes.

Next morning there seemed to be a lot more activity. Aircraft were taking off and flying low and slow around the aerodrome, while several groups of men seemed to be inspecting the fence and the dumps. The Lieutenant was still far from fit but crawled out of his sleeping bag to watch with us, as trucks began delivering huge coils of barbed wire around the perimeter, which squads of men then opened out inside the original fence to make a barrier we couldn't hope to cut through quickly with our simple hand tools. To make our day complete, as darkness fell every aeroplane on the field started up, taxied to the runway and took off until there wasn't one left.[37]

The substitute teams had already attacked other airfields on the island, hence the extra precautions now being taken. With his main objective now dispersed, reluctantly Feebery decided to switch his attention to his secondary target, a railway line. He continued:

We had been carrying six men's issue of explosive for several days and I was glad to be getting rid of it, even if it was only under a lousy railway line. We planed it all along half a mile of track, then set off in the last of the darkness to put some distance between ourselves and the milk train. It was the morning of 11 July and we had forty of so miles to travel ... Five days later Noriega and I climbed the last ridge between us and the sea. We hadn't eaten for six days now and were living in hope that the submarine would be where it was supposed to be to pick us up. We both collapsed, sound asleep until six in the morning, then set off on the last leg of the journey to the rendezvous. We were walking in a daze. Noriega was showing signs of malaria and I was wondering when my turn would come ...We walked straight into a squad of Carabinieri. Never even saw them. Their officer was very excited. I found out later ... that they had been waiting for us at the RV. The officer had his men surround us while he searched us.[38]

For Feebery the war for now at least was over. Major Verney's statement continues:

I saw Feebery a month later at Maddelena, where we were both waiting to be shipped to Italy. 25 O/Rs from the Special Boat Squadron were with him, and although they were ill from malaria and under-feeding, Feebery had them admirably under control and was keeping them both as smart and as cheerful as could have been expected. Their morale, thanks to his splendid leadership, was quite amazing, and it was amusing to note the respect the Italian guards treated them with, evidently terrified of some sudden *coup de main* by Feebery.

I was not surprised to hear that when Italy collapsed, Feebery led all his men out of their POW camp in one party and then split them up into smaller parties to make for the British lines. Many have now returned safely, including Feebery himself.[39]

~ 0 ~

North-West Europe 1944-45

The D-Day landings and the bitter fighting that followed in Normandy and North-West Europe bore witness to a large number of acts of bravery. As it was widely believed by the German high command that ordinary German soldiers would surrender readily to the British and Americans, these troops were sent instead to fight the Russians, who were known to treat prisoners harshly. Some of the most committed and fanatical Nazi troops were posted to fight in the west, and the British casualty rate sustained in the advance through Normandy in June 1944 actually exceeded that on the Somme in July 1916. Montgomery was able to make progress more rapidly than his predecessor Haig, mainly because the by now all-powerful Royal Air Force was on hand to smash a path through German defences. The Germans were adept at using the terrain to their advantage; the Normandy bocage favoured the defenders, and the German armour - Tigers and King Tigers - still outclassed and outranged much that the British brought against them.

On the right flank of Montgomery's advance through Normandy was the 49th Division, which included the 4th Battalion, the Lincolnshire Regiment. On 26 June Montgomery launched Operation Epsom, his drive to capture Caen, the German stronghold in Normandy. The day prior to the offensive, however, the 49th Division were to launch a preparatory attack to secure high ground on the right flank of the advance of the 15th Scottish Division. The high ground and the villages on and near it (Rauray, Fontenay-le-Pesnel, Tessel-Bretteville, Juvigny) were held by elements of the 26th SS Panzer Grenadier Regiment and the 12th SS Panzer Regiment. Both were well dug in.

Twenty-nine-year-old Private George Henry Sneesby of Grantham, serving with the 4th Battalion the Lincolnshire Regiment, received the DCM for a fine individual act of bravery during this offensive. The recommendation states:

> On 25th June 1944, during the Battalion attack on Fontenay the above named soldier, a pioneer by trade, was attached to one of the assault Companies. Under extreme difficulties of opposition and obscurity this Company made good its objective. As it was re-organising a party of Germans, mounted in six half-track vehicles, endeavoured to break out of the position and escape. Thick mist over hung the vicinity.
>
> Private Sneesby, who was nearby, realised at once that an individual act on his part alone would prevent their escape. As the leading vehicle drove up towards him the six Germans inside rained a hail of smeiser fire down the track to their front. In full face of this fire Private Sneesby ran up to the leading half track armoured car and threw a grenade into the driver's compartment. At this stage he was wounded in his thigh and his back by fire directed at him from the following vehicle. In spite of this he whipped out another grenade and threw it into the back of the leading track disabling the occupants. Having silenced this party he blew the engine up with another grenade, thereby blocking the exit for the following vehicles. Refusing to be deterred by his severe wounds, he then in a most determined manner advanced against the occupants of the second vehicle. So cowed were they by this man that they surrendered to him. It was not until joined at this stage by more men from the Company that Private Sneesby allowed his wounds to be treated.
>
> By this superb act of individual gallantry, Private Sneesby himself accounted for the capture or death of some 10 Germans and was entirely responsible for preventing the escape of the six vehicles and their 30 occupants. This magnificent example of courage had a high morale effect on the Battalion.[40]

The battle for Normandy was one of the severest in the western theatre of operations, and British, American and Canadian troops fought on through the summer to secure their objectives. 0500 hours on 8 July 1944 found Sergeant August (Augie) Herchenratter of the Highland Light Infantry of Canada (HLIC) dozing fitfully in a foxhole near the French village of Vieux Cairon. He was woken from his slumber by an intense artillery barrage. Dawn was yet to break on what would be a beautifully warm and sunny summer's day, but already thousands of shells were exploding on the German-held positions less than a mile away. The intensive artillery barrage signalled the launch of Operation Charnwood, a major attack by three divisions, again with the objective of seizing the ancient Norman capital of Caen and its nearby airfield.

The Canadian 3rd Division together with the British 3rd and 59th Divisions faced a well-prepared and determined enemy force holding an 8 mile front. Herchenratter was the 24-year-old leader of number 18 platoon, the only non-commissioned officer designated that day to command one of the three platoons of 'D' Company, HLIC. The attack was scheduled to begin at 7.30am, and the objective of the HLIC that day was to secure the village of Buron.

As he waited anxiously for the signal to advance, Herchenratter must have reflected on his life up to that point. Perhaps he recalled happy days growing up the youngest of three brothers and two sisters at his parents' home on Park Street, Kitchener, Ontario, and attending King Edward School in the town. Whilst there Herchenratter played hockey on the school's outdoor rink. A natural athlete, he excelled at the sport. Money was short in the 1930s and he left school early to help put food on the family table. He caddied at Westmount Golf and Country Club and, although never having golfed before, within a year achieved a zero handicap and was hired by the club as an assistant professional. He also played on local factory hockey teams. It was not long before he was recruited by the New Jersey Rivervale Skeeters. Herchenratter played one season for the American League's Springfield Illinois Indians before being hired by the Philadelphia Flyers as a right winger. He was with the Cleveland Barons when they won the league championship in 1941. That same year, he placed fifth in American League scoring.

On 4 February 1942, Herchenratter was called up for active military duty. He had gone overseas as a sergeant in August 1943, and was transferred to the 1st Battalion, the HLIC. There he met a number of his old friends from Waterloo County. The HLIC landed in the second wave of amphibious landings on Juno Beach, Normandy, on D-Day, 6 June

1944, as part of the 9th Canadian Highland Brigade. Although expecting heavy resistance by German defenders, the landing was surprisingly smooth. Herchenratter recalled:

> We saw a bunch of German prisoners and some bodies but the guys ahead of us had pretty well cleaned out German defences near the beach.[41]

The battalion moved forward to an area near Villons-les-Bussons, where they dug in for the better part of a month, waiting orders. They would soon be embroiled in one of the bloodiest battles of the Normandy campaign. About a mile to their front was Buron, a village of about eighty small buildings 4 miles northwest of Caen. A month earlier, in the initial landings, Allied troops had overrun Buron, but a strong German counter-attack had forced their withdrawal. In the ensuing weeks, the Germans reinforced their defences around Buron. Defending the village now were about 800 *HitlerJugend* (Hitler Youth). The Canadians had encountered these soldiers before. Between 7 and 15 June 1944, members of the infamous 12th SS Panzer Division, comprised of fanatical seventeen and eighteen-year-old *HitlerJugend* and led by battle-hardened veterans, had murdered 156 Canadian prisoners who they had captured in the D-Day landings.

Now, at 0730 hours the Canadian artillery barrage stopped, and the battalion's pipers played a rallying tune, which could be heard over the explosions and shouts of company commanders ordering the troops forward. Herchenratter led his three sections of riflemen along the battalion's right flank, toward the anti-tank ditch. He continues the story:

> We were taking a hail of fire from machine guns, mortars and 88 mm self-propelled guns. A number of my guys were hit within the first few minutes. When we got to the anti-tank ditch it was wider and deeper than we thought. The Germans were well dug in and had to be cleared out using rifles and grenades or knives and bayonets in hand-to-hand fighting. It was really tough going because we had to cross almost a mile of flat farm land to reach our objective.[42]

Reaching the first anti-tank ditch, Herchenratter hit the ground right in front of it. He found himself lying against a small bank of earth in front of the ditch; He could hear the German soldiers in the ditch only a few feet away from him, but they were not aware of his presence. Herchenratter pulled the pin on a grenade, counted a few seconds, then dropped it over the bank into the trench in front of him ... Nothing happened; the grenade was a dud. He frantically grabbed another and repeated the process, while the German voices were getting louder and clearly trying to establish where the grenade had come from. The second grenade was also a dud. The third grenade was not. After the third grenade exploded, Herchenratter jumped into the trench and cleared it, eliminating any opposition. The dud grenades, it transpired, were probably ruined by the sea water when coming ashore on D-Day, but Herchenratter continues the story:

> And when we got past the anti-tank ditch there were a number of well dug in machine gun nests that had to be eliminated ... The Hitler Youth kids dedicated their lives to Hitler. They obeyed orders blindly and fought ferociously to their death.[43]

By the time he reached the village only five of his twenty-eight men were left standing. Leading his platoon, Herchenratter organized the attack each time a machine-gun nest was encountered, one of which he wiped out alone. By 11:30am all four companies had reached and taken their objectives. 'D' Company's ninety men had been whittled down to one officer and thirty-eight other ranks. The HLIC war diary records that 'D' Company, first into the village, had to smash its way through alone and clean out all the trenches that comprised the German defensive system.

Buron was the HLIC's first and biggest fight as a battalion in the Second World War. The unit had been badly blooded, but won the day. After Buron, Herchenratter fought in the battle for the Falaise Gap, pursued the German army across France and took part in the battle for the Scheldt Estuary. Unwounded throughout the fighting, he became a casualty in October 1944 when his hand was crushed accidentally while riding in a Bren gun carrier. He was sent to England for rehabilitation. There he was reunited with his sweetheart Joanne, and they were married on 10 March 1945. At Buckingham Palace His Majesty King George VI personally presented Augie Herchenratter with the Distinguished Conduct Medal, for his leadership in the attack on Buron.

~ 0 ~

As the autumn of 1944 approached, at Supreme Allied Headquarters there was concern that the difficulty in supplying the British, American, Canadian and Free French armies in Europe was now slowing down their advance. The enforced delays in following up the retreating Germans allowed them time to regroup and prepare new defences, whilst Allied tanks were forced to sit idle waiting for fuel and ammunition. Montgomery was convinced that airborne troops could be used to speed up the advance. These forces could trap significant numbers of German troops by being parachuted in behind them, and cutting off their line of retreat. Supreme commander Dwight Eisenhower initially rejected Montgomery's plans, preferring instead to 'get Patton moving', referring to Monty's great rival, General George C Patton, whose tanks were temporarily stalled due to the supply problems.

Nevertheless, a short while later, he did sanction Montgomery's revised plan, called Operation Market Garden, which called for airborne troops to seize a number of key bridges over the lower Rhine in Holland, thus enabling Allied tanks to sweep over them and down into the Ruhr, Germany's industrial heartland. The plan had a number of flaws, not least in that it required the armoured troops to fight their way to the captured bridges along a single track road. Critics have long argued that Montgomery allowed his rivalry with Patton to cloud his judgement. Whatever the reason, Operation Market Garden was a costly failure. On 17 September 1944, 30,000 paratroopers from the British and American airborne forces attempted to seize the bridges. The British 1st Airborne Division was allocated Arnhem, the bridge deepest inside German territory. A number of mistakes were made, in dropping the 1st Airborne brigade too far from the bridge, and in making two drops instead of just one as originally planned. The paras were also unlucky in that they landed in the midst of two German SS Panzer divisions, which were resting and refitting in the Arnhem area.

A number of decorations were presented for Arnhem, one of them being the DCM awarded to Sergeant Thomas Bentley of the 10th Battalion Parachute Regiment. Bentley had enlisted before the war in the Royal Sussex Regiment and had been evacuated at Dunkirk in 1940. In 1941 he joined the Parachute Regiment upon its formation, and was Mentioned in Dispatches for bravery in North Africa. At Arnhem he was part of the second drop, which was forced away from the bridge by the Germans. His recommendation reads:

> At Oosterbeke on 20 Sept. 44 Sgt. Bentley, who had already shown conspicuous bravery in much hard fighting since he dropped on 18 Sept, was in charge of a detachment of mortars, using the top floor of a house as O.P. in the hard pressed North Eastern corner of the Div. Perimeter. The position was held by remnants of the Bn, about 50 strong, constantly under fire and frequently heavily attacked. From his O.P. he not only directed telling fire on the enemy, but

secured information vital to the defence, which he was obliged to take back in person to his C.O. under fire from close range on each occasion. When the side of his house was blown in by a self-propelled gun at point blank range he fell from top floor to basement, but crawled out and carried on from another. He was located and shot out again more than once that day, but set a magnificent example of determination to carry on, and during the afternoon was responsible for the discovery and repulse of a dangerous infiltrating movement from an unexpected quarter. Soon after another attack overran the battalion HQ houses: the C.O. was wounded, and the few men there captured. The mortars were lost. That night Sgt. Bentley led a patrol into the enemy occupied area and brought the mortars out, operating them from then on, often under heavy fire, under the personal direction of the Brigadier, for whom they were the last two 3 inch mortars in the Brigade. It is difficult to praise too highly this NCO's courage, coolness and competence, not to overestimate his contribution, both material and moral, in a difficult operation.[44]

Here is a clear example of a soldier going beyond the call of duty, exposing himself to the danger of fatal wounds, and by his actions influencing the course of a battle. This particular DCM must surely rank as a near-miss for the Victoria Cross. Bentley stayed in the Army after the war. In 1960 he became the sergeant major in charge of recruitment in Nottingham, and was made an MBE in 1971. When he finally left the Army in 1975, he was the last serving soldier who had dropped at Arnhem. Bentley died in Nottingham in 1982.

After the defeat of Market Garden, the Germans continued to offer heavy resistance as the Allies battled their way through Holland toward the Rhine. One of the outstanding troop leaders in this campaign was Bob Macgregor of the 1st Battalion Royal Tank Regiment. Brigadier H B C Watkins MBE, formerly a lieutenant in the 1st RTR remembered:

'A' Squadron of the 1st were fortunate in having many outstanding men. 'Paddy' McKee, Les Allen, Johnny Johnston and Joe Pitt, all Sergeants, spring instantly to mind. All were past masters of the art of tank and troop commanding, and as a young officer in their company you were very much on your mettle. After five years of hard fighting they weren't inclined to suffer fools gladly. Amongst all these outstanding leaders, Bob Macgregor was in a class of his own.[45]

Macgregor's DCM citation speaks for itself:

On 30 Sept. 1944, S.S.M. Macgregor was in command of a troop of tanks which was ordered to attack Middlerose village (MR 3942 Sheet S'Hertogenbosch) in conjunction with a section of carriers and a platoon of infantry. As soon as the advance started the enemy brought down heavy observed shellfire on the attacking troops and after 300 yards the infantry and carriers were brought to a halt by M.G. fire. Realising that the whole attack was in danger of being held up and knowing full well the risk attached to advancing in such close country without infantry support, S.S.M. Macgregor moved forward with his troop, destroyed the M.Gs holding up the infantry and one anti-tank gun which he met face to face at 50 yds range and reached the centre of the village. The infantry then came up and S.S.M. Macgregor moved to a position from which he could shoot the enemy withdrawing from the village and observe the enemy's main position. He remained in this position under continuous shellfire and mortar fire and sniping for seven hours directing artillery fire on the enemy guns. During this action S.S.M. Macgregor's troop destroyed 2 anti-tank guns and 2 M.Gs and took 20 PoWs, besides killing a number of enemy and forcing 200 to withdraw from the village. This W.O.'s coolness, courage and judgement were entirely responsible for the success of the action and had it not been for his leadership and handling of the situation both his own troop and the infantry would have undoubtedly suffered severe casualties without reaching their objectives.[46]

After having been commissioned in the field, and surviving so many close shaves in the deadly game of chance that was tank warfare, by a bitter irony Lieutenant Bob Macgregor was killed in a friendly fire incident just before the close of hostilities in the West. He was aged just twenty-six. Major Freddy Pile MC, Commanding Officer of 'A' Squadron, 1st RTR remembered:

A gun in another tank of his troop was loaded when it should not have been and it was accidentally discharged into the back of Bob's tank. He was the best troop leader I ever had the good fortune to serve with; and he had been through the whole desert campaign as well as that of North-West Europe.[47]

Bob Macgregor is buried in Becklingen War Cemetery, north of Hannover, in Germany.

~ 0 ~

Another young Canadian who had landed on D-Day was 23-year-old Private Léo Major, of La Régiment de la Chaudière. Major was a French-Canadian, born and brought up in Montreal. He was the second oldest of ten brothers and sisters and first gained a reputation for daring deeds aged just sixteen, when he rescued two young women from drowning at St Jerome. He was also an outstanding athlete in his youth. Quick on his feet and alert, he was employed in his battalion as a scout. In the early days of the Normandy fighting he showed what he was made of by single-handedly capturing a German halftrack containing a radio and secret German codebooks. Some days later he was wounded in the face by a phosphorous grenade and partially blinded in one eye. Nevertheless he refused a medical evacuation and continued fighting with his regiment. He had already played a significant part in the fighting in Holland when he captured ninety-three German soldiers with the aid of a passing Canadian tank in September 1944.

After being wounded again, he returned to his regiment in March 1945. At the beginning of April, La Régiment de la Chaudière were approaching the Dutch city of Zwolle, which was believed to be a centre of German resistance. His commanding officer asked for two volunteers to reconnoitre the German positions before the artillery began firing at the city. Major and his friend, Willie Arseneault, accepted the task. They were ordered to observe the strength of the German garrison, and attempt to make contact with the Dutch Resistance. Arseneault was killed early on in the proceedings, but Major waged a one-man war on the city, attacking a German headquarters, capturing prisoners and causing confusion among the defenders. He also managed to raise the Dutch Resistance and between them, the city was cleared of Germans. He related his own account of the events thus:

> In a few seconds I got rid of the ones responsible for his [Arseneault's] death. After that I had one fixed idea and it was to liberate Zwolle no matter what I was going to meet in the streets. A thousand Germans or much less - I didn't care. My heart was boiling but I was full of energy. I went back to Willy to grab his machine pistol and his grenades ... Before leaving for this patrol, the Colonel had promised me he would send all his fighting companies to occupy the farm lands that are close to the town at 0100 hours on 14 April. Having that in mind, I decided to wait until that time in case I got caught with some prisoners and not know what to do with them, as I am not a murderer. It's not like Normandy where there were no prisoners taken alive. They were S.S. I was already inside Zwolle so

I decided go inside a house. I wanted to study more a big map of Zwolle I had in my jacket ... After going over the city map, I left the house to start my plans for getting the upper hand against the enemy.

My first encounter came as I was advancing cautiously on a road leading out toward the country. I came close to what I could see was an enemy position. I could see clearly with my right eye that night like always. I was an expert at night fighting. There were soldiers in trenches manning a machine-gun. I came behind them in complete surprise. In a flash, with three grenades and a burst of my machine pistol, I had ten prisoners which I walked away to one of our leading companies. I came back down the same road, now having in mind to go everywhere in Zwolle. It was still early that night when I captured 12 stragglers in one of the streets. A burst of fire, a couple of grenades and a lot of loud noise. That was my aim. Again I walked back and got rid of them by giving them to another of our fighting companies. Again I went back inside the town doing one street after another. Four more times during the course of the night I had to force myself into a home. Each time the same story - the people were afraid of me but in no time I was able to prove who I was and I quickly made life-long friends. When I went in houses like I did, it was to give me more strength to go forward. I remember in each house I did not stay more than a few minutes before continuing patrolling the streets ... On a road near the river, I caught my last stragglers, which again I brought to an outpost that was much nearer the railroad crossing.

On my way back to the city, I met Frits Kuipers, a tall policeman, and two other men. From Mr. Kuipers' wife, who spoke fairly good English, and a few words in French, I learned the men were from the Resistance. I was very happy to learn that. They were unarmed but I quickly remedied that. Then I told them all: your town Zwolle is completely liberated from the Germans. I know very well – I was the one who made all that noise during the night. That must have frightened them away across the river. I asked them to come with me to the middle of the town and to pass the word around to all the population to come out of their homes, that they were at last free.[48]

Major was awarded the Distinguished Conduct Medal, and at the end of the war was demobilised, returning to his old job as a pipe fitter in Montreal.

~ 0 ~

The Far East
In December 1941, Japan had attacked the United States Naval Base at Pearl Harbor, and the British colony of Hong Kong. In early 1942 she turned her attention to other British possessions in the Far East. On 12 February, just over two months after the attack on Pearl Harbor, the Japanese launched an assault on Malaya. Stationed there, as part of the defences of the colony was the 1st Battalion Leicestershire Regiment. As the Japanese fought their way south through the rubber plantations the Leicesters managed to hold them several times, but each time the Japanese were able to outflank their enemy by seaborne assault. John Meredith enlisted in the Leicestershire Regiment in 1923, and quickly rose through the ranks. Serving with the 1st Battalion in India in the late 1930s he held the rank of company sergeant major. By the time war broke out in 1939, he was Regimental Sergeant Major (RSM) of that battalion. His obituary states:

> When the 1st Battalion arrived in Malaya he had already several times declined a commission, preferring to remain the RSM - in which rank he was quite outstanding in peace, in war and as a POW. In the depressing retreat down the length of Malaya he never lost the offensive spirit and was quite fearless, paying no attention to enemy bullets, shells and bombs, and organising and leading local counter-attacks with battalion headquarters personnel ... The smoothness and success of the amalgamation of the Leicestershire and East Surrey Regiments into the British Battalion was largely due to his tact and his quiet but determined strength as RSM.
>
> In the very difficult conditions of POW life he was able, through his personality, to maintain discipline and never lowered his standards. He commanded universal respect and admiration from all with whom he came into contact. Everyone knew that he was scrupulously fair to everyone and that he was not afraid of the Japanese guards. After the Japanese had separated the Officers and Other ranks in base camps, Mr Meredith was in a large camp when the Japanese called for 300 volunteers to go back up river to repair some railway bridges which had been destroyed by Allied bombing. There were only about 30 volunteers. Then it became known that Mr Meredith had volunteered to go in charge of the party and at once seven or eight hundred more volunteered. It was a most remarkable tribute to his character and qualities as a leader. Since these volunteers came from about 30 different units.[49]

After capture on Singapore, Meredith never hesitated to stand up to the

Japanese in endeavouring to obtain better treatment for the prisoners. He continued to do this even though he knew it was likely to result in him being beaten up, which at times happened. Upon his return home in 1945, Meredith was awarded the DCM, in recognition both of his work during the doomed defence of Malaya, and for his fortitude during the dark days as a POW of the Japanese. After the war he was appointed RSM of the regimental depot, but the years of captivity had taken their toll upon him, and he died aged just fifty-seven in February 1964.

Also taken prisoner at the fall of Singapore was Sergeant Charles McCormac of No 205 Squadron RAF, a Consolidated Catalina flying boat squadron based in the Far East. McCormac, a ground crewman, was placed in a labour camp with other service personnel and civilians. With them he was put to work at Singapore harbour. From sympathetic Malays he learned that the intention of the Japanese was to dispose of their captive labour force, once they had outlived their usefulness. With nothing to lose, McCormac and his fellow captives plotted to escape from their camp by fusing the electric lighting system, thus creating a diversion. McCormac wrote of his experiences in *You'll Die in Singapore* - armed with makeshift weapons, on the night of the escape, the prisoners waited anxiously for their guard to flick the switch of the sabotaged lighting system:

It can only have been a couple of minutes before we saw him strutting cockily across, but to each of us the minutes seemed like hours. We tried not to look at him, but I for one, each time I tried to look away, felt my eyes slide back to the short, bespectacled little man who would, in a matter of seconds, open for us the road to freedom.

He stared at us and seemed to sense that something odd was happening; then shrugging his shoulders he disappeared into the power-house. Almost as one man, in the gathering darkness, we started to edge towards the gate. We were none of us prepared for what happened next. We heard a generator start up, then a sudden, blinding flash lit up the hut, silhouetting its broken supports, its windows and its disintegrating walls. The sharp crack of an explosion echoed across the compound. The roof caved in and burst into flames.

For perhaps a couple of seconds we stood rooted to the spot, staring in disbelief. One man swore softly, another let out a ghastly cackle of laughter.

'Now!' shouted Don, and we tore towards the gate. Men shrieked in pain as the vicious coils of wire lacerated their hands, but we lifted the bamboo bar out of its socket and flung the gate up and over. At the same moment a handful of Japanese rushed out of the guard-hut. For a second they wavered, then came the staccato crackle of tommy-guns, ending abruptly as we threw ourselves on them. I was lucky. I got Pigface. I saw him tearing towards me, his teeth bared, his bayonet swinging back; with all my strength I smashed the lump of wood down and onto his face. As he dropped, I lashed at him again. I heard the bone splintering and his skull felt oddly soft. I dropped my club, grabbed his bayonet and sprinted for the rubber trees. Behind me, the outline of struggling men stood out sharply against the glare of the burning hut. No going back we had said. I tore on. I passed Donaldson; he was struggling and jerking at what looked like a dead body.

'Come on, Don!' I yelled at him. Behind us machine-guns were chattering angrily. I dared not stop. I was running now through tangled undergrowth, dodging quickly from one tree to another. Then I was in the open, and felt the sharp blades of grass whipping against my legs. On and on I rushed, my lungs heaving like bellows, until at last I could run no further. I slowed down to a walk. But already someone was catching up with me. I could hear him crashing his way through the rubber plantation. I stopped at a little hollow, and crouched there, waiting. It was Don. He almost tumbled headlong over me, but at the last moment spotted me in the flickering light from the guard-hut, now some quarter of a mile behind us.

'All right, Mac?' he panted.

'Uh,uh.' I squatted there gasping for breath. 'My wind's gone.'

'Don't wait, for Christ's sake.'

We went on, zigzagging whenever we were able, sometimes running, sometimes trotting, sometimes stumbling. Behind us the sounds of fighting grew fainter and finally died away. Both of us were breathing heavily and raspingly. But we were exultant.

'Why on earth were you hanging about outside the gate?' I panted as we slowed down to a walk.

'Fatarse had my bolo.'

'Good Lord, man! Why ever did you stop for that?'

'I dunno. The ball had stuck in his head and wouldn't come out. I left it in the end and took his bayonet.'

'Much the same as me,' I grunted. 'I got Pigface. And I took his bayonet, too.'

Don laughed. 'Well that's two of them at any rate. And two of the nastiest at that. Mac, boy, we're out! Do you realise it? We're out! We're free men!'

'I wouldn't crow yet. We're not out of the wood by a long chalk.'

'Worst part's over though.'

'I wonder.'[50]

McCormac's dramatic escape was just the start of a remarkable journey, which saw him not only leave Singapore island in a commandeered boat, but also cross some 2,000 miles of enemy held territory to reach safety in Australia. For his remarkable exploits, like the RAF personnel who escaped in Europe, he too was awarded the Distinguished Conduct Medal.

One of the final DCM awards of the Second World War was also one of the most extraordinary. Jack Wong Sue was a Chinese Australian who grew up in Perth. Australia in the depression of the 1930s was a tough place for anyone, but at this time the Australian Government had an official 'white Australia' policy, making life even harder for those who were ethnically Chinese. Even though Wong Sue was a fiercely patriotic young man, eager to enlist and fight for his country, his first attempt to join the Royal Australian Navy resulted in him being rejected on the grounds of his ethnic background. This humiliation simply made Jack Wong Sue more determined than ever to enlist. Next he tried the Royal Australian Air Force, which took a much more enlightened view of the situation. He was enlisted as a lowly Aircraftsman Second Class. However, Wong Sue's fluent knowledge of Chinese, together with his boyhood interest in canoeing and diving, and his oriental looks, which meant he could easily pass for a Malay, led to his promotion to sergeant and selection for training with the Z Special Force, the forerunners of the Australian SAS.

Wong Sue became part of a team trained to operate behind Japanese lines in Borneo in the closing stages of the war in the Far East. His citation for the award of the DCM reads as follows:

> From 3 March 1945 to 15 August 1945 this NCO displayed leadership, gallantry and cold-blooded courage of the highest order. On 3 March 1945 Sergeant Wong Sue was a member of a small party of 4 officers and 3 NCOs who entered British North Borneo well knowing:
>
> (a) that there was a large price on the head of the leader of the party as a result of his previous mission into the area (enemy posters were found bearing his portrait and offering a reward of $15000 dead or alive).
>
> (b) that having left the submarine there was no chance of withdrawal.
>
> (c) that the coast was strongly held by the enemy and continuously patrolled by land and sea.

The landing was made by rubber boat and canoe midway between two strong enemy posts at Tegahanf and Pura Pura three miles apart. Owing to the hostility of the natives, 250 miles were travelled by canoe at night before finding a friendly contact enabling the party to move inland. The cold blooded courage required to make a landing of the type above described is worthy of the highest commendation.[51]

Dressed in commando jungle greens, with American leech-proof lace-up jungle boots and sub-machine-guns, the party looked more American than Australian. However, once ashore, they soon swapped this garb for native sarongs, the better to blend in. The task before Jack Wong Sue and his comrades now was to gather information about Allied POWs on Borneo who had been taken there on a 'death march' by their Japanese captors, in order to build an airfield. His other task was organising local people into guerrilla bands to make hit and run raids on the Japanese positions. He describes his first encounter with local Dyak people, who hated the Japanese as much as the Australians did:

Breakfast over, plans were discussed to form a guerrilla force, develop a DZ (dropping zone) and defences for the Kampong. The Hadji then invited us to accompany him to view some of his wartime collection of Japanese items. Leading the way, he walked out on to a ... veranda adorned with numerous earthenware jars ... Without any hesitation or further word, Hadji removed the cover and invited us to peer inside. I half expected to see a conglomeration of Japanese side arms, weapons, uniform buttons, match boxes etc that were in evidence in almost every kampong in Borneo. Imagine my shock and revulsion when I was confronted with about 7 or 8 Japanese skulls, complete with green moss or something similar to moss growing on what must have been slime, still clinging to the obviously decapitated skulls, the odour of which was absolutely horrendous ... I fought hard to show no weakness as such behaviour would have been frowned upon by these warriors.[52]

After a number of encounters with the Japanese, described in his book *Blood on Borneo*, in May 1945 Jack Wong Sue was extracted by Catalina flying boat to provide information to the Australians in advance of the liberation of Borneo. 9th Australian Division, which was tasked with clearing the Japanese out of the island, required further intelligence and Jack volunteered to go back in behind enemy lines. On 31 May 1945, it was discovered that the Chinese stationmaster at Bongawan was anti-Japanese, and held valuable information. The DCM citation continues:

> In a particularly daring operation, covered at close range by the party leader and the other NCO, Sgt Wong Sue entered Bongawan railway station staffed and guarded by Japanese and in broad daylight extracted [him] from the station for the party leader to interrogate. During the next 8 days this NCO ... at great personal risk watched hundreds of Japanese move down the railway line.[53]

Jack Wong Sue continued to operate in Borneo behind Japanese lines until the end of the war. He returned home from active service about six weeks before his twentieth birthday, suffering badly from war neurasthenia (nervous exhaustion or 'shell shock') and malaria. Within a short time, he was placed under psychiatric treatment and was advised to purchase land in the hills area east of Perth. Here he could find inner peace by returning to his first love, which was the study of nature. Jack's sister remembered many years later:

> We were thankful to see him return after the war was over, safe but very nervy and he spent some weeks in Hollywood Repatriation Hospital with a malaria attack ... Jack was very unsettled for a long time when he came home, having made so many important decisions while away and was not keen to work for a boss ... On arriving home from Borneo, he placed a Japanese skull prominently in his museum. Thereafter, my father - being Chinese and therefore highly superstitious - refused to enter Jack's museum.[54]

Eventually, Jack did re-adjust to civilian life, starting a highly successful family business, W A Skin Divers, which retailed diving equipment and also ran diving tours. A keen naturalist, he was also a talented musician. Though a civilian, in the years after the Second World War he advised and trained the Australian SAS. He died in 2009.

~ 0 ~

Awards to foreign nationals

As in the First World War, a number of honorary DCMs were awarded to the personnel of Allied forces fighting alongside the British Army. It is believed that fifty-three such honorary DCMs were awarded to men of the United States Army in the Second World War.[55] One of these awards was made to Raymond F Kommer, who entered military service in Ohio and was serving in the 121st Infantry Regiment, 8th Infantry Division, United

States Army, when awarded the American DSC for bravery in operations in the Ardennes offensive in December 1944. These same deeds most probably resulted in his being awarded the honorary DCM. The official citation for the former award states:

> On 25 December 1944, in Germany, Sergeant Kommer, a squad leader, moved ahead of his pinned-down squad in the face of artillery, mortar and machine-gun fire toward enemy positions. With complete disregard for his own personal safety, he moved to within an arm's length of the enemy machine-gun position and when the enemy gunner momentarily halted his fire, Sergeant Kommer reached into the nest and pulled the gun from the gunner's hands. This daringly courageous act so demoralised the enemy that they immediately retreated through their escape trenches. The extraordinary heroism and courageous actions of Sergeant Kommer reflect great credit upon himself and are in keeping with the highest traditions of the military service.[56]

Awards were also made to members of the resistance forces fighting within the occupied countries of Europe. These men and women faced perhaps the greatest hazards as if captured they could expect no mercy. Usually their awards were not gazetted for reasons that are obvious. One remarkable story of courage is that of 'Kit' Colfach, a Dane. His true name was Herluf Colfach, Kit was a codename which stuck. He had just completed high school and had commenced medical studies at the University of Copenhagen when the Nazis invaded. He was 19 years old and joined a group of intellectual resistance workers. He carried an enormous medical work, in the pages of which a cavity had been made for a small pistol. His first task was to gather information and produce and distribute illegal newspapers. With the Germans closing in he escaped to England, by stowing away and later jumping ship into freezing waters. In England he joined MI5, where he trained in sabotage and other techniques, and returned to Denmark. Captured by the Gestapo, he was subjected to brutal torture and was beaten unconscious. In an extraordinary escape, he snatched a sub-machine-gun from a guard and shot his way out of a Gestapo prison, killing three of his guards in the process.

After the war, Colfach returned to medicine, becoming a surgeon. He also set up clinics in poorer parts of the world. An accomplished writer, director and photographer, he made a total of fifty-three films. Colfach died in 2002.

Chapter 4

Local Difficulties

As the Second World War drew to a close, independence movements developed in many British overseas colonies. This was particularly true of those parts of European empires in the Far East that had been occupied by the Japanese, who had done much to fan the flames of anti-European feeling.

The communist-inspired uprising against British rule in Malaya began in 1948, and was not fully defeated until the late 1950s. Many of the insurgents in Malaya were actually ethnically Chinese, trained and supported by the Communist government of Chairman Mao. British tactics in Malaya consisted of ruthlessly hunting down the terrorists using all the skills of jungle warfare learned the hard way in the Burma campaign, coupled with a well-planned hearts and minds campaign. Loyal villages were protected from intimidation by terrorists, whilst medical and other resources were made available in exchange for information. The fact that many terrorists were of different ethnicity from the native Malay population also helped the British cause. The war was fought across scattered rubber plantations, frequently miles from any form of civilization, and often by small teams led by NCOs. Just fifteen awards of the DCM were made for the Malaya confrontation.

Corporal (Acting Sergeant) William Ernest Carruthers was awarded the DCM for a sustained period of good work in the Malayan Emergency, the citation reading:

> As a sub-section Commander of 42 Commando, Royal Marines, acting Sergeant Carruthers has over a period of 11½ months, shown outstanding leadership, courage and initiative in operations in Malaya. He has been on operations continuously and has always shown a magnificent example to all ranks. As a result, his sub-section has had a series of major successes and has been responsible for killing four, capturing three and wounding three bandits in the last six months.

In November 1950 Sergeant Carruthers' sub-section was involved in a night action against heavily armed and well organised bandits in the Tyrone Estate near Batu Gajah. Sergeant Carruthers was personally responsible for rallying his subsection against superior numbers, and himself wounded and captured a well known bandit. In April, 1951, in the Bota Forest, his subsection was heavily attacked by a strong party of bandits. Sergeant Carruthers rapidly organised an attack by his out-numbered sub-section. By this action Sergeant Carruthers certainly saved the life of a comrade. By further efforts he was able to rally his men and drive off the enemy, whom he then pursued.

On 8th May, 1951, Sergeant Carruthers led a patrol of five Marines to an occupied camp on Harewood Estate, himself stalking and shooting the sentry and then leading the attack on the defended camp.

At all times his devotion to duty and his example have been outstanding, and an inspiration to the men whom he leads so well.[1]

A similar situation developed in Kenya in the 1950s, when a terrorist organisation was defeated by unorthodox and unconventional military tactics, though in this case of course the anti-colonial movement known as Mau-Mau was not born directly out of the war. The principal issue was over land. Long-standing grievances escalated as much of the territory traditionally occupied by the Kikuyu tribe in the central highlands of Kenya was taken over by white settlers, forcing the Kikuyu into smaller and smaller reserves. The political unrest over the land issue had begun in the 1930s, initially as a moderate and peaceful movement, but in consequence of colonial intransigence, it came to the boil after the war as an armed revolt. This was the period of the Mau Mau rebellion. A state of emergency was declared in Kenya by the Governor, Sir Evelyn Baring, early October 1952, following the murder of Africans loyal to the government by members of the Kikuyu tribe; the eight years of guerrilla warfare and terrorist activities that followed led ultimately to Kenyan independence.

In 1953, army officer Frank Kitson (later General Sir Frank Kitson) was seconded to the Kenya Police Special Branch. He was heavily involved in setting up an intelligence network for counter-terrorist operations against the Mau Mau. This was essentially an undercover unit. Although it worked with the more regular armed forces, due to the nature of its work it more often planned and executed its own independent operations. In early 1954 Miller joined Kitson's small operational team as a FIA (Field Intelligence Assistant). Kitson wrote later:

> At last I had received a reasonable number of new F.I.A.s ... [including] Sergeant Jacky Miller ... He was slightly unusual in that he had not lived all his life in Kenya but had arrived five years before at the age of sixteen. He was small and had fair hair and vast blue eyes with long lashes. At the time he looked no more than seventeen and he always spoke as though he had left school the day before and couldn't quite decide what all the grown-ups were doing. He seemed so innocent that no one ever suspected that he could harbour an unkind thought, even against the Mau Mau ... It would never have occurred to me, had I met him just once or twice, that he would have been the least bit of use in the job. Luckily I met him often in my first four months and discovered that underneath there was a relentless man who would not allow anything to get between him and his purpose. I sent Miller to Thika to look after the southern half of the District where the population were primarily Kikuyu from Kiambu District[2]

Frank Kitson devised what was to prove a successful, if very dangerous, method of infiltration into the Mau Mau regime; with no official sanctioning Kitson started to create a 'pseudo-gang'; initially it was made up of two or three loyal Africans, who would attempt to infiltrate larger Mau Mau gangs by posing as rebels. The scheme was a success but the amount of information gathered was limited. The approach had tremendous potential but for the greatest chance of success it was decided that a European operative needed to be present when the genuine Mau Mau gangs met. The pitfalls of this were obvious, for example how would a white man unable to speak the Kikuyu language pass himself off as a Mau Mau terrorist in close confines? As the idea developed it was also decided to use turned Mau Mau terrorists as part of the 'pseudo-gangs'. This also was inherently dangerous. Apart from gut instinct, Kitson had no idea whether the pacified terrorist would act out his part, or instead betray the rest of the 'pseudo-gang' to certain death at the first opportunity that came his way.

Eventually it was realised that posing as a senior Mau Mau leader would get the white operatives around the problem of being unable to speak Kikuyu. The Mau Mau were very hierarchical and on that basis only another senior Mau Mau would be able to talk directly to him. This enabled his turned Mau Mau to do the talking for him, while he stayed at the edge of the meeting, apparently aloof from the lesser men. Burnt cork or boot black were used for darkening the skin of the white operatives to make them look like Africans, together with ragged overcoats and strings of beads to complete the Mau Mau 'uniform'.

In May 1954 the methods devised by Kitson began to be used on a wider scale, with FIAs infiltrating gangs in their respective areas. Kitson describes the following events that led to Miller being awarded the DCM:

> During the course of our activities we had obtained a lot of information about Thika which we passed to Jacky Miller ... Miller decided to exploit this information in order to destroy a particularly elusive gang. His plan is of interest in that it shows what immense trouble we often had to take in order to get one good contact.[3]

By setting up a pseudo-gang, Jacky Miller was able to send out feelers to a hostile gang operating in his area offering to co-operate with them. Kitson continues:

> Miller did not attend all the meetings of the committee ... There was no need for him to do so. Even when he did attend he would have worked through one of his team, who would act as leader, while Jacky himself hung on the edge of the group as sentry or scout. Day by day he told me about the most recent developments. The big decision would be when to act.
>
> Throughout the scheme I was in a constant state of worry about Miller ... Consequently whenever he said that he would be meeting a few members of the gang that night I would urge him to spring the trap and be satisfied with the leader and one or two others. Jacky was determined to get the lot.[4]

Finally the moment arrived when the whole of the real gang were due to attend a meeting. Having set up an ambush with trusted local police officer, Miller attended the meeting in a nearby village hut. At a pre-arranged signal the police raided it; in order to preserve their cover, Miller and his men got their fair share of bruises from police rifle butts when they broke into the hut! The operation was a complete success and with fifteen captured and two killed, the Mau Mau organisation in that part of Kenya was completely undermined.

Acting Warrant Officer Class 2 John Austin 'Jacky' Miller was born in England, and in 1950 went to study agriculture in Kenya; Miller enlisted in the Kenya Regiment to carry out his National Service, and was awarded the DCM in the *London Gazette* of 19 July 1955, the only one granted for the Kenya Emergency. The citation simply stated that it was:

In recognition of gallant and distinguished services in Kenya during the period 21.10.1954-20.4.1955.[5]

This modest one-line citation belies one of the most extraordinary stories of counter-terrorist infiltration and subversion. The original recommendation sheds a little more light on Miller's activities and states:

By the beginning of February it had been discovered that a large Mau Mau organisation existed on certain farms in the Thika Settled Area. It was decided to establish a mock gang in the area with a view to obtaining the enemy's secrets and breaking up his organisation. The execution of this plan was left for the most part to Miller.

During the period 1 February-21 March Miller, disguised as a terrorist, attended, with his mock gang, a number of meetings of the top Mau Mau Committee. He also managed to eliminate some active terrorists, including one well-known leader. In addition, he was responsible for the recovery of two precision weapons.

On 21 March he again attended a meeting with all the senior Mau Mau office holders in the course of which he successfully directed a police patrol onto the scene so that all fifteen Mau Mau members were killed or arrested.

For the whole period Miller showed immense courage combined with careful planning and resource. One slip at any moment would have resulted not only in the failure of the scheme but obviously in the death of Miller and his party which was always very weak in numbers. In addition the danger of directing a Police party onto a meeting in which he was taking part should not be underestimated.

It is felt that Miller's conduct was of the highest order throughout, and rivals in cold-courage anything achieved by the Security Forces during the Emergency. These incidents, moreover, crown a highly successful career as an F.I.O. and are by no means the first occasions on which his courage has been noted.[6]

Miller's National Service ended in 1955, but he decided to stay in the country by joining the Kenya Police. He would ultimately reach the rank of chief inspector.

~ 0 ~

The biggest military commitment for British and Commonwealth forces since the end of the Second World War came in Korea. It was the first conflict of the Cold War, and the first test of the willingness of the United

Nations to resist aggression. The war in Korea broke out in 1950. The former Japanese satellite had been partitioned at the end of the Second World War into a communist North and pro-western South. Egged on by the Soviets (who were keen to get their hands on US airbases in the South) North Korea launched an unprovoked attack on its neighbour. With US and UN support, the South managed to drive the armies of the North back over the 38th parallel. When the total collapse of North Korea appeared a serious prospect, her neighbour, the Peoples' Republic of China, became alarmed by the possibility of a US client state right on her border. The Chinese then intervened on behalf of the North Koreans. After a series of major set piece battles, the war settled into a stalemate of trench warfare not unlike that of the Western Front in 1915 to 1918.

Fusilier Ronald Crookes had been awarded the Military Medal with the Durham Light Infantry (DLI) in the Second World War. Crookes, who was born in 1924, was awarded the decoration after an action in September 1944, as the DLI fought its way up Italy. After he was demobbed in 1950, he joined the Royal Northumberland Fusiliers and was awarded one of only thirteen Distinguished Conduct Medals granted during the Korean War. In Korea, Fusilier Crookes was a Bren gunner in Z Company, 1st Battalion, the Royal Northumberland Fusiliers. On 24 April 1951, Z Company was sent to hold a ridge that, if taken by the enemy, would have meant the encirclement of the battalion. The situation around a pinnacle of rock became so critical that the company commander reinforced it with a number of men including Fusilier Crookes. Crookes took his stand in the centre of the rock with his Bren gun and for more than two hours dominated the scene, firing his Bren gun from the hip, and when the gun was temporarily out of action, throwing grenades or firing a rifle that he had acquired. The original recommendation continues:

> Eventually just after first light the inevitable happened and Fusilier Crookes was severely wounded in the chest. Even then he refused to leave his post and continued to engage the enemy from a lying position until the attack was finally driven off.[7]

Ronald Crookes DCM MM died in Leeds in 1998. Commonwealth forces also fought bravely in Korea; Corporal William Rowlinson was decorated with the DCM for his actions in the Battle of Kapyong, between 23 and 25 April 1951. He was born at Balgowlah, New South Wales, in 1919. He saw service in the Second World War, and later with the 3rd Battalion Royal Australian Regiment in Korea. He citation reads as follows:

On 23rd and 24th April, 1951, 3rd Battalion The Royal Australian

Regiment was defending the area MOKTON-NI and D Company was assigned the role of right flank protection on feature 504 and the ridge line to the North East. 12 Platoon of which Lieutenant (then Corporal) Rowlinson was a Section Leader had the left forward section of this forward Platoon. During the first night of occupation 23rd April, 1951, enemy probing patrols endeavoured to penetrate his section position and were repulsed. On the morning of 24th April, 1951, enemy of platoon strength maintained continuous attacks against this section position for a period of from five to six hours and were again driven back sustaining heavy casualties. During these attacks Corporal Rowlinson and six members of his section were wounded. The wounded were evacuated but Corporal Rowlinson remained on duty and continued to lead his section until his section were ordered to withdraw. Corporal Rowlinson although wounded displayed leadership of a very high order and outstanding courage by holding the section together during the continuous attacks on his section position and thereby securing the company position vital to the successful conduct of the battalion defence. It is estimated that during all these attacks the enemy threw in approximately 150 men and suffered twenty-five known dead, killed in front of Corporal Rowlinson's section.[8]

Rowlinson was awarded an almost unprecedented bar to his DCM for a second act of bravery at Hill 317 (Maryang San) in October 1951, the citation for this action reading:

On the morning of 5th October, 1951, D Company 3rd Battalion The Royal Australian Regiment attacked the ridge leading to Hill 317. This necessitated four separate attacks in three of which 12 Platoon D Company was physically involved. In the early stages of the first attack the Company Commander was wounded and was replaced by the Officer Commanding 12 Platoon; Sergeant Rowlinson assuming command of 12 Platoon. 12 Platoon was immediately committed to the attack to bolster up the assault and Sergeant Rowlinson's quick cool and inspiring leadership contributed largely to its success. During the attack on the second feature in the face of heavy small arms, machine gun and 3.5 Bazooka fire he personally led his Platoon in the assault, displaying initiative and directing fire with firm control. Early in this action, he was wounded in the left leg, but without seeking medical aid he continued to follow the plan of attack and lead his Platoon in a further assault on the third feature in the face of continued heavy small arms and machine gun fire. At this stage he quickly re-organised on the third objective and contacted his Company Commander by wireless and informed him of enemy dispositions on the fourth ridge. His quick thinking and appreciation enabled the Company to successfully conclude the operation on the fourth objective. Sergeant Rowlinson's Platoon accounted for 32 enemy dead and took 14 Prisoners of War. Throughout the operation Sergeant Rowlinson showed complete disregard for his own personal safety and inspired his Platoon by his example. Sergeant Rowlinson was previously recommended for Distinguished Conduct Medal by this unit in April, 1951, and again has proved himself an outstanding, brave and intelligent soldier.[9]

In early 1952 Rowlinson was commissioned as a lieutenant in the regular army, but later in the year, while giving instruction in the use of Gelignite, he was seriously injured in an explosion, his right hand and forearm being amputated as a result. He recovered from his injuries, remaining in the Army until 1957, and reaching the rank of captain. Unsurprisingly, Rowlinson's DCM and bar are now held by the Australian War Memorial in Canberra.

When the United Nations requested military support for South Korea, Canada was among those nations quick to assist, and she began to recruit an all-volunteer force to go to Korea. In the Provence de Quebec, the Royal 22e Regiment (R22eR), the famous 'Vingt-deux' or 'Van Doos' began recruiting among French Canadians who had already seen service in the Second World War. Among those approached and who agreed to sign up once more was Léo Major DCM, who had been decorated for the liberation of Zwolle in 1945. This time, Major was to serve as a corporal, and he reached Korea in the spring of 1951.

By the autumn of that year, the R22eR were to take up a position on the extreme right flank of the 1st Commonwealth Division's front. Here they would link up with the 3rd US Infantry Division to the east who held Hill 355, Kowang San, also nicknamed 'Little Gibraltar'. At this point, the front line curved southward around the height, requiring the R22eR to hold an awkward position with 'A' and 'D' Companies on the western slopes, separated by a small valley from the remainder of the battalion. 'D' Company was the most vulnerable as it occupied the most northerly position, a low saddle between Hill 355 and Hill 227 to the west, exposed on both the northern and western fronts.

As the Panmunjong truce talks seemed to be close to reaching agreement, the Chinese decided to launch a final offensive that would improve their hand in any post-war settlement. They made one last-ditch attempt to seize as much terrain from the UN forces as possible; with the very real prospect that the Chinese might even roll the United Nations line back across the Imjin River, there was still everything to play for.

As the R22eR were just settling into their new positions on 22 November 1951, the Chinese opened up with a massive artillery barrage, engulfing Hill 355 in smoke and flying debris along with the Vingt-Deux. On 23 November, enemy attacks intensified, with two Chinese divisions directed against Hill 355, and one whole battalion attacking 'D' Company. For the next two days, desperate fighting occurred as the Americans lost Hill 355. As soon as they had captured Hill 355, the Chinese were then able to occupy Hill 227. This left 'D' Company practically surrounded, but it managed for the time being to drive off all enemy attacks. Noon of 24 November brought a lull to the fighting but, late in the day, the Chinese launched a new attack with two companies from Hill 227 against 'D' Company, and by 1820 hours had overrun Number 11 platoon on the left flank.

The situation was serious, but the commanding officer of the R22eR, Lieutenant Colonel Dextraze, was unflappable. He refused to consider conceding ground, and while the Americans assembled a counter-attack force on his right, Dextraze decided to launch his own counter-stroke. He planned to regain Number 11 platoon's lost position, and thus relieve the pressure on 'D' Company.

His best reserve was the battalion's scout platoon. He used it to assemble an assault group, under the command of Corporal Léo Major, and including a signaller to maintain a link directly with battalion HQ. Major equipped a large portion of his men with Sten sub-machine-guns, and wearing running shoes to mask the sound of their movement, they set out at midnight over the snow-covered hills. Proceeding slowly, in small groups, they followed an indirect route in order to come onto the objective from the direction of the enemy's own lines. Once near the summit, at a signal from Major, the scout platoon opened fire as one. The sudden weight of fire was enough to panic the enemy and by 0045 Major's force had successfully occupied its objective.

However, about one hour later, the Chinese launched a counter-attack and Dextraze ordered Major to withdraw from the hill. He refused, saying he would pull back only some 25 yards to some shell holes that offered some cover. From here, Léo Major directed mortar and machine-gun fire onto the Chinese. He did this throughout the darkest hours and bitter cold of the morning, at times bringing the mortar fire down almost on top of himself. The commander of the mortar platoon, Captain Forbes, wrote later in his own autobiography that Major was:

> an audacious man ... not satisfied with the proximity of my barrage and asks to bring it closer ... In effect my barrage falls so close that I hear my bombs explode when he speaks to me on the radio.[10]

Forbes increased his rate of fire until the mortar barrels turned red from the heat. He finally had to cease-fire as the tubes were in danger of suffering permanent damage. Major was awarded a bar to his DCM already gained in Europe, the citation reading:

> so expertly did he direct the fire of supporting mortars and artillery that the platoon was able to repulse four separate enemy attacks. Running from one point of danger to another, under heavy small arms fire from his flank, he directed the fire of his men, encouraging them to hold firm against overwhelming odds. Against a force, superior in number, Corporal Major simply refused to give ground. His personal courage and leadership were beyond praise. Filling an appointment far above his rank, he received the full confidence of his men, so inspired were they by his personal bravery, his coolness and leadership.[11]

By dawn, Major's force had withdrawn 200 yards to the east, reporting that the former positions of Number 11 platoon had been totally destroyed by mortar fire. Despite being attacked by overwhelming numbers, Major's platoon had repulsed all attacks and succeeded in denying possession of the position to the Chinese. Léo Major was a truly extraordinary man. Extremely modest about what he had done during his service in two wars, he was without doubt a true Canadian hero. He died in Montreal on 12 October 2008.

The hill known as Kowang-San was to witness another DCM action just over a year later, when this time an Australian, Sergeant Jack Morrison, would be decorated for his bravery here. Morrison had served overseas with the 2nd/1st Machine Gun Battalion of the 2nd AIF during the Second World War from 1941 to 1945, seeing service in 'the islands', as the Australian Pacific campaign against the Japanese was known. In 1951 he re-enlisted in the Australian Regular Army, and was awarded a DCM for an action in Korea. At Hill 355, Kowang-San, on the night of 24/25 January 1953, Morrison was the commander of a fighting patrol, tasked with moving deep behind enemy lines and to return with a prisoner for interrogation. By this stage in the Korean War, the situation had reached a stalemate, with fixed trench lines strongly reminiscent of those of the First World War in France. As Morrison's patrol reached its objective, a communication trench some 1,500 yards inside Chinese-held territory, they were spotted by two enemy soldiers who raised the alarm. The citation states:

> Sergeant Morrison himself killed both of the enemy and then withdrew his patrol under machine-gun and rifle fire coming from a second enemy position.
>
> As Sergeant Morrison was withdrawing from his objective a neighbouring patrol was attacked by an estimated enemy company. Sergeant Morrison immediately contacted a third patrol and taking command of the composite force of eighteen men went to the assistance of the other patrol. Whilst going towards the firefight a further enemy party of twenty approached from his rear. Sergeant Morrison ordered his men into a fire position and withholding his fire until the enemy were no more than eight feet away opened fire with such devastating effect that all twenty of the enemy were killed without their firing a shot. So close were they in fact that the leading enemy fell dead among the patrol.
>
> At this stage the hill feature occupied by the first patrol was completely overrun and the enemy diverted his force towards Sergeant Morrison's group. Sergeant Morrison then moved on to higher ground and waited the enemy approach. A party of six enemy approached from the rear and sergeant Morrison and one NCO killed all six at hand combat range.
>
> The enemy then commenced a series of attacks up the ridge towards Sergeant Morrison's group at the same time endeavouring to outflank the patrol with a second force. Each time the enemy attacked, Sgt Morrison personally led a charge of all automatic weapons into the enemy attacking force, then, in spite of the respite that this attack afforded quickly moved his patrol further ridge line to counter the enemy encircling movement. Each time he moved, Sgt Morrison picked up his wounded and carried them on.
>
> After the fourth attack the enemy broke contact and Sgt Morrison led his patrol safely back to his own lines having killed 50 of the enemy.
>
> By the exercise of most skilful, cool, and aggressive leadership,

Sgt Morrison was able to extricate his patrol from a perilous position and withdraw it to safety, while his superb personal courage and splendid example inspired his men to continue to inflict heavy casualties on the enemy throughout the action.[12]

British and Commonwealth troops left Korea later in 1953, having held back the advance of the communist Chinese and North Korean forces, but in spite of their individual bravery, not having achieved decisive victory. A truce was signed, and Korea partitioned again along the ceasefire line, but no formal peace treaty was ever signed, and the Korean War remains – technically – still in progress.

~ 0 ~

The port of Aden, at the mouth of the Red Sea, was well known to generations of seafarers. It was another corner of the British Empire that, by the mid 1960s, was yearning for independence. Internal warfare between the two main rival factions, together with sporadic attacks on British forces and interests, led to a declaration of a State of Emergency by the British Government and troops were deployed there to try to contain the situation. On 20 June 1967, a Sioux helicopter of the Queen's Dragoon Guards was detailed to remove a Royal Northumberland Fusiliers piquet from the high ground of Temple Hill, overlooking the settlement of Crater. The pilot, Sergeant Martin Forde QDG, had lifted one man out and was returning for the remaining two. As the helicopter lifted off, it was fired upon by a sniper. Forde was hit in the knee, and tried to land the helicopter again. As he did so, it slipped off the edge of a ravine and burst into flames. Fusilier John Duffy, one of the men aboard, received the DCM for his subsequent actions. Part of his citation reads:

In the crash Fusilier Duffy was slightly hurt but Corporal Keithley lost a leg severed below the knee and had the other leg completely shattered. Fusilier Duffy, under fire, despite the danger that the aircraft was burning, with the danger of a fuel explosion, helped the pilot out of the wreckage clear of the aircraft. He then returned to the aircraft and dragged Corporal Keithley away, He returned a third time, retrieved the radio from the wreckage, set it up and informed his base about the incident.

But for Fusilier Duffy's action, both Sergeant Forde and Corporal Keithley would certainly have perished in the wreck. His action with the radio resulted in a quick evacuation of the wounded to hospital.

By his calmness and determination Fusilier Duffy saved the lives of two soldiers under the most dangerous conditions and is worthy of recognition.[13]

~ 0 ~

For those readers born and brought up in Great Britain, the scale of Australia's involvement in the Vietnam War of 1964 to 1975 may come as something of a revelation. The Labour government of Harold Wilson resisted American overtures for British troops to participate in the conflict on the South Vietnamese side, supposedly in retaliation for the lack of US support for the Anglo-French attack on Egypt at Suez in 1956. Australia and New Zealand, however, had their own alliance with the United States (the ANZUS treaty) and with the Southeast Asian country being a much nearer neighbour, did commit troops to the conflict in support of the government of South Vietnam. These troops naturally qualified for gallantry medals such as the Victoria Cross, Distinguished Conduct Medal and Military Medal, the Commonwealth at that time still having a unified system of honours and awards. Some forty-one awards of the DCM were made to Australian troops during the Vietnam War.

The demagogue of communist North Vietnam was Ho Chi Minh. The wily old guerrilla leader had fought against the Japanese when they had invaded French Indochina, and had later defeated the French Foreign Legion at Dien Bien Phu in the 1950s. After the departure of the French, Vietnam was partitioned, and his dream was to see Vietnam reunited once more. South Vietnam had suffered from incursions from its northern neighbour since the late 1950s and these infiltrations increased during the 1960s. In the early part of the war these attacks had been carried out by a guerrilla movement known as the Viet Cong. Well supplied, politically motivated and well used to the hardships of the jungle, the Viet Cong were a formidable enemy. As the war progressed, incursions by regular North Vietnamese forces also increased. Australian involvement in the conflict largely mirrored that of the United States. The first Australian troops had gone merely as advisors to the Army of the Republic of Vietnam (ARVN). As the situation escalated, however, more and more troops were drawn in and the Australian Army's role changed from that of advisor to one of full-scale armed combatant against the northern forces. In one respect, however, the Australians did differ from the US forces, and that was in the fact that they had far more extensive experience of jungle warfare, having been recently involved in the Malaya and Borneo confrontations.

An early DCM award was the bar granted to Warrant Officer First Class Jack Morrison, of the Australian Army Training Team. Morrison was from Glover Street, South Melbourne, and, it will be recalled, he had already received the DCM for an action in Korea. Morrison is remembered with affection by a soldier who served with him:

> A truly amazing senior NCO. Many of us quailed under his acidic language ... sprinkled liberally with f.... and c....!! [14]

Morrison's was in fact the last bar ever awarded to a DCM holder. The citation for the bar reads as follows:

> During the night 8/9 December 1964, headquarters personnel of the 3rd Battalion of the 3rd Regiment of the Army of the Republic of Vietnam, supported by two field guns, were in a defensive position on Hill 159 in Quang Tin Province. With this force were Lieutenant B.K.Skinner of the United States Army and Warrant Officer Morrison.
>
> At approximately midnight, a Viet Cong force estimated at a reinforced battalion attacked the hill. During the attack, although severely wounded by grenades, Warrant Officer Morrison by leadership and example, sustained and rallied the small group in defence. Eventually, at 0330 hours with the defence pushed back by overwhelming numbers he organized a withdrawal to the artillery position where further defence was made with small arms and with the artillery firing at point blank range.
>
> As dawn was breaking, the artillery position was lost and at extreme personal risk both the advisors reconnoitred the Viet Cong disposition on top of the hill for a counter-attack. During this reconnaissance Lieutenant Skinner was killed and Warrant Officer Morrison again wounded.
>
> The defence by this small force was sufficient to delay the Viet Cong and permit the arrival of a relief column which, with daylight, retook the hill. The whole operation resulted in most severe losses to the Viet Cong and permitted highly successful follow up action.
>
> Although severely wounded, Warrant Officer Morrison displayed outstanding qualities of leadership, bravery and devotion to duty. [15]

Evidence of the quality of the troops sent by Australia to the Vietnam conflict comes from the DCM citation of Sergeant Ronald Allen, a Queenslander from Mount Isa serving with the 7th Battalion Royal Australian Regiment. It reads:

> On 27th November 1967 during Operation 'Forrest', D Company attacked a fortified enemy base camp which was occupied by the Chau Duc District Company. During the close combat that followed Sergeant Allan, the platoon sergeant of 12th Platoon, gained the initiative over the enemy and with a small party of men seized an enemy occupied bunker from which the Viet Cong were engaging elements of 10th Platoon.
>
> While the company was reorganising the enemy counter-attacked using rockets. Seeing the heavy enemy fire had caused casualties in his platoon, Sergeant Allan rushed forward without regards to his personal safety and began dragging the wounded into the comparative safety of a captured bunker. There is little doubt that without Sergeant Allan's brave actions the mortality rate during this action would have been much higher as the casualties in the open would have been exposed to friendly artillery and mortars. Sergeant Allan assumed command of the platoon when his platoon commander was wounded. ... Over many operations Sergeant Allan has displayed outstanding leadership qualities and gallantry. He has continuously been an excellent leader, dependable in all situations, calm and daring in emergencies. He has been an inspiration to his platoon and company and all who have served with him.[16]

Ronald Allen's original recommendation for the incident of 27 November 1967 was for the Military Medal, but such was his bravery in the face of heavy Viet Cong fire that day, that the award was subsequently upgraded to the DCM.

Warrant Officer Reginald Jones joined the Australian Regular Army on the 13 February 1953. After many regimental and training appointments, he was posted as Company Sergeant Major of 'C' Company, 2nd Battalion, The Royal Australian Regiment, on 11 May 1964. His citation for the DCM reads as follows:

> On the 26 January, 1968, during Operation COBURG in Bien Hoa, 9th Platoon C Company assaulted and occupied an enemy camp. It was soon apparent that the enemy force was larger than first estimated and it was necessary for Company Headquarters and 8th Platoon to reinforce them. After the reinforcements arrived the enemy made two determined counter-attacks and subjected the force

to heavy harassing fire from five machine guns and small arms. Throughout these attacks WO Jones moved around the camp giving encouragement to the members of the company and placing them in positions which afforded them maximum protection and from where they could engage the enemy. WO Jones continually exposed himself to the heavy fire sweeping the camp to perform these tasks. During the heaviest attack at 1825 hours a section commander was mortally wounded. Disregarding his own safety WO Jones moved forward under fire and rendered first aid to the soldier.

At 0800 hours on the 27 January, heavy automatic fire was again received in the camp and a sentry was wounded. The company medical orderly was mortally wounded in going to his aid. Again with complete disregard of the enemy fire WO Jones went forward and attempted to drag both wounded men to safety. The first attempt failing, he fashioned a shelter, rallied a bearer party and went forward a second time still under fire. He evacuated both men to safety and then proceeded to organize a helicopter evacuation of the dead and wounded.

At all times during this action WO Jones showed a complete disregard for his personal safety and his actions were undoubtedly instrumental in saving more lives in the company. His coolness under heavy fire and the professional manner in which he performed his duties were a source of great encouragement to the men of his company. His personal bravery and encouragement to the younger soldiers of the company were in the highest traditions of the Australian Army and reflect great credit on himself, his battalion and the Australian Forces in Vietnam.[17]

The penultimate DCM awarded in Vietnam was granted to Private Denis Horrigan and this was unusual, firstly because it was uncommon for a private soldier to be awarded this decoration in the Southeast Asia conflict; it was widely considered a senior NCO's award, as the thirty-two DCMs awarded to warrant officers or sergeants out of a total of forty-one granted in Vietnam testify. What made Horrigan's award doubly unusual, however, was the fact that he was not a regular soldier but a National Serviceman. Whilst it was not unheard of for a 'Nasho' to be decorated in Vietnam, it was highly unusual for one to receive a DCM, rather than perhaps an MM.

Denis William Horrigan was selected by ballot to join the Australian Army, and was enlisted on 28 January 1970. He was posted to the 2nd

Battalion, Royal Australian Regiment and joined them in Vietnam on 10 September 1970. His citation reads:

> On 31st March 1971 Private Horrigan was the forward scout of his platoon which had penetrated unseen into an enemy occupied bunker position. Private Horrigan signalled that he had sighted a group of enemy and indicated that the forward section should deploy while he crawled toward the enemy. Private Horrigan engaged the enemy and directed the fire of the remainder of the section into the area. During the initial burst of fire, five enemy were seen to fall. The enemy reacted by deploying strong flanking forces and by reinforcing those disabled in the initial burst of fire. This reaction placed Private Horrigan in an exposed but effective fire position which he maintained until his ammunition was almost expended.
>
> Realising that the ammunition of the remainder of his section was also running low, Private Horrigan moved back to the rear, secured a further supply of ammunition and then moved forward to replenish each man before resuming his original position. Throughout the course of his movement he repeatedly exposed himself to enemy fire.
>
> When ordered to withdraw, Private Horrigan again exposed himself to enemy fire to assist in the recovery of the platoon radio set. With two other members of the platoon he remained forward while the casualties were withdrawn, halting by accurate controlled fire a follow up launched by the enemy. Throughout the course of the contact which lasted more than three hours, Private Horrigan displayed remarkable courage in the face a determined numerically superior enemy. His personal conduct, and his complete disregard for his own safety were a great inspiration to the remainder of the platoon. His actions on that day were in the finest traditions of the Australian army.[18]

However, with the growing unpopularity of the Vietnam War among the Australian public (in particular the ballot for compulsory military service in the conflict) and anti-war demonstrations on the streets of Australian cities, Australia began a phased withdrawal from South East Asia. The last Australian combat troops were gone by 1973.

As the Australian Army's involvement in the Vietnam conflict was coming to a close, that of the British Army in Ulster was gathering pace. Northern Ireland had been a simmering cauldron of violence since its creation in 1922. There had been sporadic outbreaks of IRA activity in the province in the 1940s and 1950s, but in 1969, 'the troubles', as they became known, erupted with renewed ferocity. A re-invigorated IRA began launching attacks on the police and on Protestant targets, in the wake of a protest movement campaigning for civil rights for the north's Catholic minority. With the Royal Ulster Constabulary unable to contain the escalating tension, British troops were ordered onto the streets. Initially welcomed by Catholics as peacekeepers, British soldiers soon became the target of Republican paramilitaries themselves. The IRA's 'long war' was to last until the Good Friday Agreement of 1993.

One of the earliest Distinguished Conduct Medals for Operation Banner (as this campaign was known) was awarded for bravery in August 1972 to Corporal Michael Rattigan, Royal Green Jackets. The DCM was announced in the *London Gazette* of 24 July 1973, the full text giving an illuminating insight into the kind of urban warfare prevailing in Ulster at this time. It reads:

> On the afternoon of 28 August 1972 LCpl Rattigan was a member of a foot patrol in the Beechmount area of Belfast. Beechmount Avenue is notoriously dangerous as it gives gunmen and snipers long fields of fire and easy escape routes. At 1530 hours the patrol reached Beechmount Avenue and split up; one section moved on across the Avenue and up Beechmount Grove; the other carried on along the Avenue prior to taking up a parallel route up Beechmount Pass.
>
> At this stage LCpl Rattigan's Section Commander stopped and searched a passer by. He was about to release him when six high velocity shots were fired at the patrol from the western end of Beechmount Avenue. The patrol returned fire and, under the direction of the Platoon Commander began to manoeuvre out of their extremely exposed position on the Avenue and into the building site. The Section Commander had been fatally wounded in this first burst of fire. As soon as he realised this, and saw that the Section Commander was being given such medical assistance as was possible, LCpl Rattigan immediately took over command of the section, nominated a Rifleman as his second in command, and supervised the move to better fire positions. In order to locate the gunmen and to improve individual fire positions LCpl Rattigan exposed himself to fire several times. He acted decisively and with considerable courage throughout this incident and commanded his section with skill in the ensuing hot pursuit.
>
> Later that same day, at 2230 hrs, he was on patrol in Locan Street.

Two gunmen were seen at the top of St. Mary's Primary School. Under his direction the section sniper fired two shots at the gunmen. Eight shots were immediately returned. Throughout the gun battle which followed LCpl Rattigan kept a very firm grip on his section and gave excellent fire control orders.

On the afternoon of 22 October LCpl Rattigan (by now promoted to Cpl) was on a mobile patrol on the Springfield Road when he noticed three men standing by a bus stop. He thought there was something suspicious about them and decided to investigate. The first man he searched, a Protestant, was found to be carrying a loaded Luger pistol with a round up the breach. One of the other men was a Catholic. These men were subsequently screened and the Protestant duly charged. It seems likely that he was the gunman of an assassination squad and the Catholic was his intended victim who owes his life to Cpl Rattigan's alertness.

These three incidents typify Cpl Rattigan's success as a section commander. But in addition to specific acts of leadership in difficult and dangerous situations Cpl Rattigan was first class in his dealings with the local population. As a result he was held in very high regard as a tough, able but also reasonable and courteous NCO by both the Catholic and Protestant communities in his platoon and section area on the Lower Woodvale interface.

Cpl Rattigan's all round performance throughout the four month operational tour in Belfast has been outstanding.[19]

Michael Rattigan MBE DCM – 'Mick the Rat' to those who knew him – was born in Salisbury, Wiltshire. He rose to the rank of colour sergeant in the Royal Green Jackets and was enormously respected within the regiment, in particular by the many men he trained in his later years as an instructor. He is remembered as a scrupulously fair and honest NCO. After leaving the Army, Mick found adjusting to mundane civilian life difficult. He had a number of jobs, mainly in security, but in the mid 1980s worked in Saudi Arabia providing military training, and later in Mozambique, where one close shave too many convinced him that he was too old to be playing soldiers. After returning to live in Kent he managed property for a number of years. He died in Hythe in 2008.

Another early 'troubles' DCM was awarded to Corporal George William 'Sniffer' Courtenay,

For gallant and distinguished services in Northern Ireland during the period 1 May 1973 to 31 July 1973.[20]

Courtenay was serving in the 1st Battalion, Gloucestershire Regiment at the time of the award of the decoration. An indication of the type of work he undertook in this period may be gleaned from a letter received from the Commanding Officer, Head Quarters Northern Ireland, dated 17 December 1973:

> I am writing to say how delighted I am that you have been awarded a DCM for your bravery and dedication to duty whilst serving with your Battalion in the Lower Falls. I know that last year you were seriously wounded but that you have constantly displayed great leadership, courage and devotion to duty which resulted in large finds of terrorist weapons and explosives particularly during the period 29 April and 20 July this year.[21]

The 1st Battalion, Gloucestershires' Northern Ireland 'diary of events' for this period reveals stark evidence of the dangers inherent in searching properties for explosives: on 17 July 1973 two privates were killed and a corporal blinded by an IRA bomb placed on the fifth floor of a building in West Belfast. There is evidence also of fairly regular 'contacts' of one form or another, whether rocket or mortar attack, or direct gun battles with paramilitaries.

More Distinguished Conduct Medals would be awarded in Northern Ireland before Operation Banner was wound up, but in the early 1970s British troops were also fighting terrorists and insurgents in other parts of the globe, notably Oman. The conflict here developed largely through the intransigence of the Sultan and his refusal to allow any kind of reform or modernisation of this most backward Gulf state. The armed revolt against the almost medieval regime began in 1964 in Dhofar, the most deprived province of this benighted country. The rebels had left-wing leanings and were backed by communist and other similar regimes in the region, notably Aden. In the early 1970s the Sultan was ousted in a coup by his son, who attempted to cut the ground away from the rebels by a mixture of political and social reform, including healthcare provision for the remotest and poorest provinces, coupled with military action against those hard liners who persisted with the revolt. The new Sultan's 'hearts and minds' campaign won support from Edward Heath's Conservative government in Britain and military aid was pledged, in the form of SAS troops to train former insurgents now fighting in the Sultan's Armed Forces.

The first major operation to re-assert the Sultan's authority in the region known as the Jebel was Operation Jaguar, in October 1971. This gave the SAS and loyalist troops a toehold in the rebel areas. However, at dawn on the morning of 19 July, the rebels, known as *Adoo* (enemy) in Arabic, unexpectedly hit back, with 250 of their fighters attacking the small town of Mirbat on the Arabian Sea. They were heavily armed and their aim was to capture the town and kill its garrison of loyalist and British troops. In fact the town's garrison contained just nine SAS soldiers, all of B Squadron, equipped with one 25-pounder field gun from the Second World War, one mortar, a 0.50mm machine-gun and a few general purpose machine guns.

When the *Adoo* attacked, all the SAS men were in the British Army Training Team (BATT) house, 500 yards from the gun pit containing the 25-pounder, but when they heard mortar rounds and machine gun fire they moved swiftly into action. A Fijian trooper by the name of Talaiasi Labalaba ran to the gun pit and, though it normally took a three-man team to operate it, managed to open fire by himself, sighting the gun down the barrel and firing into the advancing rebels at what was almost point-blank range. When Labalaba was wounded, hit in the chin by an enemy 7.62mm round, it must have appeared that both the gun and then the garrison were about to be overrun.

However, the decisive action of a fellow Fijian SAS soldier, Trooper Sekonaia Takavesi, changed the course of this battle. With just his rifle and a few magazines, he sprinted to the gun pit and found his comrade badly injured, but still continuing to fire the gun.

Realising they needed more support, Takavesi left the gun pit, and ran to a nearby building where he persuaded an Omani gunner to join them. Labalaba and the Omani soldier now operated the 25-pounder, while Takavesi used a self-loading rifle (SLR).

Enemy fire intensified around the gun pit, and the Omani gunner was shot in the stomach. The two Fijians were on their own again, with Takavesi alternately firing at the enemy and helping to ram shells into the breach. Takavesi was hit next, a bullet sending him sprawling to the ground. Labalaba propped him up and handed him his SLR. By now, 25-pounder ammunition was also running low. Labalaba left the gun pit to try to reach a 60mm mortar positioned nearby. As he did so he received a fatal gunshot wound.

In the BATT house, Captain Mike Kealy heard the 25-pounder cease firing and feared the position had been taken. With a volunteer, Tommy Tobin, a trained medic, the commanding officer ran through the hail of bullets to the gun pit, where they found the dead body of Labalaba, face down on the ground, with the wounded Omani lying on his back, bleeding profusely. The only one still able to fire was Takavesi, who, also seriously wounded, was still propped on the sandbags, using his SLR to good effect in spite of the pain he was in. As Tobin turned to get his medical pack, he was shot in the face and fell to the floor mortally wounded.

Only Kealy and Takavesi were now able to fire back at the enemy from the gun pit, and they were in the fight of their lives. The situation was critical for the *Adoo* were now within grenade range. They would have undoubtedly succeeded were it not for two chance factors: at that moment the cloud lifted enough for two jets from the Sultan of Oman's air force to fly over the scene, strafing the *Adoo* with cannon fire and, at one point, dropping a 500lb bomb on the by now retreating rebels. Takavesi would later describe the scream of the jets as, 'the best sound I ever heard.' At the same time, 'G' Squadron SAS, who had been ready to relieve their 'B' Squadron comrades as part of a weekly rota, arrived by helicopter. The twenty-two reinforcements arrived at the critical moment and drove off the remaining *Adoo*. They left forty dead and ten wounded. Takavesi was decorated with the Distinguished Conduct Medal, for his incredible display of courage on this day, and the Battle of Mirbat has gone down in SAS folklore.

However, more fighting and more acts of heroism by the SAS were to follow. Corporal Melvill Keith Townsend, known as 'Taff', was born in Newport, Wales, in 1944. He was educated at The Mount School Chepstow and joined the Royal Signals as a junior leader, aged 15, in 1959. Early postings included 24 Signal Regiment and 216 (Para) Signal Squadron for parachute training, between 1963 and 1964. He was posted to 22 Special Air Service Regiment and passed Selection in December 1966. Townsend served initially with 264 (SAS) Signal Squadron then with 9 Troop 'B' Squadron, and also with 6 Troop 'B' Squadron, encompassing tours in Northern Ireland and Dhofar, including Operation Jaguar, under the command of Johnny Watts, from October 1971; the action for which Townsend was awarded the DCM was an ambush at Sheerishitti, Western Dhofar. The award was announced in the *London Gazette* of 20 July 1976, and the recommendation, dated 12 February 1975, states:

LCpl Townsend was a member of an SAS Squadron controlling Arab Irregulars in support of the Sultan's Armed Forces (SAF) in Dhofar from September 1974 to January 1975. LCpl Townsend was the leader of a 4 man SAS liaison patrol attached to a company of the Sultan's Armed Forces taking part in a battalion operation in Western Dhofar on 6 January 1975. The company to which he was attached was on high ground covering the move of a second company across some open country to their front. When this company was half way across the open ground between 60 and 70 enemy in prepared positions opened fire at close range with heavy and medium machine guns, mortars and rocket launchers. The fire destroyed the leading platoon, killing the company commander and badly wounding the Forward Observation Officer (FOO). LCpl Townsend's company was demoralised by the weight of enemy fire and he noticed that very little fire was being returned. LCpl Townsend ran forward with 2 other men under very heavy fire, seized the GPMGs from the Arab soldiers and returned the fire. At this stage it was almost the only fire being returned upon the enemy. Leaving the other 2 men he went back, still under fire, to the company's 16mm mortar, led the team forward, established a fire position and persuaded them to begin firing. Once more he returned to the front to try and get the soldiers to fire their rifles. In order to encourage them he openly stood on a rock firing at the enemy with bullets cracking around him until ordered to take cover by a senior SAS NCO. Having by force of his personality persuaded as many soldiers as he could to put fire down on the enemy he realized that no artillery fire had been returned. LCpl Townsend then began shouting instructions to the FOO and personally controlled the artillery fire.

The conduct and courage of this junior NCO throughout this very fierce engagement was magnificent. He undoubtedly saved the lives of many soldiers in the leading company, besides those of the company to which he was attached. It was an inspiring example of the highest gallantry and military ability.[22]

An eyewitness account of Taff Townsend's DCM action exists in the form of a letter from David Mason, a former officer with the Sultan's Armed Forces:

On 6 January 1975 Cpl. Townsend's 4-man patrol was attached to the SAF company of which I was second-in-command. For much of the action he and I were separated as he was with company headquarters, while I was in charge of a detachment on a different position about 150 yards away. A second company was to pass between our two positions and secure the high ground beyond a clearing in front of us; we were to cover their advance. The second company was ambushed while it was out in the open, and all our positions came under a tremendous weight of fire ... The open area where the ambush took place was flat and featureless, apart from a few rocks which afforded minimal cover. This was an area of cultivated grassland, and the company which was caught out there in the open stood no chance when the firing started. It was an area about 300 yards by 200, overlooked on our side by two small hills; on one of these hills was our company headquarters and on the other the platoon strength detachment which I was in charge of ... When this action started our company headquarters apparently fell into some disarray and I believe that Cpl Townsend was largely instrumental in restoring order and rallying the soldiers by his leadership and personal example. It was a very unpleasant situation which he overcame with a display of great courage, inspiring those around him by his deeds. Later on in the action, by which time I had gone forward by myself into the open area to see what could be done for the men of the other company, he led his patrol forward under heavy fire to join me and assist with the evacuation of the many wounded ... On the far side of the clearing, about 250 yards forward of the tree-line, there was a small knoll and beyond that a deep wadi (ravine). It was from near the knoll that Taff and I, and his men evacuated the wounded. On the other side of the wadi, forward and to the left, rose much larger hills; these dominated the whole area and were where the enemy had their fire positions ... Again, his cool head and leadership were an inspiration, and he helped save many lives. I don't mind admitting that I was practically at my wits' end by this stage and his arrival was a tremendous boost to my spirits![23]

~ 0 ~

Early in 1982 the Argentine dictatorship of General Galtieri attempted to distract the people of Argentina from domestic and economic problems by realising a long-held Argentine territorial ambition: the seizure of the Falkland Islands some 300 miles off the eastern coast of Argentina in the South Atlantic. The Argentines may have detected weakness in the attitude of the British Foreign Office, which it subsequently transpired had (deliberately or otherwise) allowed the Argentines to form the view that the Falklands - British sovereign territory since 1833 - would not be robustly defended. This added currency to the long cherished Argentine dream of claiming 'Los Malvinas' as their own.

The military garrison of the Falklands – consisting of a small party of Royal Marines and members of the territory's own Falkland Islands Defence Force – was no match for the Argentine invaders and quickly surrendered. However, Argentina had reckoned without Britain's Iron Lady, Margaret Thatcher, and a Task Force comprising the best that Great Britain had in terms of armed forces, including the Welsh Guards, Parachute Regiment, Gurkhas, Royal Marine Commandos, SAS and SBS, set forth to return the Falkland Islanders to the government of their choosing. It was in many ways a strange and anachronistic war; a very conventional conflict decided by infantrymen on the ground, often at the point of a bayonet, but fought in an age dominated at one extreme by the threat of nuclear conflict, and at the other by unconventional guerrilla tactics in which there was no formal enemy who stood up to fight.

The nature of the campaign would be further influenced by early Argentine successes in attacking British shipping. The loss of the *Atlantic Conveyor* in particular deprived the Task Force of all but a handful of helicopters, which were thenceforth carefully guarded. After the Task Force secured a beachhead at San Carlos Water, the infantry began to fight its way on foot across the Falklands towards the capital Port Stanley. The most serious opposition came from Argentine troops dug in on the ring of hills surrounding Stanley. These would have to be overcome by infantry, supported where possible by artillery and mortar fire.

The criteria for the award of the DCM had changed slightly since the end of the Second World War, in as much as an award could now be made if the recipient was killed in the action for which it was earned. One such posthumous DCM was granted to Private Stephen Illingsworth, of the 2nd Battalion Parachute Regiment, the citation reading:

> In the early hours of 28th May 1982, the 2nd Battalion The Parachute Regiment launched an attack on enemy positions in the area of the Darwin and Goose Green settlements on the Island of East Falkland. The enemy were thought to be entrenched in battalion strength. In the event, their numbers were far greater and fierce fighting ensued all day.
>
> Private Illingsworth was a member of 5 Platoon, which was the depth platoon in B Company's advance. At one point the advance came under heavy and accurate enemy fire, and OC B Company attacked the enemy position with his leading platoons, leaving 5 Platoon to provide covering fire. Dawn was growing stronger and it became clear that 5 Platoon was in fact exposed on a long forward

slope without protection and very vulnerable to increasingly heavy enemy machine gun and rifle fire. Its position became untenable and it was ordered to withdraw back over the crest. It was during this manoeuvre that one of their number was hit in the back.

Private Illingsworth, who had already reached comparative safety himself, immediately rushed forward in full view and fire of the enemy, accompanied by another soldier, to help their wounded comrade. In an effort to locate the wound they removed his weapon and webbing equipment, and having administered First Aid, dragged the soldier back over the crest line, despite a hail of enemy fire which miraculously missed them. Once in a position of safety, Private Illingsworth continued to tend the injured man's wounds.

The firefight continued intensively, and 5 Platoon began to run short of ammunition. Remembering that he had left the webbing equipment, with ammunition in it lying on the exposed forward slope, Private Illingsworth decided to go forward alone to collect it. Disregarding the enemy fire, which was still extremely heavy he broke cover and advanced once again down the forward slope. As he did so he was killed.

In these two acts of supreme courage Private Illingsworth showed a complete disregard for his own safety, and a total dedication to others. While his action in coming to the help of a wounded soldier may have been almost instinctive on seeing the plight of a comrade, his move forward to collect much needed ammunition for his beleaguered platoon was a display of coolly-calculated courage and heroism of the very highest order.[24]

Another soldier of 2 Para decorated that same day was Liverpudlian Corporal Dave Abols, part of whose citation reads:

In the heat of the battle Corporal Abols dashed through enemy fire to drag a wounded comrade to safety. When another Corporal was wounded he again crossed an exposed forward slope to rescue him. Later, well to the fore, he destroyed an enemy position which resulted in effective enemy resistance being ended in that area.[25]

Abols was later commissioned, and spent the latter part of his career with the Australian Army. Many years later he recalled that he had been fortunate when rushing forward to take on an Argentine position alone, for the enemy sniper covering it had already inflicted a number of casualties but was distracted by another target when Abols made his lone dash. His firing of a 66mm anti-tank rocket into the command trench effectively broke Argentine resistance on the Goose Green position, and turned the battle in the Paras' favour. A truly well-earned DCM.

The advance on Stanley continued, the next obstacle being the series of mountain ridges that ringed the Falklands capital, including the Two Sisters feature and Mount Tumbledown. 45 Commando Royal Marines had already completed a gruelling 80 mile forced march to reach Teal Inlet, even before they launched their attack on Two Sisters. 45 Commando was part of 3 Commando Brigade along with 3 Para and 42 Commando. While these two units were allotted Mounts Longdon and Harriet respectively, 45 Commando would take on the sharply rising Craggy Hill feature of the Two Sisters. The prospects for 45 Commando were bleak in the extreme. Even without the appalling weather conditions then prevailing, this was an extremely strong Argentine position. Concealed machine-gun nests were protected by minefields, and the enemy soldiers themselves were not the stereotypical Argentine conscripts but were in fact elements of that country's special forces. After careful reconnaissance a night attack was planned for 11-12 June 1982. One section of 45 Commando's Zulu Company was led by Corporal Julian Burdett. Burdett, from Somerleyton, near Lowestoft, had joined the Royal Marines aged 25. His hobby was rock climbing and mountaineering, and he had realised that the Marines would pay him to do this! Receiving his green beret in 1978, he subsequently graduated from the corps' Mountain Leaders course, becoming an instructor in mountain and arctic warfare.

On the Two Sisters, Burdett's section faced an extremely difficult 300-meter climb up sharply rising ground, before even contacting with the enemy. Indeed the ground was so broken with rocky outcrops that some members of the section were actually rendered unconscious by falls in the darkness. Hampered by their heavy Milan missile launchers (laughingly described as 'man-portable') the Marines' situation was rendered almost impossible by a devastating enemy mortar and artillery barrage that fell upon them just as they were forming up. Burdett was hit and seriously wounded, but continued amid the enemy flares and machine-gun fire to lead and encourage his men. For his courage and leadership he was awarded the DCM, the only one awarded to a member of the Royal Marines for the Falklands campaign. The citation reads:

On the night of 11-12 June 1982, on the island of East Falkland, 45 Commando Royal Marines launched a silent night attack against strongly held enemy positions on the Craggy Hill feature of Two Sisters, ten kilometres to the west of Port Stanley. As Section

Commander, Corporal Burdett was leading his Section when they came under heavy fire from enemy mortars. Two of his men were killed instantly and he himself seriously wounded. Despite these setbacks, he continued to encourage and steady his Section as they moved forward. Ignoring his wounds Corporal Burdett also continued to pass further important reports of enemy positions. Simultaneously he organised the evacuation of his wounded colleagues until he himself was carried from the scene of the fighting. Despite serious losses, Corporal Burdett's selfless and distinguished leadership inspired his men to continue their advance.[26]

After a firefight of some two hours' duration the summit of the position was finally taken by members of Z company, shouting their battle cry 'Zulu Zulu Zulu'. Burdett's own account of his DCM award fleshes out the bare bones of his citation:

As a section commander in Zulu Company I deployed from Rosyth on R.F.A. *Resource*, first to Ascension Island, then on SS *Canberra* before landing at Ajax Bay from HMS *Fearless*. [From there we] made the 'yomp' to the patrol base near Mount Kent. Before the assault on Two Sisters the Commando did several days of aggressive night patrolling on and about the ridge. My Section led a large thirty man plus fighting patrol, and cleared the smaller summit at the western end of the ridge before retiring under enemy artillery DF. The silent night assault had [involved] a difficult approach march, over large 'rock runs' (large, loose, flat rocks that dissect the boggy ground), Z and X Companies advanced the length of the ridge with Y Company coming in from the western end. The two troops in front had managed to get in close to lower crags with 9 Troop to the rear still in the open but with a good view of the front. I was observing with an IWS, after going to ground, and spotted a figure on top of a large rock. A flare exploded behind him which initiated the battle, with his shape seeming to attract fire from most of the Commando. Our forward marines were soon into the lower enemy positions but we were in a very exposed situation attracting heavy fire from several 0.5" Brownings, and the rest. It was just a sheet of tracer rounds overhead which fortunately stayed high (yes it's true you tend to shoot high in the dark) but then the defenders fired mortars which you don't hear until they land ... and [one came down] in the middle of my section, killing one (Marine

Gordon McPherson from Oban) and nearly blowing my leg off. I remember flying up in the air and landing in a heap, then getting a warm feeling down my back ... that was the blood coming from my leg wound. Our Troop did not move forward as we continued to observe enemy strong points until the Two Sisters Ridge was cleared. We had to wait for several hours before being 'casevaced' as artillery fire was too heavy for the choppers to fly. For my lift I was jammed in behind the pilot of a 'Scout', first to the RAP at Kent where I fell out when the door was opened into the arms of our Doc. His assessment took about ten seconds then he pushed me back in for the lift to Teal Inlet Field Hospital with me waking up the next day to the sound of a Chinook landing on *Uganda*. After five weeks and eleven operations four of us were the first to be flown out of Stanley in a Herc that had to refuel four times, in a dangerous diving operation, with several Victor tankers. A night in Ascension's wee hospital was followed by a smother ride home in a VC10, with some Scots Guards, landing at Brize Norton to the sound of bagpipes. They left the plane to the cheers of the crowd but we had to wait until everybody had left ... we were not to be seen by the public as decreed by the powers above. Then, secreted in blacked out buses, moved to RAF Rawton followed by a long stay in Haslar Hospital. As I was due to be married in October, I managed to get an early discharge just before the wedding. As we left the church in Glasgow a member of the press told us of my DCM award ... When I returned to Haslar a month later the telegram of the official notification was waiting.[27]

Whilst the Marines were engaged on the Two Sisters feature, elements of the 5th Infantry Brigade were closing on Port Stanley via the route across Mount Tumbledown, seven kilometres west of the islands' capital. After being helicoptered across to their start line on Goat Ridge, on the night of 13/14 June 1982, 2nd Battalion Scots Guards attacked the Argentine positions on the slopes of Tumbledown. As usual, the enemy were well dug in; it was commonly acknowledged among British veterans after the conflict that whatever other failings the Argentine armed forces may have had, they constructed impressive defensive positions. Again, the Argentine defenders were not the unwilling conscripts of popular legend but were instead professional Argentine Marines. They fought hard and contested every yard of ground. Two Distinguished Conduct Medals were awarded to the Scots Guards for their assault on this position. One of the Scots

Guards who was present at this action was Lance Corporal Graham Rennie, who later remembered:

> Our assault was initiated by a Guardsman killing a sniper, which was followed by a volley of 66mm anti-tank rounds. We ran forward in extended line, machine-gunners and riflemen firing from the hip to keep the enemy heads down, enabling us to cover the open ground in the shortest possible time. Halfway across the open ground, 2 Platoon went to ground to give covering fire support, enabling us to gain a foothold on the enemy position. From then on we fought from crag to crag, rock to rock, taking out pockets of enemy and lone riflemen, all of whom resisted fiercely.[28]

The citation for Guardsman James Boyle Curran Reynolds' DCM reads:

> During the attack, Guardsman Reynolds' Platoon came under fire from a group of enemy snipers. His Platoon Sergeant was killed instantly. A confused situation developed and his section became separated. Guardsman Reynolds immediately took command. Having located the enemy snipers he silenced several of them himself.
>
> That done and showing a complete disregard for his own safety, he moved forward to render first aid to a wounded comrade. He himself was wounded in the hand by enemy sniper fire, but continued to aid his colleague. Whilst doing so, he was killed by enemy mortar fire.[29]

Today Curran's name is recorded on a brass plaque at the summit of Mount Tumbledown, which honours the memory of the eight Scots Guardsmen who fell in the capture of the mountain. The second DCM for this action went to Warrant Officer Second Class William Nicol. Nicol had already been noted for his bravery in two earlier incidents in the Falklands War, but his citation goes on to describe his actions at Tumbledown on 14 June 1982:

> After the initial assault, the company came under constant and devastating machine gun and sniper fire. One of the platoon sergeants was wounded, and CSM Nicol went forward under accurate sniper fire to rescue him. Wounded in the hand while doing so, he continued to tend the dying sergeant.
>
> He remained cool and calm under heavy fire encouraging and exhorting his men and at the same time, advising one of the young platoon commanders how to defeat a seemingly impregnable enemy position.

He remained unperturbed by the weight of enemy small arms, artillery and mortar fire thus instilling great confidence in men who might well have been frightened. He refused to be evacuated himself, until all the other casualties in the company (26 in all) had been evacuated. CSM Nicol's distinguished conduct and conspicuous personal bravery throughout the campaign ... proved an inspiration and example to all ranks and have made an outstanding contribution to his company's exceptional achievements.[30]

Three years afterwards, William 'Bill' Nicol described this incident in Martin Middlebrook's *Operation Corporate: The Falklands War 1982* (later just *The Falklands War*, Penguin):

When we came under fire, everyone went to ground and was returning fire. There was a staggering amount of noise. I had gone off 'floating' around the left leading platoon, doing what I saw as a Company Sergeant-Major's job, giving my boys encouragement - not that they needed it. They shouted for me and I went across to Tanbini and tried to pull him back into cover; if I had tried to lift him, we would both have been exposed and hit. I suggested that he tried to push back with his feet, while I pulled him, but he said, 'Sir, I've been shot' - typical guardsman, the way he addressed me as 'Sir' - and then he died.

Someone else was screaming for me then. It was the Platoon Sergeant, he had been badly shot in the thigh. I jumped up and ran across to him and, as I got to him, I was hit. I was just about to kneel down beside him when the bullet hit the centre of my rifle which was across the front of the centre of my stomach in the approved manner, ready for action. If I hadn't been holding the rifle in the manner in which I had been teaching people for years, I would be dead now. The bullet ricocheted off the barrel and went through my right hand. Tanbini, John Simeon and I had all been shot in one line by the same sniper, I think. I had just received a letter from my wife to say she was pregnant and this went through my mind. I thought I was going to be next. There was nothing I could do about it. That sniper was good; I would like to have met him.[31]

The capture of Tumbledown, however, was the key that finally unlocked the Argentine defence of the Falkland Islands, from here on the way to Port Stanley was open, and shortly afterwards came the surrender of the enemy garrison on the islands.

~ 0 ~

Whilst Britain had suffered significant casualties in the Falklands, the war had been short and sharp and had clearly drawn a line under Argentine ambitions in the region. By contrast the IRA's 'long war' in Northern Ireland continued to rumble on through the 1980s, and whilst terrorist activity on occasions might subside, before long a new generation committed to reunification of Ireland by any means would rise through the ranks of the Provisionals, and conflict would escalate once more.

In the aftermath of the 1987 Loughgall ambush, where a number of its members were shot dead by the SAS, the Provisional IRA Army Council suspected a large degree of penetration by informers at the grassroots level of the organisation. They decided to form an experimental flying column, in order to mount a large-scale operation against a permanent vehicle checkpoint somewhere along the Ulster-Eire border. The Provisional IRA hoped this would both win back lost face among their own sympathisers, and by keeping information about future targets within a select band also prevent the leaks of the recent past. The planning of this operation was in the charge of Thomas Murphy, alleged leader of the South Armagh Brigade, and was to be conducted by East Tyrone Brigade member Michael 'Pete' Ryan. The unit would be composed of around twenty IRA terrorists, but the action properly was to be the responsibility of just eleven operatives.

Their chosen target, a Permanent Vehicle Check Point (PVCP) at Derryard, near Rosslea, was a 'soft target' consisting of a number of poorly protected portakabins, weakly held by lightly armed British troops. In the assault that took place on 13 December 1989 the IRA used two 12.7mm DShK machine-guns, eleven AK-47 assault rifles, grenades, and a flamethrower. To assure the destruction of the Army post, the flying column intended to detonate a van bomb, after the initial surprise assault. On the day in question it was in fact manned by soldiers of the 1st Battalion of the King's Own Scottish Borderers (KOSB), who staged an extraordinary fight back. After launching a number of grenades, the IRA members managed to break into the compound using a Hino flatbed lorry, which had been specially reinforced and armoured for the task. They were supported by automatic fire and the flamethrower's stream of fire. In the process they killed two soldiers, Private James Houston and Lance Corporal Michael Paterson. Corporal Law was severely wounded and later airlifted for treatment. The IRA unit left an Isuzu van loaded with 400lb of Semtex, which failed to explode. The attack was finally repulsed by a Borderers section from the checkpoint that was patrolling nearby, with the support of a Wessex helicopter. The IRA column, at risk of being surrounded, then fled in the truck, possibly toward the border. Two DCMs were awarded to members of the Borderers manning the checkpoint, Corporals R B Duncan and I B Harvey, and the incident was described in a Special Order circulated afterwards by Lieutenant Colonel C I Darnell MBE, commanding officer of the 1st Battalion KOSB. Part of it reads:

> As the enemy attack started Cpl Duncan immediately returned fire from the Command Sangar. He continued to do so until forced to withdraw by the weight of fire and flame that was splintering the sangar walls and penetrating inside the sangar through the observation ports ... As the enemy sprayed the base with gunfire and grenades and smashed the lorry into the compound, Cpl Duncan, still firing, crossed through the fire to check all the portakabins and to order his men to re-group behind cover at the rear of the base ... Following the sighting of the Hino lorry Corporal Harvey and his team were moving down towards the PVCP from the North when the attack began. Corporal Harvey's contact report at the time was critical. It was the only message received by battalion HQ until after the action. It allowed the essential re-deployment of reserves and follow-up agencies. The team rapidly made their way to the PVCP, halting on the road some 75-100 metres to the north. The rear of the lorry was visible outside the base. The terrorists were clearly identified firing into the compound. Cpl Harvey and his men opened fire hitting the rear of the lorry 5 times. The enemy immediately switched the bulk of their fire onto the patrol forcing them to dive for cover into the hedgerows to the West of the road. By skilful fire and manoeuvre, the patrol worked its way to a position adjacent to the PVCP, continuing to draw heavy fire and forcing the enemy to withdraw ... the 2 corporals, recognising that the Isuzu van was a bomb, evacuated the base and established the cordon ... This was a terrifying close quarter action which lasted some 10 minutes. It was a fight for existence. As PIRA declared subsequently they were intent on '...totally destroying the enemy position ....' Every man involved acted with exemplary courage and determination to defeat the enemy. The conduct of Cpl Duncan and Cpl Harvey and of L/Cpl Paterson was in the highest traditions of conspicuous gallantry. By their actions they saved the PVCP. By their actions they fought back at the enemy, fought to regain some initiative, and finally fought off the attack forcing the terrorists to withdraw prematurely and ensuring their failure. As PIRA also stated '... the soldiers,

despite several demands to surrender, refused to comply ... our ASU was forced to withdraw ... (hastened by the presence of) ... a sizeable British Army foot patrol ...'[32]

The scale and type of this attack had never been seen before in Northern Ireland, and the close quarter nature of the fighting, together with the nature of the enemy make the two DCMs awarded for this action among the most hard-fought, certainly in the twentieth-century history of the decoration.

~ 0 ~

The 1990-91 Gulf War was triggered ostensibly by Iraqi dictator Saddam Hussein's invasion of his small but very wealthy oil-producing neighbour, Kuwait, which also happened to be a client and close ally of the United States. Some might argue that it was the arms and support provided to Saddam by the United States that turned him into a regional bully in the first place, but in any event a remarkable coalition of Western and Arab nations was brought together with the express intention of forcing Saddam out of Kuwait. Most notable of the Arab nations was Iraq's neighbour Saudi Arabia, which had good reason to be wary of Saddam's regional ambitions.

British troops deployed to Saudi Arabia as part of Operation Granby, an adjunct to the US Operation Desert Shield. After an aerial bombardment of Iraqi positions lasting some six weeks came a ground offensive, beginning at 0100 hours on 24 February 1991, which saw the liberation of Kuwait. The ground offensive was suspended on 28 February, the Iraqi army of over half a million men having been routed, and coalition troops were ordered to stand fast on defensive positions.

With one exception, that awarded to Staff Sergeant Kevin Michael Davies, of 203 Provost Company Royal Military Police, all of the Distinguished Conduct Medals granted for Operation Granby were awarded to Special Forces personnel. A number of these awards went to members of Special Air Service patrols, tasked with finding Saddam Hussein's Scud missile sites, deep behind enemy lines in the Iraqi desert. These patrols had been operating since January of 1991, well before the conventional ground war began. Their missions were of supreme political importance, for Saddam Hussein at the time was firing Scuds indiscriminately into Israel, and causing civilian casualties, in the hope of provoking that country into unilateral reprisals. The move was a cunning one. If Israel had indeed attacked Iraq, as she was threatening to do, then the fragile Western/Arab coalition built up by the United States would have fallen apart, as the leaders of the other Gulf states could not be seen by their peoples to be acting in unison with the hated Israelis.

It was vital that the Scud sites were found and neutralised fast. Aircraft could do a certain amount, but what was required was reliable intelligence and where necessary, direct action on the ground. Half a dozen SAS patrols were inserted into Iraq, and several members of the regiment were decorated as a result of their bravery in these raids.

One DCM went to Sergeant 'Andy McNab', and the action for which it was awarded has been written up in his book *Bravo Two Zero*. This unquestionably, however, must rank as one of the most controversial DCMs ever awarded. McNab was the leader of a patrol, the Bravo Two Zero of the book's title, which in spite of strong advice to the contrary opted to go into Iraq without Land Rovers, preferring instead to operate on foot. Heavily laden, when they made contact with Iraqi civilians and were compromised, they had no effective means of a quick withdrawal. The bitter cold of the Iraqi desert at night and firefights with Saddam's men accounted for a number of the patrol and McNab himself was captured. Whilst his conduct under brutal Iraqi treatment was considered admirable, questions were later raised about incidents described in the book that were not mentioned in 'McNab's' de-brief at the SAS headquarters, Stirling Lines, in Hereford, directly after the Gulf War.

An unquestionably well-deserved and uncontroversial DCM went to Regimental Sergeant-Major (now Major) Peter 'Billy' Ratcliffe, the leader of another SAS patrol, Alpha One Zero. In an unprecedented move unique in the history of the SAS, Ratcliffe was helicoptered out to the patrol actually in the field, to take over command from a commissioned officer who was felt to be not up to the task. His brief was to get the patrol moving and bring it into action against Iraqi Scud targets.

Ratcliffe was born in Salford, then a working-class industrial district of Manchester, and in 1970, in search of an escape from meaningless dead end jobs, he joined the Parachute Regiment, before volunteering for SAS selection in 1972. He possessed a wealth of experience, having served in Oman, the Falklands and other flashpoints. His account of the patrol and the encounter that led to his DCM award appear in his book *Eye of The Storm*.

Having guided Alpha One Zero across the barren Iraqi desert, avoiding contact with potentially hostile civilians, he led the patrol on to its target, a transmissions relay station code named Victor Two. This was a communications centre for the control of Scud missiles, near the town of Nukhayb, featuring a collection of bunkers and an enormous radio mast. With only thirty-four men, and little solid intelligence as to what they were facing, Ratcliffe, devised a plan first to reconnoitre the complex and then to destroy it. Dividing his men into teams, he placed some men to give covering fire whilst he himself led one team carrying demolition charges directly into the main compound. Their first stroke of luck came when they discovered that the perimeter wall had already been breached, having been struck by a bomb or missile in an earlier coalition air raid. In spite of the fact that the relay station was more heavily guarded than they anticipated, Ratcliffe's team slipped inside undetected to place explosive charges around the base of the mast. Having set the timers, the team sprinted back towards the ragged hole in the perimeter wall. Radcliffe continues:

> At which point our good fortune took a nosedive. We were through the tangled fence and close to the gap in the wall when all hell broke loose. There were several single shots followed by a burst of automatic fire, then the enormous whoosh of a Milan going in and, seconds later, a huge explosion as the missile struck home. Then everyone seemed to let rip together. Rounds were zipping overhead and we could hear them smacking into the other side of the wall.
>
> There were bullets flying everywhere, riddling the sheeting covering the gap, while, above, tracers created amazing patterned arches. We were safe enough on our side of the wall, but not for long. Behind us, no more than ten metres away, was over a hundred pounds of high-explosive getting ready to blow in less than ninety seconds.[33]

A quick discussion followed among the SAS men as to what to do next – but there was only one obvious answer and they all arrived at it at the same time. High on adrenaline, the team set off like scalded jackrabbits, running as fast as they could back to the protection of the ridge from which they had first observed the Iraqi compound. Ratcliffe continues the story:

> We were halfway between the wall and the jumping off point when the first explosive charge blew, followed seconds later by another boom and, almost immediately afterwards, by a third.
>
> None of us stopped to watch the effects, however, for there were bullets whistling all around us. As I ran I looked to the left. The bunker there was gushing flames and smoke from its gun slits and entrance, which meant that the Milan had done its job.

The bunker on the other side was still intact, and there seemed to be a lot of the enemy fire coming from that direction. But Pat and his team on the 110s had the heavy machine-guns in action, while some of the guys with him had brought their grenade launchers to bear and were peppering the bunker with high-velocity fragmenting metal. As a result, most of the enemy fire was wild, since they were reluctant to face the streams of 0.5-inch rounds and 40mm grenades.[34]

Covered by the fire of the support team the SAS squad regrouped and undertook a quick debrief session. However, they were not yet out of danger for the Iraqis, who had been at first stunned by the speed and ferocity of the initial assault, were now beginning to recover some of their composure. A counter-attack began to develop as Iraqis fired down onto the SAS patrol from the edge of the berm or man-made bank behind which they were sheltering. Fortunately, the aim of the Iraqi conscripts was generally poor, but one or two lucky shots hit the vehicles, and the enemy fire was growing in intensity. Once again the general consensus was that discretion was the better part of valour, and firing up their vehicles the elite British soldiers made a scrambling and sliding retreat to the south. As the firing died away into the distance, about a kilometre further on they stopped to regroup. Ratcliffe again:

> Miraculously, when I asked for casualties everyone shook his head. There were no wounded. No one had even a scratch, and no one was missing. My only concern now was for Pat and his men ... Ten minutes later we heard the growl of engines as the four Land Rovers emerged out of the darkness. All their crews were intact. As soon as they drew up alongside Pat's men jumped out and suddenly everybody seemed to be hugging and backslapping everybody else. Even for the SAS, the end of a mission brings a tremendous release of tension, made up partly of relief and partly of pleasure at having performed well in a difficult and dangerous task. By some incredible miracle, and against far greater odds than we could have anticipated, we had managed to get in and out of the enemy stronghold with every member of the unit present and unwounded. In doing so we undoubtedly killed and wounded numbers of Iraqi troops, as well as firing the demolition charges on the mast. We had also thoroughly alarmed and confused the enemy.[35]

Ratcliffe did not learn of his award until June 1991, four months after his return from the Gulf. Later that summer, wearing his best uniform he and a number of other SAS personnel decorated in the Gulf arrived at

Buckingham Palace to receive their awards from Her Majesty the Queen. As usual on these occasions Her Majesty stopped for a few moments to chat to each soldier. After presenting Ratcliffe with his DCM, she asked him about his experiences in the Gulf, adding that it must have been very frightening. Ratcliffe's reply, to the effect that he had actually rather enjoyed it, left Her Majesty somewhat bemused, but was entirely typical of a man who had spent eighteen years in the toughest and most respected fighting force in the world and who had risen to become its senior non-commissioned officer.

One of the final DCMs to be awarded went to a part-time soldier of the Ulster Defence Regiment. The corporal, who cannot be named for security reasons, was involved in an IRA ambush at Mulleek, County Fermanagh. A member of the UDR since 1970, the recipient was also a local authority dog warden during normal working hours. As such, on 6 February 1992, he was called out to a remote farm close to the border with the Republic, on the pretext that the farmer's dog had attacked a person. Nevertheless, as a potential IRA target for more than twenty years, the UDR soldier had grown accustomed to never leaving home without a loaded firearm in the cab of his van. He recounted what happened next in an interview published in *Soldier* magazine:

> As I stopped in front of the house, two men came running at me from either side of my van roaring: 'IRA! Get out of the van! Get out! Get out!' One had a pistol at the passenger window so I whipped my gun up, cocked it and bang, bang, bang, out through the door. He fell.
>
> The other was at the driver's door. Seeing I had a gun in my hand, he ran. I jumped out and lay down at the front wheel of the van. One man was at the corner of the house, the other between the hedge and the wall. A shot busted the front wheel, just by my head. I knew there was no place to run without getting shot and I knew I was firing ammo too quickly. I saw a man's head coming round the corner, so I took aim as best I could, pressed the trigger but nothing happened, the magazine was empty.
>
> I knew there was a spare magazine in my coat on the passenger seat so I ran round and grabbed the coat. It must have taken them a while to realise what was wrong and two of them came running at me with their guns on automatic. That's when I was getting it in the legs. I whipped on the magazine. Bang.[36]

At this point the attackers fled, though the UDR corporal was badly wounded, his thighbone being smashed. He managed to get inside the farm, where he telephoned for assistance. He would spend a year in hospital and be medically discharged from the UDR upon his release.

In 1993, following a review of the honours system, the Distinguished Conduct Medal was relegated to the pages of history. Having a separate second level gallantry award for officers and other ranks was held, in the late twentieth century way of thinking, to be in some way elitist. Across the honours system, some awards were opened up to officers and men alike, whilst others were replaced entirely. The Distinguished Conduct Medal was replaced by the Conspicuous Gallantry Cross (CGC), which also occupied the position previously held by the Distinguished Service Order as the second level bravery award for officers (though the DSO was retained for outstanding leadership). At the time of writing, twenty–eight individual awards and one collective award (to the Royal Irish Regiment/Ulster Defence Regiment for Northern Ireland) of the new decoration have so far been made. The acts of heroism that have led to the award of the CGC, in Bosnia, Iraq, Afghanistan and elsewhere have been entirely in keeping with the high standards set by the DCM, and make the CGC a worthy successor. While British troops continue to be committed to battle, and conduct themselves with exemplary courage in trouble spots around the world, there can be no doubt that further awards of the new medal will be made. In one hundred years time, who can doubt that there will be a need for further books chronicling the deeds of heroes?

Chapter 5

Collecting Distinguished Conduct Medals and Tracing Your DCM Ancestor

The first step in tracing the story of a Victorian DCM might actually be identifying it as such! No official DCM was ever struck with an obverse bearing the bust of Queen Victoria. In almost every case, the obverse from 1854 to 1901 bore the panoply of arms, in exactly the same fashion as the Army Long Service and Good Conduct Medal. Indeed, without a ribbon, and without examining the legend on the reverse, the two medals can be difficult at first glance to distinguish. However, one DCM, described by DNW as 'a very rare trial or specimen striking', is known, bearing on the obverse the bust of the 'young' Queen. It is engraved to William Finch, Coldstream Guards, a confirmed Crimea DCM recipient. This particular medal is noted by Abbott & Tamplin in *British Gallantry Awards*. They state:

> A DCM exists which has for obverse Queen Victoria's effigy as it appears on the MSM, having no date below the bust. This medal had every appearance of being struck officially and it may have been a trial pattern. However, it is difficult to see why such a striking should have been made since when the initial order was placed with the Royal Mint on 2nd February 1855 it was made clear that the obverse was to be as for the L.S. & G.C. Medal. The medal referred to here is named in a highly suspect engraved, interrupted and irregular script.[1]

Awards made in respect of service in the Crimea or Indian Mutiny are impressed in serif capitals, regimental numbers are not given and in the infantry and cavalry the ranks of private soldiers are omitted. First names often appear, either in full or abbreviated. Infantry regiments are usually given with the number followed by REGt. Occasionally a battalion number is given. Awards for later campaigns are often found named in the style of the relevant campaign medal and some for the First Boer War of 1880-81 are engraved. In later issues, the soldier's regimental number does often appear, except in the case of cavalrymen. The soldier's rank, including that of private soldiers, also appears in abbreviated form. Most awards made after 1881 have the date of the act of gallantry added on the rim of the medal, after the recipient's name. In early photographs the DCM can often been seen worn immediately after the relevant campaign medal, as instructed in Queen's Regulations for the Army 1881. Army Order Number 181 of July 1902 gave the DCM precedence over all campaign medals, and then Army Order Number 196 of October 1905 listed it immediately after the Conspicuous Gallantry Medal in the order of precedence.

Victorian DCMs were initially recorded in a Register of Awards (which was continued until 1909) although Crimean awards to the Royal Artillery and Royal Sappers and Miners were not recorded. It appears that at some stage, after a large number of awards had been made, it was realised that no roll had been maintained and that a late effort was made to compile the Register from a variety of sources. Consequently there are discrepancies, and it has been shown that some DCMs awarded for the Crimea and Indian Mutiny had been missed from the Register.

From Army General Order Number 61 (June 1885) awards were published in the Regular Army Orders. From the *London Gazette* of 15 November 1898 onwards, all details of DCM awards and recipients were published in that newspaper, as is still the case today for gallantry awards. As mentioned previously, a bar for subsequent acts of gallantry was authorised in 1881. The bar had the date of the second act of gallantry in raised relief. This practice continued until 15 September 1916, when the standard laurel pattern bar was introduced. Eighty-six dated bars were issued during the Great War to eighty-five recipients; Sergeant G Mitchell of the Black Watch received two dated bars ('25th September 1915' and '12th April 1916') and Sergeant C Leadbeater of the Lincolnshire Regiment received one dated bar ('13th October 1915') and one laurel pattern bar.

Awards for the South African War 1899-1902 and later were impressed in plain block capitals without serifs although some of the earliest were still engraved. On the whole, Boer War DCMs can be extremely difficult to research, and unless supporting evidence from regimental journals or other sources can be found, it can often be hard to attribute a DCM to a particular action. Although the awards were published in the *London Gazette*, no citations were shown until the final months of the war. Indeed, the date of the gazette in which it appears does not appear to correspond in any meaningful way with the date of the action. In many cases, at least a year appears to have passed between the incident for which the award was made and the announcement in the gazette. At the same time, the practice of impressing the date of the deed for which the award was made on the rim of the medal itself (after the recipient's name and regiment) appears to have ended in the second half of the Boer War. Boer War DCM awards appear also to be closely linked to mentions in dispatches. Often a recipient was mentioned and received the medal for the same incident.

Although Boer War DCM citations were hardly ever published in the *London Gazette*, the various staff papers held at The National Archives (TNA) at Kew, including Lord Robert's own papers, contain operational reports that include lists of men being recommended for inclusion in despatches. There are also some good write-ups or recommendations for soldiers, which include some DCMs. It is, however, a needle-in-a-haystack situation, because it is necessary to wade through boxes and boxes of material in the hope of finding something relevant.

From the death of Queen Victoria on 22 January 1901 onwards, the bust of King Edward VII appeared on the obverse of the DCM. The King's head type was issued to some recipients who had actually performed their acts of gallantry during the Queen's reign, for example, Trumpeter W W Ayles (7th Battery, RFA), awarded for the Battle of Colenso in 1899 (gazetted 2 February 1900). Furthermore, the Register is annotated to the effect that the medal was to be replaced by the Victorian type, though this clearly never happened. Driver N Harding of the same battery also received a DCM for this action but his award was gazetted on 19 April 1901 (after the Queen's death) and is also the Edwardian type. Confusingly enough, the DCM to Corporal W Knight, 66th Battery, for Colenso, which also appeared in that same gazette, is of the Victorian type.

A large number of DCMs for South Africa were gazetted on 27 September 1901, and are of mixed Victorian and Edwardian types. Some replacements for lost Victorian type DCMs, awarded for the South African War, were made using Edwardian types, so all in all the Boer War remains a less than transparent area for investigators and researchers.

The National Archives at Kew remains the most important repository for DCM research. Victorian DCM recipients can usually be researched by tracing their discharge documents in the WO 97 series at TNA. If they are present, these documents will reveal details of a soldier's place of birth and his postings. However, they may not reveal much about the DCM beyond the bald statement that it was awarded. Pre-1886 awards can also involve a search of regimental musters in WO12 & WO16, medal rolls in WO 100, regimental histories, regimental newspapers, and officers' journals. Post-1886, muster rolls cease, but the likes of WO 108 come in to play. Also as some of these men were commissioned, it may be worthwhile looking into WO 25, WO 76 and even odd places like PIN 71. A small number of citations from the Boer War survive in WO 108, which comprises War Office correspondence and papers from that conflict.

By far the commonest obverse type of the DCM was that of HM King George V. Large numbers were awarded during the First World War, making this issue the one most likely to be encountered in the course of family history research. When researching a Great War DCM ancestor the first port of call must always be the Medal Index Cards. These are held by The National Archives online service Documents Online, and also by www.ancestry.co.uk. A search of the index cards should be made to locate that for the person under research. The card may mention the award of the DCM, but even if it does not, make a note of the soldier's service number if not already known, as this will be useful later.

Sometimes a second index card is found, containing far less detail, and a reference to LG. This is an index card for the date the award was gazetted in the *London Gazette*. The next port of call is the *London Gazette* website, www.gazettes-online.co.uk. If you have the date of the announcement, you can go straight to it. If you need to search around, be aware that the search engine is not a perfect instrument, and the easiest way to search is sometimes simply to enter surname and service number (or even just service number). If you are having problems, try switching to the *Edinburgh Gazette* as the Optical Character Recognition appears to be better in this edition. Researching a 1914-18 DCM is far easier than researching an MM from the same period, as in most cases a citation giving a description of the act of gallantry was published in the *London Gazette*. These can be extremely detailed and often tell the researcher when, where and how an award was gained. If the award was listed in the King's Birthday Honours, then there will probably not be a citation, and it may be inferred that the award was perhaps not for a single act of gallantry. The essential guide for those interested in Great War era DCMs is Howard Williamson's *The Great War Medal Collector's Companion* (2011). Of its 250 pages covering gallantry medals some thirty-five relate to the DCM. Some of the areas covered by Williamson include details of bars to DCM, including a list of recipients of dated bars (with date shown on bar), notes on naming style with font alphabet, late issues, the history of the DCM League, awards to foreign troops, DCM paperwork, and DCM ephemera found with medals, a list of DCM recipients for 1 July 1916 and a list of the *London Gazette* editions in which the dates and places were removed from DCM citations, giving the dates covered by each gazette and notes on battles covered by them.

Having dated a DCM award and found the citation, it is then worthwhile checking local newspaper archives. Often there will be a write-up about a local soldier who has been awarded a DCM, along with a photograph. If he was given a 'smoking concert' or presented with an engraved watch, then there is a strong chance this will be reported. Equally well, it is worth checking the numerous part works that appeared during the First World War. *The War Illustrated* is a case in point, as it frequently carried portraits of, or reports about, DCM recipients. Similarly, *Deeds That Thrill The Empire* often carried stories about DCM actions, certainly in the early part of the war. You may also discover that your ancestor's deed appeared on a postcard, as a series of artists' impressions were produced in postcard format.

The 'George V first type' is common to all awards for the Great War. The obverse shows the bust of the king, bareheaded and in field marshal's uniform. Excepting some early issues, these are almost always impressed with the recipient's details in plain block capitals, showing the regimental number, rank, initials, surname and unit. The battalion is often given, as are batteries or field companies for the corps. Ranks and units were denoted in abbreviated form. A notice appeared following a list of awards in the *London Gazette* of 5 December 1914, requiring all recipients who had received an unnamed medal to return them to the Deputy Director of Ordnance Stores, Woolwich Dockyard, for engraving. One such medal, presented by HM King George V (5 December 1914) to Corporal A H Sutton, Royal Field Artillery is known to be engraved in block capitals, and additionally has 'RICHEBOURG. 1914' engraved after the usual details. Official records state that one thousand DCMs were sent to Woolwich Dockyard for naming between 27 November and 10 December 1914, but it is not known what proportion were impressed or engraved. It seems likely that not all of those that were awarded un-named were returned for naming, which could account for the genuine un-named examples (rather than those which have been subsequently erased) which are sometimes encountered. From 1918 if a recipient already held another award (such as an MM) then those post nominal letters would be included in the naming. Late awards were in smaller impressed naming. The 'second type' George

V issue shows the king in robes wearing a crown. Paradoxically, it was never used during his lifetime, but examples were issued during the brief reign of King Edward VIII. Compared with the 'first type' this is extremely rare.

Second World War DCMs can be harder to research. Although the name of the soldier will be listed in the *London Gazette*, citations were not published and it is necessary to check either in George A Brown's *For Distinguished Conduct in the Field - The DCM 1939-1992* or Philip McDermott's *For Distinguished Conduct in the Field - The Register of the Distinguished Conduct Medal 1920-1992* for the original recommendation. It is also possible to find an original recommendation at The National Archives (or via its website Documents Online), in the WO 373 series. Searching the original recommendations can be an interesting and rewarding project in its own right, as there are numerous instances of soldiers who were originally recommended for a DCM, but this was downgraded and they actually received an MM. In a few cases, the opposite situation is true and an MM was upgraded to a DCM. Some regimental archives also have copies of the original recommendations. In the Second World War, regional newspapers often carried reports about local DCM recipients so these are worth searching. If the recipient of the DCM has been dead for more than twenty-five years, and this can be proved with a copy death certificate, Ministry of Defence Historic Disclosures may release the man's service record under Freedom of Information legislation.

Post-Korean War, DCM citations were almost always published in the *London Gazette* and the descriptions of the events surrounding the award are extensive. The obvious exceptions to this rule are Special Forces DCMs. In the case of some awards for the Gulf War for example, no names were ever published, let alone citations. In other cases the names alone were published together with the details of the parent regiment, but no citation.

Notes on Sources

Chapter 1

1   *The Times*, 27.12.1854
2   House of Commons Debates, 19 December 1854 vol 136 cc505-7
3   *Ibid*
4   *London Gazette* (LG), 12.12.1854
5   WO 97 (quoted DNW archive 29.06.2006)
6   Border Regiment archives (quoted DNW archive 06.07.2004)
7   Kinglake, Alexander William, *The Invasion of the Crimea*, volume VI (1880), p348
8   Farquharson, R S, *Reminiscences of Crimean Campaigning and Russian Imprisonment* (Quoted DNW archive 02.04.2004)
9   DNW archive 2.04.2004
10 Quoted in Tyrell, Henry, *The History of the War With Russia Vol I*, (nd) p333
11 George Loy Smith, *A Victorian R.S.M.* (1987)
12 *Ibid*
13 Charles Rathbone Lo, *A Memoir of Lieutenant-General Sir Garnet J Wolseley*, R Bentley: 1878, pp. 57-176
14 DNW archive 22.09.2006
15 DNW archive 04.07.2001
16 *The Listener*, British Broadcasting Corporation, December 1936
17 Hensman, Howard , *The Afghan War of 1879-80*, Allen & Co, London, 1882, p208
18 WO 97 (quoted DNW archive 01.12.2004)
19 G.G.O. 383/2 July 1880 (quoted DNW archive 27.06.2007)
20 DNW archive 27.06.2007
21 DNW archive 05.12.1995
22 LG, 03.12.1880
23 Grant, James, *Cassell's History of the War in the Soudan Vol 2*, (nd), p130
24 *Punch*, 15 March 1884
25 DNW archive 09.12.1999
26 DNW archive 17.09.1999
27 WO 97 (quoted DNW archive)
28 *St George's Gazette*, June 1899

29 *St George's Gazette*, December 1899

30 LG, 24.01.1899

31 ADM 159/24

32 Downham, John, *Red Roses on the Veldt* (2000), p46

33 LG, 19.04.1901

34 LG, 08.02.1901

35 Wilson, Heather, *Blue Bonnets Boers and Biscuits* (1998), pp28–31

36 *Morning Post*, 22.05.1900

37 Churchill, Winston S, Letter 10.12.1913 (quoted DNW archive 07.07.2010)

38 Greenhill-Gardyne, C, *The Life of a Regiment: The History of the Gordon Highlanders Vol 2* (1929)

39 Gretton, George Le Mesurier, *Campaigns and History of the Royal Irish Regiment 1694–1902* (1911), p363

40 Gretton, *op cit*, pp364–365

41 DNW archive 17.09.1999

42 Witton, George, *Scapegoats of the Empire* (1907), ch 15

43 Witton, *op cit*, ch 20

44 LG, 11.12.1900

45 *Ibid*

46 *The Antelope*, May 1908

Chapter 2

1 *London Gazette* (LG), 17.12.1914

2 LG, 19.08.1916

3 Charman, Alfred. Information printed on commercial postcard (author's collection)

4 LG, 16.01.1915

5 War Diary, 1st Battalion Bedfordshire Regiment 09.11.1914 (http://www.bedfordregiment.org.uk/1stbn/1stbtn1914diary.html)

6 Chambers, Arthur, Manuscript diary 11.11.1914 (by permission of Leeds University Library)

7 LG, 16.01.1915

8 LG, 01.04.1915

9 *Ibid*

10 Shepherd, Frederick W Letter DNW archive 13.12.2007

11 LG, 05.08.1915

12 Humphries, Edward tape-recorded recollections 1972 (by permission of Leeds University Library)

13 *Mossley and Saddleworth Reporter* 01.08.1915
14 Irvine, William (junior), recollections as given to author (author's collection)
15 *Daily Mirror* 24.04.1915
16 LG, 05.08.1915
17 *Ibid*
18 LG, 05.08.1915
19 LG, 06.09.1915
20 Evans, Reginald, manuscript recollections (by permission of Leeds University Library)
21 LG, 25.01.1916
22 LG, 25.01.1916
23 Richards, Frank, *Old Soldiers Never Die* (1933), p153
24 Richards, *op cit*, pp142-3
25 Richards, *op cit*, pp152-3
26 McClintock, Alexander, *Best O'Luck* (1917), pp70, 80-82
27 McCormock, *op cit*, pp83-85
28 McCormock, *op cit*, p88
29 LG, 22.09.1916
30 Vlok, Nicholas. *South Africa* magazine/*Rollcall* (by permission of Ian Uys)
31 LG, 22.09.1916
32 LG, 14.11.1916
33 LG, 14.11.1916
34 LG, 05.08.1915
35 LG 21.10.1918
36 Gerrard, James, manuscript recollections (by permission of Leeds University Library)
37 LG, 03.09.1918
38 *Ibid*
39 DNW archive, 21.09.2007
40 LG, 5.12.1918
41 DNW archive, 20.09.2002
42 Curran, John, service papers WO 363
43 *Ibid*
44 *Ibid*
45 *Ibid*
46 *Ibid*
47 *Melbourne Herald*, 30.05.1915
48 LG, 15.09.1915

49 LG, 05.08.1915
50 LG, 01.05.1918
51 LG, 01.03.1918
52 LG, 15.03.1916
53 LG, 27.07.1916
54 LG, 05.11.1915
55 LG, 15.07.1919
56 LG, 15.07.1919
57 WO 363
58 LG, 06.11.1936
59 Moore, Maj Geoffrey MBE, *Just As Good As The Rest* (1976)
60 *Ibid*
61 *The Green Tiger*, August 1939

Chapter 3

1   Sheppard, John, typescript recollections (author's collection)
2   DNW archive, 21.09.2007
3   *Ibid*
4   DNW archive, 2.03.2005
5   *Ibid*
6   *Journal of the Orders and Medals Research Society*, September 2006, Volume 45, Number 3 (272)
7   WO 344
8   WO 344
9   WO 344
10 Allan, James, *No Citation* (1955), p27
11 Allan, *op cit*, p28
12 Allan, *op cit*, p29
13 Allan, *op cit*, pp170–171
14 WO 373/93
15 Nabarro, Derrick, *Wait For The Dawn* (1952), pp5,10
16 Nabbarro, *op cit*, p68
17 Nabaro, *op cit*, p74
18 Nabaro, *op cit*, pp87–88
19 http://www.thesoutheastecho.co.uk/Pilots2/Wareing_P.htm
20 WO 344
21 WO 373/17
22 Richardson, Tom, mss letter (author's collection)
23 WO 373/17

24 DNW archive, 22.09.2006
25 Richards, Harry, personnel file, National Archives of Australia
26 Richards, Harry, Log of 'MV *Leaving*', Australian War Memorial 3DRL/7974
27 *Ibid*
28 *Ibid*
29 WO 373/21
30 Moore, William, *Panzer Bait* (1991), p111
31 Moore, *op cit*, p122
32 *Ibid*
33 WO 373/23
34 WO 373/2
35 WO 373/25
36 Feebery, David, *Guardsman and Commando* (2008), p146
37 Feebery, *op cit*, p97
39 Feebery, *op cit*, p100
39 Feebery, *op cit*, p147
40 WO 373/53
41 *Waterloo Chronicle*, 05.11.2008
42 *Ibid*
43 *Ibid*
44 WO 373/55
45 DNW archive, 04.07.2001
46 WO 373/51
47 DNW archive, 04.07.2001
48 DNW archive, 22.09.2006
49 *The Green Tiger*, Spring 1964
50 McCormac, Charles, *You'll Die in Singapore* (1954), p62
51 WO 373/102
52 Wong Sue, Jack, *Blood On Borneo* (2001), p139
53 WO 373/102
54 Wong, *op cit*, p355
55 Abbot and Tamplin, *British Gallantry Awards* (1981)
56 General Orders, No. 61, HQ Ninth United States Army

Chapter 4

1 *London Gazette* (LG), 19.10.1951
2 Kitson, Frank, *Gangs and Counter-gangs* (1960), pp49–50
3 Kitson, *op cit*, p165

4 *Ibid*
5 LG, 19.07.1955
6 WO 373/121
7 WO 373/114
8 Rowlinson, William, personnel file, National Archives of Australia
9 *Ibid*
10 Forbes, Lt Col J Charles. http://www.kvacanada.com/stories_trfleo.htm
11 DNW archive, 22.09.2006
12 Morrison, Jack, personnel file, National Archives of Australia
13 LG, 31.10.1967
14 Downey, Mike, correspondence with author, 15.03.2010
15 Morrison, Jack, personnel file, National Archives of Australia
16 Allen, Ronald, personnel file, National Archives of Australia
17 Jones, Reginald, personnel file, National Archives of Australia
18 Horrigan, Denis, personnel file, National Archives of Australia
19 LG, 24.07.1973
20 LG, 18.12.1973
21 DNW archive, 22.09.2006
22 DNW archive, 25.03.1997
23 Mason, David. Spink sale catalogue, Sale 9033 Lot 25, 19.11.2009
24 LG, 08.10.1982
25 LG, 08.10.1982
26 *Ibid*
27 Burdett, Julian, correspondence with author, 18.07.2010
28 http://www.devonheritage.org/Nonplace/FalklandsMemorial/FalklandsArmy2.htm
29 LG, 08.10.1982
30 LG 08.10.1982
31 Middlebrook, Martin, *Operation Corporate: The Falklands War* (1985)
32 Special Order Of The Day, 1st Battalion King's Own Scottish Borderers, undated, (private collection)
33 Ratcliffe, Peter, *Eye of the Storm* p375. (Extracts from *Eye of the Storm: Twenty-Five Years in Action with the SAS* by Peter Ratcliffe, DCM (with Noel Botham and Brian Hitchen) by

permission of the publisher, Michael O'Mara Books Limited. Copyright © Peter Ratcliffe 2000; all rights reserved)

34 Ratcliffe, *op cit,* p376
35 Ratcliffe, *op cit,* p381
36 http://www.soldiermagazine.co.uk/op_banner/pages/28_29_aug2.pdf

Chapter 5
1   DNW archive, 18.05.2011

Bibliography

Abbot, P E, *Recipients of the Distinguished Conduct Medal 1855-1909*, London, 1975

Abbott, P E and Tamplin, J M A, *British Gallantry Awards*, London, 1981

Allan, James, *No Citation*, Angus and Robertson, Sydney, 1955

Ashcroft, Michael, *Special Forces Heroes*, Headline Review, 2008

Brown, George A, *For Distinguished Conduct in the Field - The DCM 1939-1992*, Naval & Military Press, London, 1994

Brown, John, *In Durance Vile*, Hale, 1981

Clift, Ken, *The Soldier Who Never Grew Up*, Sydney, 1976

Cromwell-Martin, C, *Battle Diary*, Dundurn Group Ltd (Canada), 1994

Dunning, George, *Where Bleed The Many*, Elek Books, London, 1955

Farquharson, R S, *Crimean Campaigning and Russian Imprisonment*, W. & D. C. Thompson, Dundee, 1889

Feebery, David, *Guardsman and Commando*, Pen and Sword Military, Barnsley, 2008

Franki, George, *Mad Harry*, Kangaroo Press, Sydney, 2003

Gravel, Michel, *Tough As Nails*, CEF Books, 2005

Hamilton, John, *Gallipoli Sniper: The Life of Billy Sing*, Sydney, Pan McMillan, 2008

Kitson, Frank, *Gangs and Counter-gangs*, Barrie & Rockliff, London, 1960

Lee, John A, *Soldier*, A H & A W Reed, Wellington, NZ, 1976

Lloyd, Brian, *A Gallant Life, the story of an old soldier*, Melbourne, 1998

Mackinlay, G A, *Beyond Duty (the DCM to the British Commonwealth 1920-1992)*, James Stedman Books, Sydney, 1993

McClintock, Alexander, *Best O'Luck, How a Fighting Kentuckian Won The Thanks of Britain's King*, George H Doran, New York, 1917

McCormac, C, *You'll Die In Singapore*, Robert Hale, 1954

McDermott, Philip, *For Distinguished Conduct in the Field - The Register of the Distinguished Conduct Medal 1920-1992*, J B Hayward & Sons, Polstead, 1994

McNab, Andy, *Bravo Two Zero*, Corgi, 1994

Maze, Paul, *Frenchman in Khaki*, 1934

Millar, F N, *The Lone Kiwi*, Dublin 1948

Moore, William, *Panzer Bait*, Leo Cooper, London 1991

Nabarro, D, *Wait For The Dawn*, Cassell & Co, London 1952

Ratcliffe, Peter , *Eye of the Storm, Twenty-Five Years in Action with the SAS*, Michael O'Mara Books Ltd, London, 2000

Richards, Frank, *Old Soldiers Never Die*, Faber and Faber, London 1933

Walker, R W, *Recipients of the Distinguished Conduct Medal 1914-1920*, Midland Medals, Birmingham 1981

Williamson, Howard, *The Great War Medal Collectors Companion*, Anne Williamson, 2011

Wilson, Heather, *Blue Bonnets, Boers & Biscuits*, Heather Wilson, London 1998

Wong Sue, Jack , *Blood on Borneo*, Jack Wong Sue, Perth, Australia 2001

Index